Collaborative Crisis Management

Public organizations are increasingly expected to cope with crisis under the same resource constraints and mandates that make up their normal routines, reinforced only through collaboration. *Collaborative Crisis Management* introduces readers to how collaboration shapes societies' capacity to plan for, respond to, and recover from extreme and unscheduled events.

Placing emphasis on five conceptual dimensions, this book teaches students how this panacea works out on the ground and in the boardrooms, and how insights on collaborative practices can shed light on the outcomes of complex inter-organizational challenges across cases derived from different problem areas, administrative cultures, and national systems. Written in a concise, accessible style by experienced teachers and scholars, it places modes of collaboration under an analytical microscope by assessing not only the collaborative tools available to actors but also how they are used, to what effect, and with which adaptive capacity. Ten empirical chapters span different international cases and contexts discussing:

- Natural and "man-made" hazards: earthquakes, hurricanes, wildfires, terrorism, migration flows, and violent protests
- Different examples of collaborative institutions, such as regional economic communities in Africa, and multi-level arrangements in Canada, the Netherlands, Turkey, and Switzerland
- Application of a multimethod approach, including single case studies, comparative case studies, process-tracing, and "large-n" designs.

Collaborative Crisis Management is essential reading for those involved in researching and teaching crisis management.

Fredrik Bynander is Director of the Center for Societal Security and Chairman of the Board of the Center of Natural Hazards and Disaster Science (CNDS). Prior to this appointment, Fredrik was head of strategic planning at the Prime Minister's Office Secretariat for Crisis Coordination. His current research interests include crisis management studies, leadership succession, and foreign policy analysis. Fredrik is a member of the Royal Academy of War Sciences and the Swedish Society for International Affairs.

Daniel Nohrstedt is Associate Professor of Political Science at Uppsala University, Sweden. He studies processes of inter-organizational collaboration, learning, change, and performance in the context of crisis management and natural hazards planning. His other research interests include policy process theory (particularly the Advocacy Coalition Framework), governance, policy network theory, and collaborative public management.

"Crisis collaboration across geographical and administrative borders is a must. It is also extremely hard. Under the guidance of Bynander and Nohrstedt, crisis experts pursue the Holy Grail of crisis collaboration in an exciting set of case studies. Extremely relevant for both academics and practitioners. A welcome addition to the crisis literature!"

—**Arjen Boin**, Leiden University

"*Collaborative Crisis Management* addresses collective action dilemma in response to major crises and disasters such as terrorism, wildfires, and earthquakes in different geographies, cultures, and political and administrative settings. This timely volume provides conceptually and analytically valuable perspectives from experts in the field in applying network governance in dealing with crises and disasters. The volume is an essential resource for both scholars and practitioners."

—**Naim Kapucu**, Ph.D., Pegasus Professor & Director of the School of Public Administration, University of Central Florida

"Emergency management is, above all, a social process. This authoritative book provides a valuable structure for analyzing the participation of people and organizations in crisis response. Its coverage of hazards and geographical areas is broad and eclectic. In responding to disasters and major incidents, collaboration is becoming more and more necessary. Many different agencies are likely to be involved, and hence the inter-organizational perspective brought by the authors of this book is particularly welcome."

—**David Alexander**, Professor of Risk and Disaster Reduction, University College London

Collaborative Crisis Management

Inter-Organizational Approaches to Extreme Events

Edited by Fredrik Bynander
&
Daniel Nohrstedt

NEW YORK AND LONDON

First published 2020
by Routledge
52 Vanderbilt Avenue, New York, NY 10017

and by Routledge
2 Park Square, Milton Park, Abingdon, Oxon, OX14 4RN

Routledge is an imprint of the Taylor & Francis Group, an informa business

© 2020 Taylor & Francis

The right of Fredrik Bynander and Daniel Nohrstedt to be identified as the authors of the editorial material, and of the authors for their individual chapters, has been asserted in accordance with sections 77 and 78 of the Copyright, Designs and Patents Act 1988.

All rights reserved. No part of this book may be reprinted or reproduced or utilized in any form or by any electronic, mechanical, or other means, now known or hereafter invented, including photocopying and recording, or in any information storage or retrieval system, without permission in writing from the publishers.

Trademark notice: Product or corporate names may be trademarks or registered trademarks, and are used only for identification and explanation without intent to infringe.

Library of Congress Cataloging-in-Publication Data
A catalog record for this book has been requested

ISBN: 978-0-367-14852-2 (hbk)
ISBN: 978-0-367-14856-0 (pbk)
ISBN: 978-0-429-24430-8 (ebk)

Typeset in Sabon
by Apex CoVantage, LLC

 Printed in the United Kingdom by Henry Ling Limited

Contents

Acknowledgments vii
List of Figures viii
Appendices ix
List of Tables x
List of Contributors xi

1 Collaborative Crisis Management: Inter-Organizational Approaches to Extreme Events 1
FREDRIK BYNANDER AND DANIEL NOHRSTEDT

2 Upscaling Collaborative Crisis Management: A Comparison of Wildfire Responder Networks in Canada and Sweden 13
DANIEL NOHRSTEDT, JULIA BAIRD, ÖRJAN BODIN, RYAN PLUMMER AND ROBERT SUMMERS

3 Secure Summits: Collaborative Crisis Management Before and During Global Government Conventions 27
SANNEKE KUIPERS AND MARIJ SWINKELS

4 Managing Extraordinary Influx of Migrants: The 2015 Migration Crisis in Sweden 43
EDWARD DEVERELL AND DAN HANSÉN

5 Overcoming Collective-Action Problems in Collaborative Crisis Management: Meta-Governance and Security Communications Systems 57
OSCAR L. LARSSON

6 Vertical Collaboration During the 2014 Swedish Wildfire 70
FREDRIK BYNANDER

7 Collaborative Crisis Management in Turkey: Perceptions and Outcomes of Collaboration During Two Earthquakes 80
HELENA HERMANSSON

vi Contents

8 Transregional Crisis Management in Africa 92
SIMON HOLLIS AND EVA-KARIN OLSSON

9 Addressing the Challenges of Transboundary Crises: The Dutch Local
Response to the Global Surge in ISIS Supporters 104
SCOTT DOUGLAS, ALINE BOS AND MIRKO NOORDEGRAAF

10 Avoiding the Failures of Collaborative Crisis Management: Lessons from
Research and Practice 119
CHARLES F. PARKER AND BENGT SUNDELIUS

11 Under What Conditions Does an Extreme Event Deploy its Focal Power?:
Toward Collaborative Governance in Swiss Flood Risk Management 132
KARIN INGOLD AND ALEXANDRA GAVILANO

12 Lessons and Avenues for Future Research in Collaborative
Crisis Management 148
DANIEL NOHRSTEDT AND FREDRIK BYNANDER

Index 161

Acknowledgments

This edited volume comes out of a truly collective effort among colleagues to jointly advance the understanding of collaborative crisis management and how it can be conceptualized and studied in different settings. Most of us have a history of working together in different constellations but some are newfound friends. We are grateful to all of these wonderful colleagues who agreed to devote their valuable time and energy to contribute to this book and for their patience in coping with a seemingly endless stream of deadlines and reminders. We also acknowledge the financial support from several funders, among them the Swedish Civil Contingencies Agency (MSB) and the Swedish research council Formas, which made this collaboration possible.

The Center of Natural Hazards and Disaster Science (CNDS), with which many of us are affiliated, has provided a constructive forum and intellectual engine for this work. The Center for Societal Security at the Swedish Defense University has been the institutional home for many contributors to this book and has served as an important platform for us to meet and discuss this work. A special thanks goes to Publications Manager Stephanie Young for correcting our mistakes and making the manuscript readable and coherent. Nevertheless, responsibility for any remaining errors rests solely with the editors.

We are grateful to Paul 't Hart for helping us get going with the project and for being a constructive and sharp commentator along the way. Arjen Boin has been another important discussion partner for many of us throughout this process, and his influence on our thinking is noticeable across many of the chapters. This work has been inspired and influenced by meetings and interactions with many other researchers, students, and practitioners. These conversations have been an important source of ideas and a major inspiration for this book.

Carole Sargent of Georgetown University has been a generous guide to the publishing process and helped us sharpen our ideas for a book that can strive to appeal beyond crisis coordination scholarship. At Routledge, we thank Senior Editor of Political Science Natalja Mortensen, Editorial Assistant of Politics Charlie Baker, and the Production Department for their steadfast assistance and guidance in completing the manuscript and making it presentable.

We do feel that the time is right for a concerted push toward a better understanding of the mechanisms of collaborative crisis management, and we hope that this volume can work as an inclusive and fertile ground for the continuous evolution of this research community.

Figures

9.1	Overview of the actors involved in the crisis response	110
9.2	Overview of a typical local case review process	113
11.1	Paradigm shift in Swiss flood prevention	138
11.2A	Number of deaths	140
11.2B	Geographical outreach (number of cantons affected)	140
11.2C	Economic damages in millions of Swiss Francs	141

Appendices

Chapter 3	Appendix I: List of respondents	42
Chapter 11	Appendix II: Table of regulations and legal texts taken into account for paradigm shift identification	146

Tables

1.1	Chapter focus and topics	8
3.1	Assessment of success of G20 and NSS	29
3.2	Characteristics of the high security events	33
3.3	Outcomes in terms of experienced unrest	34
3.4	Overview of main findings	39
5.1	Number of subscriptions/prognosis	65
5.2	Categories of users and number of subscriptions	65
8.1	Mapping transregional capacity	94
8.2	Description of major topics discussed in subregional meetings, 2014–2016	95
8.3	Percent of topics discussed in subregional meetings and events, 2014–2016	97
8.4	Number of *ad hoc* and formal transregional meetings or events, 2014–2016	98
8.5	Number of meetings devoted to sharing, analyzing information, and decision making, 2014–2016	98
8.6	Number of subregional meetings or events used for discussing acute crisis events, 2014–2016	98
8.7	Acute crisis topics discussed in transregional meetings and events, 2014–2016	99
9.1	Theoretical categories for understanding a crisis and observations from the case	106
9.2	Theoretical categories for responding to a crisis and observations from the case	108
9.3	Observations from the case on responding to a transboundary crisis	112
11.1	Selected flood events	135

Contributors

Julia Baird is Canada Research Chair and Assistant Professor in the Environmental Sustainability Research Center and the Department of Geography and Tourism Studies at Brock University. Her research focuses on resilience and the human side of water management and environmental governance, including the structure and function of networks and how they influence individual perceptions and actions.

Örjan Bodin is Associate Professor of Environmental and Sustainability Science at Stockholm Resilience Center, Stockholm University, Sweden. He is studying different challenges and opportunities in governing natural resources, and much of his research bridges the natural and social sciences.

Aline Bos works as Senior Consultant and Researcher at Utrecht University School of Governance (USG). She conducted research for many government and civil society organizations, including the Dutch Ministry of Justice, for which she examined topics of anti-terrorism policy and exploitation of minors.

Fredrik Bynander is Director of the Center for Societal Security at the Swedish Defense University and Chairman of the Board of the Center of Natural Hazards and Disaster Science (CNDS). Prior to this appointment, Fredrik was a special adviser at the Prime Minister's Office Secretariat for Crisis Coordination, and in 2011–2012, he was its head of strategic planning. His current research interests include crisis management studies, collaborative crisis management, leadership succession, and foreign policy analysis. Frederik is a member of the Royal Academy of War Sciences as well as the Swedish Society for International Affairs.

Edward Deverell is Assistant Professor of Political Science at the Swedish Defense University. His research focuses on topics such as organizational learning from crises, institutional crisis management, crisis decision making, and public agency communication.

Scott Douglas is Assistant Professor of Public Management at Utrecht School of Governance (USG). He specializes in the performance management of collaborations, with a particular focus on collaborations addressing wicked problems such as radicalization, obesity, and illiteracy. He is cofounder of the Collaborative Governance Case Database, a common pool resource for sharing high quality case studies.

Alexandra Gavilano is Research Scientist at the Center for Development and Environment and the World Overview of Conservation Approaches and Technologies at the University of Bern. She is also the founder and Vice-Director of Pyrolysis LLC and board member of Climate Protection Switzerland (Klimaschutz Schweiz). Her research focus is on sustainable land and water management with special interest in environmental impacts due to climatic changes and related socioeconomic consequences.

xii Contributors

Dan Hansén is Associate Professor of Political Science at the Swedish Defense University. His research interests include policy-oriented learning in relation to crisis experience and crisis making. Empirically, he has foremost focused on the law and order sector.

Helena Hermansson is currently Associate Senior Lecturer at the Swedish Defense University, working in collaboration with the Center for Natural Hazards and Disaster Science. Her research interests include collaborative and network governance, disaster management, and crisis management, with a particular focus on cases about Turkey.

Simon Hollis is Assistant Professor at the Department of Security, Strategy and Leadership at the Swedish Defense University. His research interests include international disaster studies, disaster resilience, and crisis management.

Karin Ingold is Associate Professor at the Institute of Political Science and the Oeschger Center for Climate Change Research. She is furthermore the head of the research group "Policy Analysis and Environmental Governance" at the Eawag in Dübendorf. She is interested in policy processes and their evolution related to complex environmental issues such as transboundary water quality management or climate change adaptation.

Sanneke Kuipers works at the Institute of Security and Global Affairs, Leiden University, where she received her Ph.D. in 2004. Sanneke teaches and conducts research on crisis management, accountability and blaming, comparative politics, and public administration. She is Chief Editor of the journal *Risk, Hazards and Crisis in Public Policy* (RHCPP) and leads the Leiden University Crisis Research Center at the Institute of Security and Global Affairs. Also, she is Associate Editor of the upcoming *Oxford Research Encyclopedia of Crisis Analysis*.

Oscar L. Larsson holds, since 2015, a Ph.D. in Political Science from Uppsala University. He is currently a postdoctoral researcher (2017–2019) at the Swedish University of Agricultural Sciences (SLU). Oscar's main research interest is network governance, and he explores such related themes as democracy, legitimacy, participation, power, and domination. He has previously published articles on network governance in *Critical Policy Studies* and *Regulation and Governance*, on neo-institutionalism in *Critical Review*, and on collaborative crisis management in *Risk, Hazards and Crisis in Public Policy*.

Daniel Nohrstedt is Associate Professor of Political Science at Uppsala University, Sweden, where he also serves as research coordinator in the Center of Natural Hazards and Disaster Science (CNDS). He studies structures and processes of inter-organizational collaboration, learning, change, and performance in the context of crisis management. His other research interests include the policy process, policy networks, and collaborative governance.

Mirko Noordegraaf is Professor of Public Management at Utrecht University School of Governance (USG) and Vice Dean for Societal Impact, Faculty of Law, Economics and Governance (LEG). He focuses on governance, public organizations, public managers, and public professionals, in relation to tackling societal issues. Earlier, he published *Public Management: Performance, Professionalism and Politics* (2015).

Eva-Karin Olsson is Professor and Head of the Department of Security, Strategy and Leadership at the Swedish Defense University. Her main research areas include political science with a focus on crisis management and international collaboration, journalism, and media.

Charles F. Parker is Associate Professor of Political Science at the Department of Government and serves as the Deputy Chair of the board for the Center of Natural Hazards and Disaster Science (CNDS). His research has focused on climate change politics, leadership, crisis management, and the origins and consequences of warning-response problems.

Ryan Plummer is Professor and Director of the Environmental Sustainability Research Centre (ESRC) at Brock University in Canada. His multifaceted program of research broadly concerns resilience and governance of social-ecological systems.

Robert Summers is Director of Sustainability and Associate Director of the Urban and Regional Studies Program at the University of Alberta. His research interests include institutional approaches to exploring the transition to sustainability and urban and regional planning.

Bengt Sundelius has been Professor of Government at the Uppsala University and the Swedish Defense University. He serves as Strategic Advisor to the Swedish Civil Contingencies Agency (MSB) and has published many scholarly works and policy reports related to crisis management issues.

Marij Swinkels is a Ph.D. candidate and lecturer at the Utrecht University School of Governance. In her research, she aims to understand how the beliefs of political leaders permeate crisis decision making.

Chapter 1

Collaborative Crisis Management
Inter-Organizational Approaches to Extreme Events

Fredrik Bynander and Daniel Nohrstedt

Doing things together in order to protect society from harm is a self-evident activity in most societies and cultures. Yet, the study and practice of collaboration in relation to crisis management is a minefield of false starts, conceptual confusion, and practical difficulty. Collaboration, and its many related concepts (e.g., cooperation, coordination, co-management), has come to signify everything from coexisting at an accident site to long-term co-planning and investing in generic capabilities to mitigate and manage transboundary hazards across national borders. The effect of the catchall nature of the concept of collaboration has been to diffuse expectations of common behavior in the crisis preparedness arena and create standards for participating actors that are extremely hard to meet in practice. When forging the public blueprint for collaborative crisis management in a country or region, administrative realities, operating procedures, resource allocation, and a number of other practical and organizational factors must be reconciled with expectations of public administration activities that are inflated and oftentimes unrealistic.

Recent advances in political science, public administration, public management, and related disciplines and subfields have significantly increased our awareness and knowledge of collaborative governance and management on many important fronts (Nohrstedt et al. 2018). There is also a growing recognition among policy actors, stakeholders, and practitioners that complex policy problems have to be managed by initiating and maintaining various organizational architectures to facilitate collaboration among actors working together across organizational boundaries spanning sectors, jurisdictions, and levels of authority. But despite these insights and experiences, there are still important lessons that can be learned about collaborative governance in different problem settings.

This book focuses on collaborative approaches to crisis management ("collaborative crisis management," in short), which we define broadly as involving joint efforts of multiple autonomous actors to work across organizational borders, levels of authority, and sectors to prepare for, respond to, and learn from risks and extreme events that disrupt our modern society. In policy circles and academic discourse, there is a strong emphasis on the advantages and benefits associated with collaboration but also recognition of barriers, hurdles, and pitfalls. One dominating paradigm suggests that because the risks and hazards that face modern society are so complex and uncertain, there is a need for institutional arrangements and governance approaches that enable flexible solutions and responses based on capacities to innovate, improvise, and adapt to rapidly changing circumstances and complex problems. Traditional hierarchical bureaucracy might still be apt to meet known contingencies (so-called "routine emergencies") but more complex and large-scale crises generally require mobilization of more diverse networks of organizations that pool different mandates, resources, skills, and capabilities (Nohrstedt 2016). In this perspective, safety and security are contingent upon the aggregated capacity of diverse sets of actors and stakeholders to work together across organizational boundaries to ensure swift mobilization of knowledge and expertise, both of which are required to cope with events that outstrip the capacity of single organizations. Ideally, these collaborative arrangements and networks should also be capable to adapt by retaining abilities to learn and adjust procedures and working methods in the face of experience (Farazmand 2007).

At the same time, the historical record testifies to the difficulties involved with realizing these governance ideals in practice. Multi-organizational crisis responder networks often underperform, or even break apart, due to difficulties to develop common understandings and achieve effective coordination, sharing of information, and joint decisions. Individuals with different organizational backgrounds, experience, knowledge, resources, and skills will face considerable transaction costs that have to be overcome to enable fruitful collaboration. Oftentimes it is difficult to find proper levels of overlap between networks of organizations that work together to plan and prepare for crises and those networks that emerge in response to acute events. Another common problem is that the circle of participants is drawn too narrowly, which can lead to the exclusion of organizations with relevant expertise and other resources required for an effective response (Boin and 't Hart 2010). Waugh and Streib (2006, 132) succinctly capture the challenge:

> On the one hand, emergency response requires meticulous organization and planning, but on the other hand, it is spontaneous. Emergency managers have to innovate, adapt, and improvise because plans, regardless of how well done, seldom fit circumstances. Blending these conflicting needs is no easy task.

These demands and expectations concerning streamlined collaborative approaches to risks, hazards, and security have been shaped by broader strategic developments in society. For one, in the post–Cold War world, the strategic focus shifted gradually from territorial integrity and national security to a notion of *societal security*, which rests on the premise that security is about "safeguarding the critical functions of society, protecting people, and upholding fundamental values and structures of democratic governance" ('t Hart and Sundelius 2013, 445; see also Buzan 2008). Second, many governments have adopted a *whole-of-society* approach for societal security, promoting continuous cross-sectoral collaboration between public organizations and nongovernmental partners and stakeholders outside the sphere of government (Lindberg and Sundelius 2012). Third, the guiding principle for the whole-of-society approach for societal security is societal *resilience*, referring to the capacity of any given system to "withstand" or "bounce back" from disturbance, which necessitates collaboration on a broad scale and over time to build trust and collaborative skills among multiple stakeholders to ensure adaptation to increase societies' readiness to respond (Comfort, Boin, and Demchak 2010). A fourth trend is the emergence of the *risk reduction* paradigm (Smith 2013), which places the emphasis on long-term plans and strategies for identifying and reducing vulnerability and risk ("flood risk management" and "drought risk management" being vivid examples). In this perspective, collaboration is depicted as a means to reduce risk and vulnerability by community-based participation to facilitate integration of information, knowledge, and experiences (Thomalla et al. 2006).

While collaborative approaches for crisis management have become a key priority around the world, issues of collective-action in response to risks, threats, and extreme events have long been on the social science research agenda. Already in the 1960s disaster sociologists began studying *coordination* in disaster and emergency, with a focus on "the cooperation of independent units for the purpose of eliminating fragmentation, gaps in service delivery, and unnecessary (as opposed to strategic) duplication of services" (Gillespie 1991, 57). These studies advanced the understanding of community coordination in relation to crisis management operations "on the ground" (Drabek 2007). Two central insights emerged from this research. The first is that coordination structures and processes designed to cope with "routine emergencies" do not work particularly well in the context of major disasters, which rather tend to produce alternative coordination mechanisms. This observation spurred additional comparative work on coordination in different types of organizational systems (Quarantelli 1966; Dynes 1978) including:

- established organizations – the first-line of response to an unfolding acute emergency
- extending organizations – dealing with the economic, social, and psychological impacts of crises and disasters on the lives of victims/communities
- expanding organizations – human services organizations within and outside government that have crisis management as a key (though not core) component of their mission, yet they have the majority of their personnel routinely committed to other tasks
- emergent organizations – emerging spontaneously and unexpectedly, often in reaction to hitherto unplanned needs or perceived deficiencies of the existing response efforts, e.g., victims' groups, recovery networks.

Horizontal cooperation between such different responding parties is easily undermined by both technical and cultural communication problems. They are likely to entertain different notions of the meaning and necessity of coordination. Disaster research has demonstrated some recurrent fault lines between these four types of response organizations (Boin and 't Hart 2012).

Professionals Versus Amateurs

The well-trained first responders – often eager to show that they are ready – may be shocked or dismayed (or both) with the perceived lack of speed and experience that "bureaucrats" from extending organizations can display during a crisis. While first responders have their "feet in the mud," they see how the "bureaucrats" fail to "ramp up" to high-speed, high-volume processing requirements. They wonder aloud how the "do gooders" of expanding organizations can deliver ("we will have to find something for them to do"). The "bureaucrats," in turn, will try to explain that their organizations were doing the best they could, given the impossible tasks at hand. The volunteers of expanding organizations are astounded to learn that their contributions are not being valued.

Operational Versus Strategic Perspectives

In the thick of crisis, first responders tend to be solely and urgently concerned with the safety and survival of (potential) victims. This is their mission; it is what they train to do. This operational perspective, and the total lack of concern with the long term (the here and now is the only thing that matters), conflicts easily (and often rapidly) with the perspective that extending organizations bring to the scene. Other values – fairness and accountability, for example – enter the decision-making arena. Conflicting values can give rise to vehement disagreements that play out on-site, fueling already existing misperceptions about underlying motivations. As the crisis unfolds, the search and rescue dimension of disasters tends to lose importance quickly, making the other organization types more relevant and important. This can lead to frustration among first responders, which feeds mounting disrespect ("we have done our job, why can't you?"). The operational fixation and apparent blindness to the bigger policy picture and long-term considerations beyond the incident at hand tend to confound members of the other organizational types.

Local Versus Wider Interests

Members of expanding organizations typically enter the response network from "outside." They are volunteers who rushed to the scene, leaving behind families and jobs ("we're here to help"). Appreciation for these volunteers may not last long ("nobody here asked you to help"). When outside organizations establish themselves in the arena and claim authority, locals may resist. They may not immediately recognize the competence, ability, or legitimacy of these incoming organizations. This perception can be further strengthened if expanding organizations play to their funders, sticking to an action repertoire that is in line with their mandate and refusing to take on additional tasks – or worse, when expanding organizations start fighting each other for "turf," performing in the lights of TV cameras.

These are but three examples of potential fault lines; empirical research suggests there are more. Other studies – e.g., Auf der Heide (1989); Gillespie and Colignon (1993); Perry and Lindell (2003) – point at the intricate relationship between preparedness activities and disaster response and map the coordination challenges that flow from it. We do not mean to suggest that coordination problems will always play out along these fault lines, but we do propose that those who will be held responsible for coordination failures should consider these types of fault lines.

The second key finding from disaster sociology was that the need for coordination increased demands on the professional emergency manager to take on the role as the "community coordinator" that actively interacts with government officials and representatives of the broader disaster relief community (Waugh and Streib 2006). This insight turned the spotlight on managers as "facilitators" and the strategies that enhance interagency coordination as well as barriers to coordination (Drabek 1987). While emergency and disaster response operations were the dominating focus of these studies, some work was also conducted on coordination processes in relation to recovery operations, mitigation, and vulnerability reduction.

The vast academic literature that has evolved in the recent decades confirms the growing importance of collaborative arrangements and processes as a strategy to cope with a range of complex policy issues and societal challenges on different scales and in different parts of the world. This work spans a variety of theoretical and empirical fields and has evolved into an interdisciplinary endeavor where scholars apply different cases, concepts, assumptions, theories, and research methods. But despite these overlaps, studies rarely exploit the potential benefit of examining parallel literatures (O'Leary and Bingham 2009; Nohrstedt et al. 2018). Consequently, the literature on inter-organizational collaboration lacks a common framework of analysis and clear definitions to specify the meaning and measurement of collaboration.

Collaborative public management and crisis management have previously been connected in various ways in the literature. One example is the notion of "collaborative emergency management," which turns the spotlight on inter-organizational communication, information technologies, and mechanisms for fostering joint decision making (Kapucu, Arslan, and Demiroz 2010; Mendonça, Jefferson, and Harrald 2007; Patton 2007). A similar conceptualization (McGuire, Brudney, and Gazley 2010) emerged around "the new emergency management," involving cross-sectoral collaboration in emergency response operations. This work set the focus on issues such as professional competencies of emergency managers, criteria for assessing performance, and conditions for building theory around collaborative crisis management. In another study, Ansell, Boin, and Keller (2010) chartered a research agenda to address the "transboundary dimensions" of crises and disasters with four boundary-spanning mechanisms that constitute an effective transboundary crisis response: *distributed sensemaking* (merging conflicting problem definitions), *networked coordination* (institutional design to support cooperation), *surge capacity* (overcoming problems of supply logistics), and *formal scaling procedures* (clarifying decision-making structures and procedures).

These separate contributions are useful starting points for advancing our understanding of collaborative crisis management, but more work clearly remains to be done to define and investigate the drivers, structures, processes, and outcomes of collaborative crisis management across settings (Nohrstedt et al. 2018). In this book, we contribute to this effort by studying a selection of multi-organizational arrangements and efforts to prepare for, respond to, recover, and learn from extreme events that exceed the capacity of any single organization to manage alone.

Conceptual and Analytical Dimensions

Throughout the different chapters of this volume we highlight five conceptual dimensions that are helpful to unpack and systematically examine collaborative approaches to extreme events and crisis management. First, we take a broad *temporal perspective* on crisis management. Our definition of collaborative crisis management is not confined to reactive behaviors and processes limited to the acute phase of crisis management, including joint decision making and collaboration in the midst of urgency and uncertainty. Although we are indeed interested in advancing insights regarding multi-organizational responses to acute crisis episodes – situations characterized by a combination of uncertainty, threat, and limited response-time – we adopt a broader analytical perspective on crisis management that also includes efforts associated with planning, preparation, lesson drawing, and crisis-induced policy change and reform. In addition, we take a relatively broad view of planning and preparation, which includes crisis preparedness as well as collaborative approaches associated with risk reduction measures. Hence, we seek to enhance knowledge of collaborative management in the various temporal phases typically associated with crisis management.

Second, we seek to capture a broad selection of *different crisis trajectories*, which has implications for the nature and purpose of collaboration. Our perspective departs from the insight that extreme events follow different dynamic patterns based on the speed of development (fast versus slow) and pace of termination (abrupt or gradual). Using these dimensions and borrowing from 't Hart and Boin (2001), we discern four ideal-types of crisis trajectories including: (1) the "fast-burning crisis" (sudden onset, sharp closure), (2) the "cathartic crisis" (long and gradual onset, abrupt termination), (3) "the slow-burning crisis" (incremental escalation, fades away rather than being resolved), and (4) "the long-shadow crisis" (sudden occurrence, followed by drawn-out political or institutional crisis). These trajectories are analytical simplifications but nevertheless helpful to delineate what types of organizations and actors take active part in collaboration and also the specific objective of collaboration.

Third, we consider a *range of collaborative arrangements and efforts*. Based on the insight that organizations pursue different notions of collaboration, we adopt a relatively inclusive understanding of collaboration spanning the range of collective arrangements and efforts in which organizations engage. For instance, we consider different types of collaborative institutions, ranging from institutionalized venues (more or less formalized forums or arenas (Fischer and Leifeld 2015) where stakeholders participate regularly over time to formulate and work toward some common goal) to *ad hoc* multi-organizational arrangements (temporary forums or areas where stakeholders work together to jointly address a specific problem or situation). In addition to the arrangements where collaboration takes place, we are interested in the different goal types that guide collective-action during disruptive crisis situations, including exchange of information, formulation of joint goals, coordination of activities, sharing of resources, and so on. Oftentimes any given area is likely to consist of multiple interconnected collaboration networks that pursue partially overlapping goals and that are bound together by people, knowledge, and resource dependency (Kapucu and Hu 2014; Bodin and Nohrstedt 2016). Together these overlapping networks create a complex "ecology" of actors and institutions. Although these "networks of networks" are part of the reality that many stakeholders face every day, this is an area where research lags behind (Lubell 2013).

Fourth, we investigate collaborative crisis management along *different spatial scales* – from the local to the international level as well as cross-level networks and interactions. Our starting point is the insight that crises increasingly transcend organizational boundaries (Ansell, Boin, and Keller 2010) across sectors and levels of authority, raising the need for approaches to enhance the understanding of information sharing, the alignment of expectations and actions across organizations, and the willingness and ability of managers, policymakers, and stakeholders to do so (Drabek and McEntire 2002). Trends associated with increased interdependency between social, political, economic, and ecological systems increase the importance of understanding horizontal (within levels) and vertical (across levels) collaboration, which is often nested within complex and multileveled "polycentric" governance systems (Galaz et al. 2017). In this perspective, we exemplify patterns of collaboration on different scales of government, from relatively localized phenomena to events and processes of interaction at the international level.

Fifth, a final important distinction concerns the type of actors that are engaged in collaboration, which include a *range of different constellations* that occur within and between states, private actors and interests, and communities. At the state level, various inter-agency networks are important to coordinate public resources and actions (Kapucu 2005). In addition, scholars stress the importance of collaboration among political officeholders, agency leaders, and other public executives at the strategic level ('t Hart and Boin 2010; Nohrstedt et al. 2018). While crisis and emergency management is subject to increasing professionalization (Waugh and Streib 2006), there is also a parallel trend of security privatization to "outsource" security issues to private firms and interests (Bryden and Caparini 2006). As a consequence, increasing demands and expectations are imposed on these diverse interests to develop collaborative skills and competencies to interact with a variety of collaborators. The same goes for community actors, such as nonprofit organizations (Simo and Bies 2007; Demiroz and Hu 2014) and voluntary associations (Brudney and Gazley 2009). Finally, collaborative crisis management also hinges on social ties forming across these actor categories, including co-management between state and community actors (Næss et al. 2005), public-private partnerships between state and private interests (Koliba, Mills, and Zia 2011), and private-social partnerships involving communities and private interests (see Lemos and Agrawal 2009).

Modes of Collaboration in Crisis Management

One implication of the conceptual dimensions outlined earlier is that we need a way of discriminating different "modes" of collaboration, which differentiates between types, goals, and levels of intensity of interactions among stakeholders. However, even if there has been an explosion of research on collaborative governance and management in recent years, the term "collaboration" still lacks a common definition. There is also a broad variety of indicators and benchmarks to guide empirical research and evaluate effectiveness and performance, yet little consistency regarding the application of these measures across cases and contexts. As the concept of "collaborative governance" has been discussed extensively elsewhere (e.g., Ansell and Gash 2008), we settle here with a relatively common basic distinction between three types of interactions that are helpful in unpacking the notion of collaborative crisis management.

Obviously, there are numerous ways of categorizing and scaling "modes of collaboration," but ours is quite straightforward: it assesses the amount and complexity of interaction needed to make joint outcomes compliant to the mandates, interests, and repertoires of influential actors and stakeholders while satisfying the "problem-solving priorities" of each organization (Bryson and Crosby 2008; Gray 1989). This results in a qualitative scale between combinations of tasks associated with **cooperation** (communication in order not to get in each other's way and to foster a suitable division of labor around commonly agreed upon problems and objectives), **coordination** (demanding dialogue and negotiation to settle priorities between organizational goals and societal values), and **collaboration** (generating new structures, defined relationships, resource-sharing, and continuous communication in pursuit of jointly defined goals). In this conceptualization, collaboration "is best examined as a dynamic or emergent process rather than a static condition" (O'Leary and Vij 2012, 508; see also Nohrstedt and Bodin 2014). The implication of making this rather crude distinction in the context of crisis management is to balance the "supply side" of collaboration (which level and quality of collaboration can the actors achieve) with the "demand side" (which level and quality of collaboration does the situation demand). Collaborative structures are currently much too tailor-made for specific problem sets; in fact, there is room to develop and fine-tune structures and processes of collaboration that are more efficiently adapted to a wider spectrum of hazards. The chapters presented in this book will each probe a set of problem-defining factors and the way the response units collaborate to meet them.

Chapter Summaries

Together, the contributions to this book illustrate the idea that findings in collaborative governance and management are applicable to risks, threats, and extreme events and their fast-evaporating room for action in relation to different challenges and political contexts. Public organizations are increasingly expected to cope with crises under the same resource constraints and mandates that make up their normal routines, reinforced only through *collaboration*. Our book explores how this panacea plays out on the ground and in various decision-making contexts and how insights regarding collaborative practices can shed light on the outcomes of complex inter-organizational challenges across cases derived from different problem areas, administrative cultures, and political systems. It hereby places modes of collaboration under the analytical microscope by assessing not only the collaborative tools available to actors, but also how they are used and to what effect.

This introductory chapter has provided a common conceptual framework for studying very different contexts in which collaboration takes place. The authors have combined deep empirical knowledge of their cases and the contexts in which they evolved, with a shared objective to extract processes and qualities significant of collaborative practice and ways in which that may change over the period of study. Thus, the dynamic qualities of how collaboration evolves in each case will inform our findings and produce a more nuanced understanding of collaboration in relation to different types of extreme events.

Table 1.1 gives an overview of the range of empirical cases and how they contribute to the book theme. The categories present themes for summarizing current areas of emphasis in collaborative crisis management research. It should be noted that the categories detailed in Table 1.1 are on a continuum with blurred boundaries; hence, the classification of each chapter is based on dominating emphases.

Table 1.1 Chapter focus and topics

Case thematic and geographical focus (authors)	Temporal perspective	Crisis trajectory	Arrangements and efforts	Spatial scale	Actor constellations
Wildfire response, Sweden and Canada (Nohrstedt et al.)	Crisis response	Fast burning	Pre-planned collaboration, low-fidelity	Cross scale	First responders to local and regional authorities
International summits, Canada and the Netherlands (Kuipers and Swinkels)	Planning and preparedness	Slow burning	International collaboration, national lead, high-fidelity	Cross scale	National coordination of several national agencies
Migration crisis, Sweden (Hansén and Deverell)	Crisis response	Cathartic crisis with rapid escalation	*Ad hoc* collaboration, over-burdened lead agency	Cross scale	National coordination of local authorities
Security communication system, Sweden (Larsson)	Preparedness and emergency communication	All trajectories	Organizing response organizations, high-fidelity	National coverage	Government infrastructure
Wildfire crisis management, Sweden (Bynander)	Crisis response	Fast burning	Low-fidelity to *ad hoc*	Local to regional	Public and private
Earthquakes, Turkey (Hermansson)	Crisis response	Fast burning	Hierarchical, centralized	Specific locations	National/local
Transregional crisis management, Africa (Hollis and Olsson)	Crisis response	Fast burning	Low-fidelity, diplomatic	Multilateral	Governments
Counterterrorism, the Netherlands (Douglas, Bos, and Noordegraaf)	Preparedness, mitigation	Slowburning	Intelligence based	Cross scale	Law enforcement, social workers
Avoiding CM failures (Parker and Sundelius)	Preparedness, lesson-drawing	All trajectories	Organizing response organizations	No specific scale	Government policy planning
Flood risk management, Switzerland (Ingold and Gavilano)	Lesson-drawing	Long shadow	Policy process	National-local	Government, public administration

Source: Table Created by Authors

The chapters in this book serve as an illustration of the different analytical approaches and methods that can be employed for empirically studying collaborative crisis management in different countries and contexts. In the field of crisis management there is a strong tradition of utilizing in-depth single case study approaches to reconstruct crisis events and situations as a basis for understanding and explaining behaviors and responses. Crisis management scholars have also frequently resorted to cross-case comparisons to uncover similarities and differences across cases. Both these approaches are exemplified in the contributions to this book. Chapters utilizing a single case study approach include the 2015 migration crisis in Sweden (Hansén and Deverell, this volume), the 2014 Västmanland wildfire (Bynander, this volume), the Dutch response to the ISIS threat (Scott, Bos, and Noordegraaf), and secure communication systems in Sweden (Larsson, this volume). Comparative case studies include wildfire responses in Canada and Sweden (Nohrstedt et al., this volume), global summits in Canada and the Netherlands (Kuipers and Swinkels, this volume), experiences of crisis management failures and proposed prescriptions (Parker and Sundelius, this volume), and the "within-case comparison" of earthquakes in Turkey (Hermansson, this volume) and collaborative governance in Swiss flood risk management (Ingold and Gavilano, this volume). Finally, the chapter on transregional crisis management in Africa (Hollis and Olsson, this volume) is an illustration of a comparative approach involving a larger number of cases and observations. In addition, the chapters also illustrate the breadth of data collection methods employed to retrieve information about actors, events, and processes and structures for collaboration. The main data sources include interviews, various public documents, and news media reports, which have enabled detailed insight into the structures and processes of collaborative crisis management.

Enhancing the understanding of collaborative crisis management – including its drivers, practices, and consequences – depends on empirical research to inform theory and practice. We share the impression by many other scholars that the field of collaborative governance is rich on concepts and theory while empirical application still lags behind. Hence, we agree there is a need for more systematic empirical work to shed light on the usefulness of our concepts and to probe the descriptive and explanatory validity of our theories in this area. Offering a theoretically informed empirical perspective on collaborative crisis management is a key ambition and key goal of this book. Each chapter can thus be read as a stand-alone story of a particular event, phenomenon, or case, which may serve as a guide for practical and theoretical lesson drawing. But in addition, each individual chapter also adds to an overarching story of collaborative crisis management, which hopefully can help advance the scientific knowledge frontier and also provide some useful lessons for crisis management practitioners.

We encourage and challenge the readers of this book to contemplate what the most important message is from each chapter and the book as a whole to the broader field of collaborative governance, as well as to the emergent field of collaborative crisis management. Hereby we can promote a collective effort to build new knowledge by identifying the most relevant research questions and engaging in empirical work to answer those questions. The concluding chapter (Nohrstedt and Bynander, this volume) serves the purpose of summing up some of the lessons and insights that have emerged from each chapter, as well as some general patterns that we see across cases.

References

Ansell, Chris, Arjen Boin, and Ann Keller. 2010. "Managing Transboundary Crises: Identifying the Building Blocks of an Effective Response System." *Journal of Contingencies and Crisis Management* 18 (4): 195–207.

Ansell, Chris and Alison Gash. 2008. "Collaborative Governance in Theory and Practice." *Journal of Public Administration Research and Theory* 18 (4): 543–71.

Auf der Heide, Erik. 1989. *Disaster Response: Principles of Preparation and Coordination*. Toronto: Mosby Company.

Bodin, Örjan and Daniel Nohrstedt. 2016. "Formation and Performance of Collaborative Disaster Management Networks: Evidence from a Swedish Wildfire Response." *Global Environmental Change* 41: 183–94.

Boin, Arjen and Paul 't Hart. 2012. "Aligning Executive Action in Times of Adversity: The Politics of Crisis Co-Ordination." In *Executive Politics in Times of Crisis*, edited by Martin Lodge and K. Wegrich, 179–96. New York, NY: Palgrave Macmillan.

———. 2010. "Organizing for Effective Emergency Management: Lessons from Research." *Australian Journal of Public Administration* 69 (4): 357–71.

Brudney, Jeffrey and Beth Gazley. 2009. "Planning to Be Prepared: An Empirical Examination of the Role of Voluntary Organizations in County Government Emergency Planning." *Public Performance and Management Review* 32 (3): 372–99.

Bryden, Alen and Marina Caparini, eds. 2006. *Private Actors and Security Governance*. Münster: LIT Verlag.

Bryson, John and Barbara Crosby. 2008. "Failing Into Cross-Sector Collaboration Successfully." In *Big Ideas in Collaborative Public Management*, edited by L. Blomgren Bingham and R. O'Leary, 55–78. New York, NY: M.E. Sharpe.

Buzan, Barry. 2008. *People, States and Fear: An Agenda for International Security Studies in the Post-Cold War Era*. Colchester: ECPR Press.

Comfort, Louise, Arjen Boin, and Chris Demchak. 2010. *Designing Resilience: Preparing for Extreme Events*. Pittsburgh, PA: University of Pittsburgh Press.

Demiroz, Faith and Qian Hu. 2014. "The Role of Nonprofits and Civil Society in Post-Disaster Recovery and Development." In *Disaster and Development*, edited by Naim Kapucu and Tom Liou, 317–30. London: Springer International Publishing.

Drabek, Thomas. 2007. "Community Processes: Coordination." In *Handbook of Disaster Research*, edited by H. Rodriguez, E. Quarantelli, and R. Dynes, 217–33. New York, NY: Springer.

———. 1987. "The Professional Emergency Manager: Structures and Strategies for Success." In *Program on Environment and Behavior Manograph*, Vol. 44. Boulder, CO: University of Colorado, Institute of Behavioral Science.

Drabek, Thomas and David McEntire. 2002. "Emergent Phenomena and Multiorganizational Coordination in Disasters: Lessons from the Research Literature." *International Journal of Mass Emergencies and Disasters* 20: 197–224.

Dynes, Russell. 1978. "Interorganizational Relations in Communities Under Stress." In *Disasters: Theory and Research*, edited by E.L. Quarantelli, 50–64. London: Sage Publications.

Farazmand, Ali. 2007. "Learning from the Katrina Crisis: A Global and International Perspective With Implications for Future Crisis Management." *Public Administration Review* 67 (1): 149–59.

Fischer, Manuel and Philip Leifeld. 2015. "Policy Forums: Why Do They Exist and What Are They Good For?" *Policy Sciences* 48 (3): 363–82.

Galaz, Victor, Jonas Tallberg, Arjen Boin, Claudia Ituarte-Lima, Ellen Hey, Per Olsson, and Frances Westley. 2017. "Global Governance Dimensions of Globally Networked Risks: The State of the Art in Social Science Research." *Risk, Hazards and Crisis in Public Policy* 8 (1): 4–27.

Gillespie, David. 1991. "Coordinating Community Resources." In *Emergency Management: Principles and Practice for Local Government*, edited by Thomas Drabek and Gerard Hoetmer, 55–78. Washington DC: International City Management Association.

Gillespie, David and Richard Colignon. 1993. "Structural Change in Disaster Preparedness Networks." *International Journal of Mass Emergencies and Disasters* 11 (2): 143–62.

Gray, Barbara. 1989. *Collaborating: Finding Common Ground for Multiparty Problems*. San Francisco, CA: Jossey-Bass Publishers.

Kapucu, Naim. 2005. "Interorganizational Coordination in Dynamic Context: Networks in Emergency Response Management." *Connections* 26 (2): 33–48.

Kapucu, Naim, Tolga Arslan, and Fatih Demiroz. 2010. "Collaborative Emergency Management and National Emergency Management Network." *Disaster Prevention and Management* 19 (4): 452–68.

Kapucu, N., Qian Hu, and Sana Khosa. 2014. "The State of Network Research in Public Administration." *Administration & Society* 49 (8): 1087–120.

Koliba, Christopher, Russell Mills and Asim Zia. 2011. "Accountability in Governance Networks: An Assessment of Public, Private, and Nonprofit Emergency Management Practices Following Hurricane Katrina." *Public Administration Review* 71 (2): 210–20.

Lemos, Maria and Arun Agrawal. 2009. "Environmental Governance and Political Science." In *Governance for the Environment: New Perspectives*, edited by M. Delmas and O. Young, 69–97. Cambridge: Cambridge University Press.

Lindberg, Helena and Bengt Sundelius. 2012. "Whole of Society Disaster Resilience: The Swedish Way." In *McGraw-Hill Homeland Security Handbook*, 2nd ed., edited by D. Kamien, 1295–319. New York, NY: McGraw-Hill.

Lubell, Mark. 2013. "Governing Institutional Complexity: The Ecology of Games Framework." *Policy Studies Journal* 41 (3): 537–59.

McGuire, Michael, Jeffrey Brudney, and Beth Gazley. 2010. "The 'New Emergency Management': Applying the Lessons from Collaborative Governance to Twenty-First-Century Emergency Planning." In *The Future of Public Administration Around the World*, edited by R. O'Leary, D. Van Slyke, and S. Kim, 117–28. Washington, DC: Georgetown University Press.

Mendonça, David, Theresa Jefferson, and John Harrald. 2007. "Collaborative Adhocracies and Mixed-and-Match Technologies in Emergency Management." *Communications of the ACM* 50 (3): 45–49.

Næss, Lars Otto, Guri Bang, Siri Eriksen, and Jonas Vevatne. 2005. "Institutional Adaptation to Climate Change: Flood Responses at the Municipal Level in Norway." *Global Environmental Change* 15 (2): 125–38.

Nohrstedt, Daniel. 2016. "Explaining Mobilization and Performance of Collaborations in Routine Emergency Management." *Administration & Society* 48 (2): 135–62.

Nohrstedt, Daniel and Örjan Bodin. 2014. "Evolutionary Dynamics of Crisis Preparedness Collaboration: Resources, Turbulence and Network Change in Swedish Municipalities." *Risk, Hazards, and Crisis in Public Policy* 5 (2): 134–55.

Nohrstedt, Daniel, Fredrik Bynander, Charles Parker, and Paul 't Hart. 2018. "Managing Crises Collaboratively: Prospects and Problems-A Systematic Literature Review." *Perspectives on Public Management and Governance* 1 (4): 257–71.

O'Leary, Rosemary and Lisa Bingham, eds. 2009. *The Collaborative Public Manager*. Washington, DC: Georgetown University Press.

O'Leary, Rosemary and Nidhi Vij. 2012. "Collaborative Public Management: Where We Have Been and Where We Are Going." *American Review of Public Administration* 42 (5): 507–22.

Patton, Ann. 2007. "Collaborative Emergency Management." In *Emergency Management: Principles and Practice for Local Government*, edited by W. Waugh and K. Tierney, 71–84. Washington, DC: ICMA.

Perry, Ronald and Michael Lindell. 2003. "Preparedness for Emergency Response: Guidelines for the Emergency Planning Process." *Disasters* 27 (4): 336–50.

Quarantelli, Enrico. 1966. "Organization Under Stress." In *Symposium on Emergency Operations*, edited by R. Brictson, 3–19. Santa Monica, CA: The RAND Corporation.

Simo, Gloria and Angela Bies. 2007. "The Role of Nonprofits in Disaster Response: An Expanded Model of Cross-Sector Collaboration." *Public Administration Review* 67: 125–42.

Smith, Keith. 2013. *Environmental Hazards: Assessing Risk and Reducing Disaster*. 6th ed. New York, NY: Routledge.

't Hart, Paul and Arjen Boin. 2001. "Between Crisis and Normalcy: The Long Shadow of Post-Crisis Politics." In *Managing Crises: Threats, Dilemmas, Opportunities*, edited by U. Rosenthal, A. Boin, and L. Comfort, 28–46. Springfield, IL: Charles C. Thomas Publisher.

't Hart, Paul and Bengt Sundelius. 2013. "Crisis Management Revisited: An Agenda for Research, Training and Capacity Building Within Europe." *Cooperation and Conflict* 48 (3): 444–61.

Thomalla, Frank, Tom Downing, Erika Spangler-Siegfried, Guoyi Han, and Johan Rockström. 2006. "Reducing Hazard Vulnerability: Towards a Common Approach Between Disaster Risk Reduction and Climate Adaptation." *Disasters* 30 (1): 39–48.

Waugh, William and Gregory Streib. 2006. "Collaboration and Leadership for Effective Emergency Management." *Public Administration Review* 66: 131–40.

Chapter 2

Upscaling Collaborative Crisis Management

A Comparison of Wildfire Responder Networks in Canada and Sweden

Daniel Nohrstedt, Julia Baird, Örjan Bodin, Ryan Plummer and Robert Summers

Introduction

Crisis management involves making strategic decisions about what actors should be involved in efforts to mitigate harm and restore order, as well as clarifying their mandates and responsibilities. These decisions are relatively unproblematic in cases where the scope of the crisis is relatively predictable, which often is not the case. Rather, many crises feed uncertainty about the appropriate scope of the response organization and ways to achieve effective collaboration among diverse stakeholders. This begs the question of how collaborative crisis management is organized to support collaboration among multiple stakeholders, which is the focus of this chapter.

Most countries have emergency response systems that seek to enable flexibility to match a broad range of risks, crises, and hazards (the "all-hazards approach"). In these systems, complex emergencies – such as major wildfires – will initially be managed by local organizations, yet at some point responsibility and capacity for organizing the emergency response needs to be "scaled up" to a larger organizational setting. However, the process of up-scaling brings challenges concerning appropriate organizational forms and distribution of responsibility.

In this chapter, we report results from a series of interviews[1] with managers involved in the response to two major wildfires: in Västmanland, Sweden in 2014, and Fort McMurray, Alberta, Canada in 2016. We seek to answer three empirical questions:

1. What was the formal process for upscaling the crisis response organization?
2. How did the process of upscaling play out in practice?
3. How did the actors perceive the performance of the collaborative crisis responder network?

The analysis is positioned in relation to the different designs of the emergency response system in Canada (greater centralization) and Sweden (less centralization), respectively. We discuss whether and how these institutional preconditions may shape strategic decisions about crisis response organizations supporting collaboration.

Our analysis sheds light on the tension between diversity and coordination. Complex crisis events raise the need to bring together individuals with different responsibilities, resources, skills, and knowledge that exchange information in a collaborative fashion (Waugh and Streib 2006). While such interactions benefit from preexisting relationships (e.g., established through joint training and preparedness activities), oftentimes crisis responder networks are more *ad hoc* – particularly in the context of unprecedented events

(Mendonca, Jefferson, and Harrald 2007). Collaborative crisis management thus brings significant costs associated with developing and maintaining relationships among actors from different organizations with different cultures, responsibilities, and working methods. Research illustrates the difficulties involved with overcoming these transaction costs during normal conditions and obviously the challenges are even greater in the midst of a crisis when there is limited time to locate, cultivate, and maintain interpersonal contacts (cf. Schneider et al. 2003).

We discuss interactions between institutional preconditions, the dynamic nature of crisis events, and strategic decisions related to the establishment and evolution of joint crisis response organizations. Prior research pays limited attention to the dynamic nature of crisis responder networks; that is, how they evolve and change through time (Nohrstedt and Bodin 2014). Hereby, our study sheds light on how rapidly evolving crisis events influence decisions about crisis responder organizations and how these organizations are perceived by the actors involved in the response.

Canada: The 2016 Fort McMurray Wildfire

On May 1, 2016, a fire was identified by a provincial fire crew member 7 km from the community of Fort McMurray in northern Alberta, Canada. Fort McMurray is an urban service area with a population of approximately 67,000 (Statistics Canada 2017). It is situated in a forested region of the province (in the Regional Municipality of Wood Buffalo) and many of its inhabitants work in the oil and gas industry, which is prevalent in the region. The fire increased in intensity and severity very quickly – called "The Beast" by the municipal fire chief and firefighters (Markusoff, Macdonald, and Gillis 2016) – and a mandatory evacuation of the majority of the community and some surrounding areas, approximately 88,000 people (KPMG 2017), occurred on May 3. Despite the quick escalation and little warning prior to the evacuation notice, no deaths were attributed to the fire itself. The fire, at its height, spanned more than 500,000 hectares and destroyed more than 2,400 structures, with an anticipated $9 billion in damage (KPMG 2017). Several residents lost their homes and even more were displaced for a minimum of one month, even if approximately half of the evacuees returned in early June (The Globe and Mail 2017).

Formal Process of Upscaling

In Canada, the authority for emergency management response rests with the lowest level of government appropriate. This is usually the local (i.e., municipal) level, except in circumstances where assets or resources are held by the provincial or federal governments. As emergencies escalate in severity, other levels of government become involved through a formal process of declarations of emergency and upon request from other governments.

In the province of Alberta, the *Emergency Management Act* (2000) provides authority for municipalities to create bylaws for emergency management and also sets out the role of the provincial agency responsible for emergency management (Alberta Emergency Management Agency, or AEMA) as well as other actors managing emergencies at the municipal and provincial levels. In Alberta, there are four operational levels for emergency management organization between the local and provincial governmental bodies (Government of Alberta 2016):

> *Routine:* no incident or a low-level incident that is being managed at the local level. The provincial government is briefed on any incidents by field staff or emergency responders and remains aware of any potential for escalation.

Augmented: an incident has occurred or may occur that has the potential to disrupt community functioning. The provincial government makes determinations, based on reports provided at least once per day, about whether further escalation is needed.

Mandatory key provincial government coordination: a significant incident is about to occur or has occurred that will disrupt community functioning. The provincial government formally coordinates a response and reports are provided at least twice a day, and incident action plans are prepared and modified as needed. Relevant ministries are brought into the emergency response.

Mandatory full provincial government coordination: a very significant event is causing full disruption of a community. Emergency responders are deployed from all levels of government (federal, provincial, municipal) and incident action plans are prepared and modified as needed with reports provided at least three times per day. All ministries are engaged in the emergency response. The provincial government holds formal authority at level 4.

The province may request the assistance of the federal government, if required. As the operational levels increase, more actors become involved in the response and reporting becomes more frequent.

Municipal and provincial responses to wildfires operate under the Incident Command System (ICS) (MNP 2017). It is a system that unifies organizations under a single chain of command, with the intention to simplify reporting and command structures to ensure common understanding of the situation and an efficient and effective response (MNP 2017).

At the municipal level in Fort McMurray, the regional emergency operations center (REOC) operates as required, when an emergency occurs, staffed by municipal employees. A provincial operations center (POC), tasked with serving as a communication and response coordination center, is located in the capital city of Edmonton and is staffed 24/7 (AEMA 2017). When the POC is activated, as the operational level increases, it becomes staffed by all ministries and other relevant organizations (e.g., industry, nongovernmental organizations, city emergency management representatives, and emergency social services) (Respondent 2). Close and frequent interaction between the REOC and the POC remains critical during the escalation of the operational level and throughout the emergency response.

Upscaling in Practice

The Regional Municipality of Wood Buffalo (within which Fort McMurray is located) began organizing the emergency response upon identification of the wildfire on May 1 by declaring a State of Local Emergency (KPMG 2017) and continued to coordinate and implement response measures from their REOC (which had to be moved several times), including the evacuation (MNP 2017). The provincial government, upon learning of the wildfire on May 1, quickly made the decision to escalate their operational level to 2, which can be made by the Director of Central Operations and results in a few extra people in the POC and heightened awareness (Respondent 1). The subsequent decisions to escalate the operational level to 3 and then 4 on Wednesday, May 3, occurred in a matter of hours and were authorized by ministerial orders. This was all a matter of formal protocols in place and occurred accordingly.

Upscaling the response became difficult in terms of how authority was distributed between the municipal and provincial levels as the operational level escalated. While municipalities are tasked with managing emergencies in their jurisdiction, they also may request assistance from the province when needed. Those in the POC found it difficult to navigate this phase where, from their perspective, the municipality needed help but was not requesting it:

> It's not right for us to just go and push our way in and say we're going to fix this; you're not going to do it. You can't handle this. We have to wait for them to ask. In this case . . . we kind of had to push our way in . . . We started pushing things towards them. They hadn't asked for help yet.
>
> (Respondent 1)

The delegation of authority in relation to the Provincial State of Emergency was a particular challenge. One provincial actor explained,

> What we did was we delegated a lot of the powers, a lot of the authority to them [the municipality]. That was political to a degree because we don't want it to be seen that the province is coming in and taking over. We're working together. That I agree with too. But when we delegated some of those authorities down, we were not necessarily very clear.
>
> (Respondent 2)

This was confirmed in a post-incident assessment report, which recommended greater clarity around the delegation of authority (KPMG 2017).

The province dispatched Can Task Force 2 (a mobile unit of approximately 200 volunteers that provides assistance and resources in emergency situations) to Fort McMurray as one of their initial efforts to assist the municipality in terms of capacity and to "ground truth," or provide perspective that is objective for the province (Respondent 2). However, the municipality did not initially appreciate the presence of the Task Force (Respondent 3), and one provincial actor noted that this was likely because of a lack of communication with the Task Force regarding its specific role, and the Task Force was also unsure of exactly what it should be doing (Respondent 2).

A provincial representative was dispatched shortly thereafter to Fort McMurray to assist the municipality and to facilitate collaboration between the municipality, Can Task Force 2, and the province. He was given the purview to take over regional operations if needed and stated that he was unsure of what situation he would be faced with when he arrived. He found his job difficult initially on two fronts. First, to ensure information was flowing to the province in a timely way:

> When folks are on the ground, and things are really, really hectic, it's hard to take the time to even make the phone call to say, 'Here's what's happening.' So you're striking this – well, you're trying to strike a balance of the information that comes in, how accurate is it? Is it truly verified or verifiable? And then you've got to package that to move it along to the executive and senior leadership of the government.
>
> (Respondent 2)

Second, to alleviate tensions between the Task Force and the municipality and facilitate collaboration between them: He stated that his role for the first 48 hours was to build bridges and explain the situation and the implications of calling a Provincial State of Emergency. He explained the nuances of this role, where the province technically held authority,

> but we made sure that it was theirs, and with . . . all the support that came in, it was 'we're here to help you'. And that took about four days for most of them to understand, okay, this is a good thing.
>
> (Respondent 3)

Reflecting on the upscaling process, a provincial government actor noted that it requires some "cobbling together" of people to create the units required for the Incident Command System used by the province in Provincial States of Emergency because it is rarely used. However, he also noted that, in general, it worked extremely well and attributed it to "the processes that we use, the communications, the collaboration, the training that was done prior to, the networking that was done to build those relationships of trust all happened. That set the conditions for that success" (Respondent 2).

Responder Network Performance

The necessity of the province's assistance, at what point in time it was needed, and the nature of that assistance were all perceived differently by the municipality versus the province. The municipality, in the first few days, believed it could manage the emergency response on its own:

> When we did declare it a Provincial State of Emergency, it was chaotic for them [the municipality]. He [the Director] was still trying to manage it. The man had no sleep, he's exhausted, and he's been up for hours. It's his and he's determined he's going to fix it on his own. He doesn't need our help.
>
> (Respondent 1)

The province, on the other hand, believed that the nature of the fire warranted provincial assistance and took action:

> We had to put our arm around him and say you know what, you actually need some sleep, you need some rest, you can come back. I'm telling you it's not in your best interest or the community's best interest to do this.
>
> (Respondent 1)

Ultimately, the province's belief that the emergency response effort was not sufficient led it to become engaged in it. The functionality of the response network was compromised initially due to a lack of acknowledgement of the need for the network to extend to other actors outside the REOC and then by the tensions between the province's resources shared with the municipality (Can Task Force 2 and provincial support). However, the ability of the provincial actor dispatched to Fort McMurray to facilitate understanding of the situation, the available resources, and available support and to do so in a manner that did not threaten the autonomy of the municipality appeared to be key to upscaling success over time.

As the province became involved of its own volition, tensions were evident between the municipal and provincial actors. The dispatch of Can Task Force 2 resulted in substantial tension between it and the municipality. According to one provincial actor,

> I think part of it was because the help had not necessarily been – the context for the help was not necessarily understood by him [the Director]. And I would argue that that's probably more attributable to him being fatigued and not taking things in. So he seemed to take this professional organization coming in to create structure and given them some form – I think he initially took great offense at this, as did a number of his key subordinates.
>
> (Respondent 3)

Another provincial actor reflected on the province's approach to the state of emergency, how authority was delegated, and the role of collaboration in emergency response: "You've got to work together, you've got to be collaborative, but in response, there were certain things where you don't have time to do that" (Respondent 2). Ultimately, however, those in the REOC did acknowledge their fatigue and created space for provincial actors to step in (MNP 2017).

Communication was a major hurdle and theme in terms of the process of upscaling. There was a lack of communication at first from the municipality to the province regarding its needs and situational awareness. Once the province declared the Provincial State of Emergency, communication again broke down between the municipality and the province related to how authority was to be delegated and the roles of the provincial and federal assets and actors (e.g., Can Task Force 2) in the emergency response. One respondent summed this challenge up the following way: "It was chaotic. I'd say it went well but it was still chaotic. Every emergency I've ever been in, every emergency, one of the areas of growth and development is always communication" (Respondent 1).

Sweden: The 2014 Västmanland Wildfire

The Västmanland wildfire started on July 31, 2014, on the border between Sala municipality and Surahammar municipality, during ground preparation work in a cutover area. The fire escalated quickly and within a week it covered an area of approximately 15,000 hectares covering four municipalities: Sala, Surahammar, Norberg, and Fagersta. Over 1,000 people were evacuated, and another 4,500 residents were considered for evacuation as the fire threatened the city of Norberg, with a population of 7,000 people. The fire was initially dealt with by local rescue services in accordance with the "principle of responsibility," which prescribes that actors that are responsible for activities under normal circumstances maintain that responsibility – including initiating collaboration – during major crises. As the wildfire continued to spread, rescue service leaders realized that the local organizational structure was insufficient to effectively contain the situation. As a result, a decision was made on August 5 to shift the responsibility for the crisis response operation from the municipalities to the County Administrative Board of Västmanland (regional level). Following an escalating need for coordination, an *ad hoc* "headquarters" organization was established (located in the community of Ramnäs in Surahammar municipality), which was modeled and based on experiences from crisis simulation exercises to coordinate the crisis response among multiple organizations including the municipalities (Asp et al. 2015).

Formal Process of Upscaling

In Sweden, responsibility for civil emergency planning, including responding to major crises and emergencies, resides in those organizations that are responsible for any given activity during "normal" conditions. This is the "principle of responsibility," which prescribes responsibility for minimizing risk and impacts of major emergencies, societal preparedness, and coordination across sectors and areas of responsibility. Organizations at the local, regional, and national levels are formally responsible for civil emergency planning within their functional and geographical domain including taking action to facilitate and support collaboration across sectors and levels of authority.

In 2014, crisis management at the national level in Sweden was regulated by the *Crisis Preparedness Act*, which prescribed that any government agency that would be affected by a crisis should retain capacity to collaborate with other organizations. Thus, in practice

Sweden does not apply any by-laws for crisis management but relies on ordinary laws for managing crises.

At the local level, the municipality executive board is the highest civilian authority responsible for crisis management, supported by the County Administrative Board, which coordinates crisis preparedness activities at the regional level. The formal process for shifting responsibility for large-scale crisis management operations is regulated by the *Civil Protection Act*, which contains provisions for placing the responsibility for emergency management on a County Administrative Board or some other government agency in situations when the magnitude of the event outstrips the coping capacity of the local actors. In those cases, the County Administrative Board (or some other government agency) becomes formally responsible for appointing the incident commander.

In Sweden the formal structure for orchestrating inter-organizational coordination and collaboration is regulated through regional agreements. This is partially a consequence of Sweden's constitutional structure that gives considerable autonomy to the municipalities, which in turn have developed different types of institutional forums to support collaboration (Nohrstedt 2018). The county of Västmanland has in place a regional forum called "USAM," which is an arrangement based on a formal agreement among 18 organizations (including municipalities, government agencies, and regional authorities and associations) for facilitating collaboration during major crises. USAM does not take over the responsibilities of the member organizations but provides a forum to enhance communication and coordination (e.g., by supporting situation awareness), which in practice takes place through a coordination group of regional and national level organizations; this group is summoned when one of the member organizations calls for it.

Upscaling in Practice

Although the fire was not under control during the first day, rescue services representatives believed that the fire did not pose a threat to nearby communities. During the second day (August 1) the response (focusing primarily on fire extinction) was organized in two geographical areas and although contacts were taken between regional and local authorities, the response was primarily limited to coordination between the rescue services (with some logistical support from the Swedish Armed Forces). The County Administrative Board perceived a need to summon a meeting with the USAM, but the rescue services disagreed. In the meantime, the trajectory of the fire was becoming increasingly uncertain.

Since USAM was not summoned, the situation was handled through informal contacts within the region and between the regional and the local levels. These contacts intensified during the third and fourth day (August 2 and 3). On day four, several decisions were made that shaped the structure of the crisis responder organization. First, by 3:00 pm on August 3, the incident commander requested the support from the County Administrative Board to help coordinate information to the general public. The request was followed by a decision by the county governor to launch a regional crisis management organization, which essentially was staffed by five individuals with key functions in the County Administrative Board. Second, following a request from the incident commander a decision was made about 3:00 pm on August 3 to summon the USAM to share information and discuss situation awareness, which was unclear at the meeting. Efforts to develop a regional common operational picture were further delayed by the fact that the municipalities did not supply their operational pictures. Third, as the incident operation center was located too close to the wildfire, the incident commander made a decision to move the location to a hotel in Ramnäs.

August 4 was described as "Hellish Monday" following the rapid escalation of the fire. USAM had three additional meetings that day to agree on a strategy for coordinating information. As the city of Norberg was under urgent threat of evacuation, it was decided during USAM's final meeting in the evening to expand the incident operations center in Ramnäs with functions for information and evacuation. It was also decided to immediately summon the staff in Ramnäs. At this point, the fire had spread across four municipalities and the local rescue services no longer had the resources to contain the fire. At the staff meeting, the incident commanders therefore requested that the responsibility for local rescue services should be taken over by the County Administrative Board. After the decision was made, Lars-Göran Uddholm, fire chief from Södertörn, was appointed new incident commander and charged to organize the incident operations center in Ramnäs. In turn, decisions were made to place representatives from the County Administrative Board in the Ramnäs headquarters.

Based on the insight that the situation had escalated "from a wildfire to a societal crisis," steps were taken to ensure that the headquarters were properly organized and staffed to support swift decision making and transparency. One of the first steps was to form a coordination unit within the headquarters. Initially, however, the headquarters were relatively disorganized and needed a more structured organization. For example, representatives from several government authorities were present in the headquarters but most activities still focused on fire extinction. It was also unclear what responsibility the municipalities had, and technological support systems were lacking. To address these problems, a decision was made to structure the headquarters organization into six functions – leadership support, planning, voluntary groups, information, personnel, and incident command – each with a staff and an appointed leader.

The Ramnäs headquarters was essentially an *ad hoc* organization formed as the result of trial and error. Initially, in the startup phase it was perceived as a welcome contribution to the crisis response. In this regard, the timing for setting up the headquarters was essential; at the time, most of the staff was exhausted and there was a shortage of ideas on how to cope with the escalating wildfire. Therefore, the startup of the headquarters was perceived as a fresh start of the crisis response.

Responder Network Performance

One crucial step in the crisis response was to upscale the local operation involving several municipalities to a more coordinated regional response. Here it seems that different actors had different views of the necessity of upscaling. One example involves the issue of whether or not to summon USAM to enhance coordination. As described earlier, the decision to activate USAM or not was discussed during the initial phase of the wildfire. Regional authorities repeatedly passed on the request to the rescue services, who responded that a meeting through USAM was not necessary. Part of the explanation as to why USAM was not initially summoned, it seems, is that different actors had different understandings of the need for coordination. Some regional actors had the view that the rescue services did not ask for any help because they view a wildfire as something that they should be able to cope with without external support. Also, there was a concern among some regional actors that the rescue services would disapprove if USAM was summoned without them asking for it, which would risk undermining collaboration (Asp et al. 2015, 24).

A related issue is what role and responsibility the County Administrative Board actually had during the response and within the crisis responder network. One regional manager (Respondent 4) testified that the role of the County Administrative Board was clear:

"Our role is to coordinate and collaborate. It [our instruction] says that we shall promote necessary collaboration and I think that we do this through USAM." A local manager (Respondent 5) representing one of the affected municipalities had a different view: "It felt like we lost the idea behind USAM. The idea is that USAM is summoned when something happens but this did not happen. . . . We actually did not see our own County Administrative Board." These differences in opinion might be partially explained by the *ad hoc* nature of the headquarters organization. In fact, there were some different views within the County Administrative Board concerning the status of the Ramnäs headquarters; whereas some individuals saw it as part of the County Administrative Board and headed by the county governor, others saw it as an independent organization (Asp et al. 2015, 37).

Some tensions arose between some of the local and regional actors concerning the operation of the Ramnäs headquarters. Some evidence suggests that frictions occurred due to differences in background and experience. One local manager (Respondent 6) argued that

> it was quite common that people did not understand each other and we tried to assist in communication. I have never experienced a situation like this where wires got crossed at this level. People misunderstood and misinterpreted things and sometimes you thought it was even intentional.

This view can be contrasted with a regional manager (Respondent 4) who described the headquarters in more positive terms: "It was a way to create the common operational picture and contacts. It was very easy to talk to people because they were in the same location." Similarly, another local manager (Respondent 7) argued that "we would not have performed as well without the Ramnäs headquarters."

Some actors expressed some discontent about the process of obtaining situation awareness (common operational picture, hereafter COP). It can be noted that the process of developing a COP was delayed initially due to the relatively chaotic situation and the lack of a clear structure to coordinate the flow of information within the headquarters and between the headquarters and the municipalities. In addition, the quality of the COPs was undermined by the fact that the rescue services did not provide any information in addition to what was shared during the headquarters briefings (Respondent 7). Another problem, it seems, was the different types of COPs that were produced and disseminated to different recipients, including the news media, landowners, and the Government Offices (Asp et al. 2015). One local manager asserted that the COPs suffered from several additional problems. For example, it was difficult to provide updated information about the trajectory of the fire. The COPs sometimes came in with a 12–15-hour time lag, so updated information was lacking. In addition, the COPs produced in the headquarters often conflicted with the local COPs, which created some confusion (Respondent 5 and 6).

The evidence reviewed here suggests that some municipality representatives in the Ramnäs headquarters called into question the way the relationship between the headquarters and the municipalities was set up. One local manager (Respondent 6) argued that: "We had individuals in Ramnäs but they got absorbed by the work there. Thereby, in practice we lost our coordination staff." A related aspect concerned the flow of information between the municipalities and the headquarters, which appears to have led to some disagreements between the municipalities and the County Administrative Board. While the municipalities perceived that they should report to the headquarters, the County Administrative Board suggested that they should also report back to their municipality (Respondent 5). This issue, it seems, may partially be explained by different perceptions regarding what role individuals representing the municipalities should have in the headquarters organization. One local manager (Respondent 5) that worked in the headquarters perceived that this role was very unclear in the early stages and that the responsibilities shifted from one day to the next. Similarly, one regional manager (Respondent 4) recognized that the responsibility and goals of the individuals that staffed the headquarters should have been more clearly defined.

Comparative Analysis

What are the main differences and similarities between the two cases regarding the dynamics of organizational upscaling? One contrast between the two cases is that although civil emergencies in both countries are dealt with at the lowest level possible, the process of upscaling is different from a regulatory perspective. In Canada, higher levels of government (province, federal) become involved in circumstances where assets or resources are held by the provincial or federal governments or when a state of emergency is declared. Also, in the Alberta provincial system, efforts to escalate crisis response operations follow four pre-defined levels of severity, which regulate distribution of responsibility between local and provincial governmental bodies. Within this system, municipalities manage emergencies within their jurisdiction but can also request assistance from the province. By contrast, the process is more informal in Sweden where the principle of responsibility provides a mandate to actors at all levels to coordinate with other organizations. Unlike Canada, the Swedish system does not include the possibility to declare a state of emergency as a means to scale up the responsibility for crisis responder operations to higher administrative levels. Whereas organizations at the local, regional, and national levels have responsibility to maintain proper resources to ensure coordination, in practice there is no template (equivalent to Alberta's operational levels) for escalating emergency management operations.

Although the basic design of the crisis management system is fundamentally different, one of our key findings is that in practice the wildfire response led to similar managerial challenges. In both cases, there was considerable uncertainty and partially also different views among the actors about the "ripe moment" for upscaling. Both cases are strikingly similar in terms of how the relationship between the regional and local levels played out in practice. In both Canada and Sweden, the regional actors (POC in Canada and the County Administrative Board in Sweden) were under the impression that the local authorities did not have sufficient resources to cope with the escalating wildfires and were also a bit frustrated by the fact that the local actors did not ask for assistance.

These experiences suggest that, regardless of the design of the crisis management system, the issue of when to upscale the crisis responder organization becomes a challenge. In both cases, this decision depended on a more or less formal request from the local actors to call for support from higher levels. Our evidence suggests that in practice, actors from the local and regional level organizations may have different views of when such upscaling is justified and needed, which in turn can feed frustration and, in the worst case, delay coordination and resource mobilization. In Sweden, these disagreements can partially be traced back to organizational cultures. One interviewee (regional level manager) expressed the view that the rescue services never ask for external support and others testified that they did not actually believe that the County Administrative Board would formally take over the crisis response operation. These examples corroborate the insight that organizations are likely to interpret crises differently depending on their mandates and areas of responsibility, which in turn bring substantial transaction costs that potentially constrain coordinated action.

Another interesting insight from the Canadian case is that the dynamics of upscaling can become subject to political risk assessments, which may inhibit coordination. During the Fort McMurray wildfire, the POC faced a delicate balancing act between providing support to the municipality without violating its autonomy. Whether the risk of violating the autonomy of the municipality was real or imminent is hard to say based on the available evidence, but, regardless, it was a factor that appeared to create some coordination problems. Specifically, in order to avoid overrunning the municipalities by violating their autonomy the regional actors delegated authority in that they did not "take over" the response but rather worked with the municipality, asking where specifically they needed extra support and capacity to maintain the image of the crisis response operation as essentially collaborative. The regional actors sought to maintain this image even after calling a Provincial State of Emergency, which technically gives authority to the provincial level and where this was formally delegated to the municipality. One insight that emerges from these observations is that hierarchically superior organizations should be careful not to violate the autonomy of lower level organizations in order to maintain viable relationships to promote inter-governmental collaboration.

The two cases illustrate the role of communication challenges, inter-governmental tensions, and the key role that individual "network brokers" play in overcoming coordination problems. Regarding communication challenges, the evidence reviewed here demonstrate the difficulties associated with reconciling problem perceptions across governmental levels. In both cases, the actors faced the challenge of how to ensure the proper exchange of information between the local and the regional levels. Part of the problem was the intensity of the situation at the local level, where the actors struggled to keep pace with the rapidly escalating wildfires. One contrast between the two cases is what solutions were promoted to address communication issues across levels. In the Canadian case, one provincial representative was sent to Fort McMurray to assist the municipality and to facilitate collaboration between the municipality and the province. Hence, the regional level placed staff on site in the municipality to ensure that information was transferred back to the provincial level. In contrast, in the Swedish case the municipalities dispatched staff in the headquarters organization to fill the need for personnel in the headquarters, whereas regional authorities had no staff on the ground in the municipalities.

Our evidence suggests that similar tensions occurred in the two cases between actors at the regional and local levels. In Sweden, there were some disagreements concerning the role that USAM should play in the response and the way that information was communicated between the Ramnäs headquarters and the municipalities. Similarly, in Canada, some tensions arose between the provincial and the local actors following the dispatch of Can Task Force 2. Nevertheless, it is important to note that despite these disagreements, most actors seemed to agree that the crisis responder networks performed well overall.

Several interviewees, in both cases, stressed the importance of preexisting relationships as a resource that facilitated collaboration, which is a recurrent finding in the literature on collaborative crisis management (Boin and 't Hart 2010; Nohrstedt et al. 2018). In the Canadian case, for instance, it was challenging to set up the units that were required within the framework of the Incident Command System. This process, however, was eventually facilitated by personal relationships that had been established prior to the wildfire through joint training, which in turn promoted trust among the actors. Such relationships also played an important role in the Swedish case, which also illustrates the different types of networks that influence collaborative crisis management (Kapucu and Hu 2016). On the one hand, there are *inter-organizational* networks based on familiarity with other organizations, their functions, capacities, and roles within the crisis management system (Respondent 4). Through these networks, several individuals are closely acquainted with other organizations but not necessarily with particular individuals, which facilitate collaboration. On the other hand, there are *interpersonal* networks that are based on close personal ties between individuals. Such close relationships facilitated communication and swift decision making during the Västmanland wildfire (Respondent 6; Asp 2015, 25). However, in contrast to these experiences, other individuals mentioned that they did not have access to preexisting relationships, which in turn raised a need for urgent action to build new relationships. For example, one interviewee (Respondent 2) from Canada estimated that approximately 30% of the individuals involved in the response to the Fort McMurray wildfire were inexperienced and required mentoring and hands-on training.

Finally, our analysis corroborates the essential role of individual "network brokers" that ease collaboration between other actors. In theory, network brokers are individuals that connect other individuals that would otherwise be disconnected (Berardo 2009). In the Canadian case, the aforementioned dispatch of a provincial representative in Fort McMurray can be seen as an effort to establish a brokerage function. The purpose was partially to facilitate collaboration between the local and provincial organizations, and the representative testified he spent a lot of time creating connections between various individuals. In Sweden, a similar challenge related to collaboration between the local and regional levels occurred in relation to the formation of the headquarters organization in Ramnäs. When the headquarters organization took form, the municipalities sent staff members to the headquarters to relay information between the municipalities and the headquarters. In retrospect, this can be seen as an attempt to create different brokerage positions to facilitate information sharing between the headquarters and the municipalities. However, there was considerable uncertainty among all actors concerning what role these local representatives actually had and in practice their presence in the headquarters did not enhance the exchange of information (Asp et al. 2015, 38–39). Thus, in practice, these brokering roles did not actually help connect the local level with the headquarters. Quite on the contrary, some municipality representatives saw their presence in the headquarters as a waste of scarce resources.

Conclusion

In this chapter we conduct a comparative case study of organizational upscaling in wildfire responder networks in Sweden and Canada. We conclude with some general observations about organizational upscaling and how it may influence collaborative crisis management in different institutional settings.

First, although crisis management in Canada and Sweden is organized in very different ways, our analysis unveiled similar managerial challenges. Comparison of the two cases suggests that regardless of a formal procedure for organizational upscaling (Canada) or more decentralized responsibility for collaboration (Sweden), actors face similar challenges. We saw examples of actors in both cases that had different views of the timing of when upscaling was deemed necessary, which fed both frustration and uncertainty. Our evidence suggests that differences in perceptions of the severity of the situation and of the sufficiency of local capacities lead to different understandings of the necessity and timing of upscaling. In Sweden, these differences can partially be explained by organizational culture; whereas the local firefighters maintained they had the fire under control, regional level managers with a broader focus on societal security were more eager to scale up the response. Similar challenges were noted in Canada, where the regional operations center was resistant to the province coming in and the province was navigating the authority to take over with the desire to allow the regional municipality to manage the response to the extent feasible.

Second, we show that upscaling will present challenges regardless of how the crisis management system is designed. In Canada, the actors had to spend considerable time and effort to set up the units required for the Incident Command System. Furthermore, they spent considerable time prior to the wildfire in training and building networks across units of the provincial government to enhance preparedness. Similarly, in Sweden, actors working to establish the headquarters organization during the wildfire had to solve a number of problems associated with staffing, organizational structure, communication technology, and leadership. Hence, the process of upscaling brings some level of uncertainty and requires coordination and innovation regardless of the design of the crisis management system.

Third, our analysis confirms insights from the literature concerning collaboration. One insight is that collaboration is needed to tackle several challenges simultaneously. For instance, actors come together to address multiple interconnected tasks related to coordination, communication, and conflict resolution. This corroborates the notion of "multiplex networks," characterized by the coexistence of multiple network forms, including social networks, knowledge networks, communication networks, and inter-organizational networks, that overlap in multiple collaborative activities (Kapucu and Hu 2016; Bodin and Nohrstedt 2016). Furthermore, we make several observations concerning the collaborative skills and qualities that are essential to cope within these complex network structures. Our analysis confirms the essential role of informal interpersonal networks among key individuals for facilitating collaboration. In practice, these networks become conduits for communication and negotiation, which in turn are essential for establishing collaboration between organizations. In both cases, personal relationships were particularly important for facilitating collaboration between local and regional/provincial level organizations.

These insights also underscore the importance of bridging social capital, i.e., connections between individuals to avoid fragmentation and enhance communication between parts of a network that would otherwise be disjoined. These connections, in turn, are enabled by individuals that take on bridging roles by establishing relationships between organizations (Berardo 2014). Both our cases show that this role fell upon certain key individuals who had previously spent considerable time and effort in building trust and negotiating conflicts. Our study is hereby a reminder that interpersonal and managerial skills that facilitate collaboration in general – negotiation, endurance, persistence, conflict resolution – also play a decisive role in facilitating organizational upscaling during disruptive crises.

Note

1. It should be noted that all individuals – in both Canada and Sweden – that were interviewed for this study were granted anonymity. Hence, we assign a number for each respondent and provide as much information as possible about them (e.g., type of organization represented) without disclosing their identity.

References

Alberta Emergency Management Agency (AEMA). 2017. *Provincial Operations Centre (POC)*. www.aema.alberta.ca/provinicial-operations-centre (Accessed 17 April 2017).

Asp, Viktoria, Fredrik Bynander, Pär Daléus, Jenny Deschamps-Berger, Daniel Sandberg, and Erik Schyberg. 2015. *Bara skog som brinner? Utvärdering av krishanteringen under skogsbranden i Västmanland 2014 [Only Trees Burning? The Evaluation of the Crisis Management of the 2014 Västmanland Wildfire]*. Stockholm: CRISMART, Swedish Defense University.

Berardo, Ramiro. 2014. "Bridging and Bonding Social Capital in Two-Mode Collaboration Networks." *Policy Studies Journal* 42 (2): 197–225.

———. 2009. "Processing Complexity in Networks: A Study of Informal Collaboration and Its Effects on Organizational Success." *Policy Studies Journal* 37 (3): 521–39.

Bodin, Örjan and Daniel Nohrstedt. 2016. "Formation and Performance of Collaborative Disaster Management Networks: Evidence from a Swedish Wildfire Response." *Global Environmental Change* 41: 183–94.

Boin, Arjen and Paul 't Hart. 2010. "Organising for Effective Emergency Management: Lessons from Research." *Australian Journal of Public Administration* 69 (4): 357–71.

The Globe and Mail. 2017. "The Fort McMurray Fire: What's Happening Now, and What You've Missed." *The Globe and Mail*. www.theglobeandmail.com/news/alberta/the-fort-mcmurray-disaster-read-the-latest-weekend/article29930041/ (Accessed 17 April 2017).

Government of Alberta. 2016. *Appendix 1-POC Operational Levels and Associated Activities*. Personal communication.

Kapucu, Naim and Qian Hu. 2016. "Understanding Multiplexity of Collaborative Emergency Management Networks." *American Review of Public Administration* 46 (4): 399–417.

KPMG. May 2017. "May 2016 Wood Buffalo Wildfire Post-Incident Assessment Report." *Alberta Emergency Management Agency*. www.alberta.ca/2016-wildfire-review.aspx (Accessed 4 January 2019).

Markusoff, Jason, Nancy Macdonald, and Charlie Gillis. 12 May 2016. "Fort McMurray Fire: The Great Escape." *Maclean's*. www.macleans.ca/fort-mcmurray-fire-the-great-escape/ (Accessed 4 January 2019).

Mendonca, David, Theresa Jefferson, and John Harrald. 2007. "Collaborative Adhocracies and Mix-and-Match Technologies in Emergency Management." *Communications of the ACM* 50 (3): 44–49.

MNP. June 2017. "A Review of the 2016 Horse River Wildfire." *Alberta Agriculture and Forestry*. www.alberta.ca/2016-wildfire-review.aspx (Accessed 4 January 2019).

Nohrstedt, Daniel. 2018. "Networking and Crisis Management Capacity: A Nested Analysis of Local-Level Collaboration in Sweden." *American Review of Public Administration* 48 (3): 232–44. https://journals.sagepub.com/doi/abs/10.1177/0275074016684585

Nohrstedt, Daniel and Örjan Bodin. 2014. "Evolutionary Dynamics of Crisis Preparedness Collaboration: Resources, Turbulence and Network Change in Swedish Municipalities." *Risks, Hazards and Crisis in Public Policy* 5 (2): 134–55.

Nohrstedt, Daniel, Fredrik Bynander, Charles Parker, and Paul 't Hart. 2018. "Managing Crisis Collaboratively: Prospects and Problems-A Systematic Literature Review." *Perspectives on Public Management and Governance* 1 (4): 257–71.

Schneider, Mark, John Scholz, Mark Lubell, Denisa Mindruta, and Matthew Edwardsen. 2003. "Building Consensual Institutions: Networks and the National Estuary Program." *American Journal of Political Science* 47 (1): 143–58.

Statistics Canada. 2017. *Fort McMurray [Population Centre], Alberta and Saskatchewan [Province] (Table): Census Profile: 2016 Census: Statistics Canada Catalogue No. 98-316-X2016001: Ottawa*. Released 8 February 2017. http://www12.statcan.gc.ca/census-recensement/2016/dp-pd/prof/index.cfm?Lang=E (Accessed 17 April 2017).

Waugh, William and Gregory Streib. 2006. "Collaboration and Leadership for Effective Emergency Management." *Public Administration Review* 66 (S1): 131–40.

Chapter 3

Secure Summits

Collaborative Crisis Management Before and During Global Government Conventions

Sanneke Kuipers and Marij Swinkels

Introduction

Anytime world leaders meet, the stakes are high: both in terms of policy outcomes as well as in terms of event security. A trip down memory lane takes us from the streets of Genova in 2001, where massive protests resulted in many injured and one death, to the recent 2017 G20 meeting in Hamburg, when the charming old harbor area turned into a downtown battlefield. Summits simultaneously represent inflammable political controversy and potential global agreement. By nature, international summits attract demonstrators and global media attention for their issues and attempts to influence negotiations between political leaders.

The presence of so many heads of government requires the most extreme security measures which makes summits high security events. Meanwhile, the national host tries to organize a successful conference in a comfortable atmosphere, arrange for the complex logistics of delegates, respect protestors' civil rights and limit the consequences of security operations in terms of mobility and restrictions for its own citizens.

Securing summits is a daunting task where things can go dramatically wrong. Violent protests during previous summits in Prague (IMF Annual Meeting, September 2000), Nice (European Council, December 2000), Gothenburg (EU Council, June 2001), Genoa (G8 Summit, July 2001), Copenhagen (UN Climate Summit, December 2009), and Seoul (Nuclear Security Summit 2012) are cases in point. Despite variation in the previous cases regarding local protest cultures and security approaches, these demonstrations all ended in violent clashes between protestors and police, resulting in hundreds of arrests, use of unprecedented force by police units, and millions of euros in damages caused by vandalism and casualties among the protestors.

As such, summits are potential "crises in the making." Yet not all summits become crises. In this chapter, we argue that much can be learned from collaboration in the crisis preparation phase and its effects on the outcome of summits in terms of security. Incident evaluations after Gothenburg, Nice, Genoa, and Prague in the early 2000s hint at a variety of organizational factors that pertain to crisis preparedness. These include a lack of cooperation between the actors involved, a lack of calibrating responsibilities and mandates, blind spots and hubris on behalf of responsible authorities, and limited (inter)national and inter-organizational learning in preparing for high security events (Cf. Hansén and Hagström 2004; SOU 2002, 122; Wallmann 2006; KAMEDO 2001).

Global summits are examples of collaborative crisis management as they are potentially disruptive events that exceed the capacity of any single organization to manage the security situation alone (see introductory chapter). Hitherto studies on security events such as summits have been confined to the domain of policing, from the perspective of "liminal events" (Boersma 2013) or to the domain of sociology with a focus on protest dynamics in the realm of social movement theory and contentious politics (see, e.g., Tilly and Tarrow 2012). A focus on summits from a crisis management perspective is new, and it can yield important clues on the prevention of and response to violent clashes.

Summits as Crises?

Arranging a secure and smoothly organized summit while respecting civil rights is a balancing act that resembles the many challenges of collaborative crisis management. The authors in the introductory chapter rightly state that crisis collaboration enjoys increasing popularity in scholarly research, but its share in published output is still limited despite its relevance (Kuipers and Welsh 2017). In a context of continuous threats, urgency and conflicting interests, a network (often *ad hoc*) has to provide public safety and reliability of critical infrastructures under conditions of high uncertainty. Summits are latent crises, and as they occur regularly, they seem more comparable than most extreme events. Authorities can prepare and plan better because summits have a lead time. Summits provide an opportunity for learning because the next event is usually scheduled before the current one is over. Summits allow us to study the conditions for collaboration in relation to security outcomes. Even though all the ingredients for a crisis to occur may be present, some summits are carried out calmly whereas others end up in chaos. Public evaluations, intense media scrutiny, and detailed bureaucratic record-keeping on each summit (calm or chaos) provide rich documentation for comparative case studies.

Judging success or failure of governance – in this case collaborative crisis governance – is of course an inherently political act, "because political actors, such as interest groups, politicians, journalists and voters are the main judges" (Bovens, 't Hart, and Peters 2001, 10). In this study, we base our review of success and failure in the cases under study on the verdicts of others, such as the previously mentioned actors for each case. Bovens et al. conclude that good government, which comes close to our idea of successful collaborative crisis governance, entails

> working one's way through a complex series of challenges in the most effective and politically sensitive manner possible. When doing so, people in governments would be working with incomplete information . . . and would be attempting to please a public with diverse and often conflicting values. These governments would also be faced with a number of internal governance problems, not the least of which is attempting to coordinate the activities of the numerous organizations working within the public sector.
>
> (2001, 657–58)

Later, Bovens (2010) presents a useful distinction to evaluate success and failure in policymaking: between how a policy came about and what it entails (the locus of the study: process versus outcome), and between success from a political or a programmatic perspective (the focus of the study: legitimacy gained versus goals attained) (Bovens 2010, 584–85).

In this study on summits, we say that the cooperation and coordination of network partners during a summit fails when either the collaborative network falls apart (process failure) or when the network collaboration produces predominantly unintended or negative results or consequences (outcome failure). Failure in terms of summit security from a programmatic perspective would be breaches to security of political executives. Failure in terms of legitimacy include civil unrest, violation of rights, eruptions of violence leading

Table 3.1 Assessment of success of G20 and NSS

	Programmatic perspective	*Legitimacy perspective*
Process	Both +	G20: +/–; NSS: ++
Outcome	Both ++	G20: —; NSS: ++

Source: Table Created by Authors

to damage and casualties in public space, use of force toward citizens by law and order authorities, and decline of trust in public authorities and their work. A combination of these would constitute a local, national or international crisis depending on the levels of governance involved and on the severity of the incident(s).

Each case can be evaluated as success or failure regarding the locus and focus introduced by Bovens (2010). We will compare a summit that could be characterized as a violent, disruptive event (G20 Toronto in 2010) to a case of similar threat, size, and scope that occurred relatively calmly (NSS The Hague in 2014). Although both summits had successful outcomes from a programmatic security perspective (all heads of state participated unhindered and returned home unharmed), they were not equally successful in terms of legitimacy.

Why is it that some collaborative networks result in failed outcomes during high profile security events whereas others do not? What we will probe into is whether the collaborative process was smooth or rugged (programmatic success/failure) and whether it was inclusive and responsive or not (legitimacy success/failure). As we will outline later, collaboration in preparation of summits brings together a set of actors similar to those cooperating in crisis and disaster response. The fault lines that impede cooperation and coordination are also similar, and variation in the cases along these fault lines can help to explain the different outcomes.

Cooperation and Collaboration in Crisis: Focus on Fault Lines

"Decades of research on the subject have demonstrated that effective cooperation under crisis conditions is unlikely to emerge by itself" (Boin and 't Hart 2012, 183). The scale and scope of the threat or damage, the fact that crises respect no territorial or functional boundaries, and above all the different types of actors involved are among the key challenges that crises pose (Bynander and Nohrstedt, this volume). Summit actors come from within and from outside government organizations, bringing different perspectives, interests and resources to the table. Many of these actors are new to the safety and security field. And yet they need to collaborate to produce an effective response to the crisis or threat at hand (Boin and 't Hart 2012). In these networks, cooperation is most likely involuntary and defined by political responsibility (Moynihan 2012). Among the involuntary networks, Kenis and Provan (2009) distinguish between the ones led by a hierarchically superior actor (the "lead organization network") and the ones coordinated by a "network administrative organization."

Cooperation between actors in a collaborative crisis network has vertical and horizontal dimensions (Moynihan 2012). Vertical relationships pertain to hierarchy between network partners: central agencies and line or niche departments, national and local or regional authorities, and chief executives with their strategic staffs as well as operational commanders and their units. Horizontal relations exist between actors that are interdependent but have no authority (formal or de facto) over each other.

Cooperation between public authorities and private actors (such as NGOs, business firms, interest groups) come to mind but also relationships between actors at an equal level of authority (such as two regional police units or two ministries that are horizontal). A Network Administrative Organization (NAO) could be helpful here (Kenis and Provan 2009).

While relating to each other along the horizontal and vertical dimensions, the actors in the network can also be fitted neatly into Dynes' boxes of established, extending, expanding, and emerging organizations in the crisis and security field (see Dynes 1970, in the introductory chapter for explanation of each category). Though Dynes originally discerned between organizations responding to disasters, the typology applies well to security networks preparing for summits. Established organizations (type I) are the routine security partners such as police and counterterrorism units. Extending organizations are those (public) organizations involved in hosting and accommodating the summit, the "type II bureaucracies" that Boin and 't Hart (2012) routinely refer to. Expanding organizations (type III) would be existing private organizations with some interest or involvement in the summit operation, organization or outcome (firms, NGOs, and interest groups). Finally, emerging organizations (type IV) are *ad hoc* groups of demonstrators, protesters, residents or other citizens that react to the summit in some newly organized form.

Boin and 't Hart (2012) identify several collaboration fault lines. We regroup them here into three categories. First, fault lines seem to occur when **cultures clash** (between different organizational styles such as type I command and control type organizations versus type II confederations of diplomats). Second, fault lines also occur when crises cross functional boundaries and tasks are not covered, and when **problem frames are set too narrow** (creating discussions between type I and II organizations on who assumes responsibility for what, or disputes between insiders – type I and II – versus outsiders – type III and IV). Third, fault lines prevail when **single perspectives rule** (short-term not long-term, national focus with disregard for local interests, and strategic considerations versus operational demands) and when actors of different types do not find common ground during the collaboration process.

What we expect to see in the cases is that the composition of the network, the cooperation between the actors, and the content of the joint planning and operations reflect how the collaborative network has dealt with the previously mentioned fault lines that are likely to occur between different types of organizations. The prevalence of fault lines in the cases is related to the outcome (violent or peaceful summit) in our analysis and discussion.

Research Design

This study is a structured, focused comparison of two cases (George and Bennett 2005). Our cases focus on the middle zone between long-term collaborations in managing public policy and the *ad hoc* prevention and management of crises. Organizing an international summit usually takes one to two years of preparation and involves threats, uncertainty, and high stakes regarding security matters. An international summit sometimes materializes into a public order crisis and sometimes not. Our cases involve the wide spectrum of security related actors and representatives from sectors affected by security measures. These actors participate in a network, and they each bring their own organizational values and interests, which may be implicit and inherently conflicting (Owen et al. 2016). Moynihan points out that involuntary participation in public service networks (such as the collaborative security networks in our study) may increase each participant organization's concerns about extra-network reputation and organizational values, as opposed to reciprocity norms that usually bind voluntary networks (Moynihan 2012, 568, 573).

We do not study the diplomatic outcome of the selected cases (i.e., the treaty content), nor did we study operational and tactical decisions during the summits. We selected two summits: one summit that – in spite of intense network cooperation – was perceived as a security drama, a civil rights nightmare, and a logistical standstill, and another summit that in terms of civil rights, logistics, and security, ran smoothly (in the eyes of media and the respondents, according to the formal evaluations). This allows us to probe into the collaborative practices in preparation of these summits to see what influenced the difference in outcome in terms of public order and security.

Of course, collaborating authorities responsible for security operations during international summits do not fully impact the security threats they face. Anti-establishment groups may or may not decide autonomously (uninfluenced by considerations regarding security measures) to demonstrate during a summit, and the intensity and size of their demonstration and ultimately rioting efforts may vary. Part of the explanation may also be anticipation: rioters decide not to mobilize because of expected police presence and security barriers. While the advanced announcement of such measures could be seen as part of successful preparation and communication by the summit's host, we cannot control for the autonomous decisions made by rogue individuals or groups.

We compare the two cases in a qualitative case study design to examine whether collaboration in the governing networks responsible for security and logistics before and during the summits reveal striking differences that may relate to the diverging case outcomes. We look into what fault lines were present in the cases, and the ways these collaborative networks dealt with these fault lines can be connected to the overall outcomes of the cases.

The outcomes of collaboration in the security management of a summit are compared on dimensions such as security, public order, civil rights, and mobility. It is important to consider all these dimensions because they are inherently conflicting. Security and public order are much easier to guarantee if constitutional rights can be disregarded (for instance when all protests and demonstrators are banned from the wider area surrounding the summit), and if all local mobility can be optimally restricted. Vice-versa, if both citizen rights and their mobility have to be respected, the risks that demonstrators or even terrorists can disturb a summit are much higher.

Data Collection

Data for the study was collected in two steps. First, a content-analysis of all relevant (public) evaluations from official government sources, media sources (through Lexis-Nexis searches) and independent inquiries were coded in NVivo to get an idea of the key characteristics of both cases in terms of the policy process and the policy outcomes of the summits in terms of (1) security, (2) public order, (3) constitutional rights, (4) mobility, and (5) resources.[1] The second step included semi-structured interviews with key respondents of both cases. In the interviews, we asked respondents about the relations between key stakeholders in the preparation phase, the prior relationships between key stakeholders, the formal structure of the summit preparation organization, the timeline, and the perceived successes and failures in the collaboration process. The 26 interviewees were identified either by their names appearing in the key documents used for the content analysis or by snowball sampling (see list of respondents in Appendix I). All interviews were recorded, transcribed, and coded by both authors independently using NVivo.

Description of the Cases: NSS The Hague Versus G20 Toronto

The G20 Toronto Summit in June 2010 was the fourth in a line of G20 meetings addressing global finance and economic issues. Its theme "Recovery and New Beginnings" referred to the aim to overcome the ongoing economic worldwide recession. The G20 Toronto Summit was combined with a G8 Summit held immediately prior in nearby rural Huntsville. Together, the summits represented the largest and most expensive security operation in Canadian history. Both summits were criticized for being many times more costly than similar events in the UK and in Japan (Chase 2010).

The Hague's Nuclear Security Summit in March 2014 was the largest security operation the Netherlands ever hosted. This NSS 2014 was the third in a row, preceded by Nuclear Security Summits in Washington DC (2010) and Seoul (2012). Though the aim of the summits was to improve global nuclear safety, the prior summit in South Korea had sparked violent protests. The NSS in The Hague was combined with a G7 summit that took place on the same premises the same week.

The cases are highly comparable in the sense that they both took place in the post-9/11 era, they were preceded by similar summits in other countries that instigated violent demonstrations, they were organized in a densely populated city center and they put similar demands on policing capacity. The summits were similar in terms of political controversy and terrorist threat. Neither of the host countries had experienced violent protests during previous summits. Both summits were hosted in metropolitan areas and preceded by a G7/G8 summit back to back to the larger summit. At both events, over 20,000 security officers were deployed during the operations, parts of the city centers (where the summits were held) were entirely sealed off with fences, and the summits paralyzed regional logistics for three consecutive days.

The Netherlands scores much higher than Canada in studies on protest demonstrations and activism, with self-reported activism among respondents scoring 32% in the Netherlands (ranking 3rd, which is comparable to Sweden: ranking 2nd with 35%) against 19% in Canada (ranking 14th), which is more comparable to South Korean scores (14%, ranking 18th) (Norris, Walgrave, and Van Aelst 2005, 199).

Yet, the Toronto Summit attracted 9,000 protesters and resulted in over 600 reported incidents and more than 1,000 arrests, whereas The Hague Summit occurred rather peacefully. The protests in downtown Toronto addressed generic issues as globalization, capitalism, and gay rights and further escalated during the summit itself. What started off as peaceful demonstrations led to increasing protests and the use of *black bloc* tactics once the summit officially started (The Star 26 June 2010). Shops and businesses in downtown Toronto were vandalized. Security was subsequently tightened, which further escalated the aggression exerted against the police officers near the temporary detention facility where 500 protesters were being detained. In total, more than 1100 people were arrested during the week of the summit. Riot police and protesters clashed, and tear gas and plastic bullets were used to push back the protesters (The Globe 28 June 2010). After the Toronto Summit, at least nine formal investigations into police operations were conducted. The costs of the G8-G20 security amounted to 930M Canadian dollars (Office of the Parliamentary Budget Officer 2010).

Table 3.2 Characteristics of the high security events

	G20	NSS
Theme	Economic recovery after the global recession	Increase global nuclear security
Dates	26–27 June 2010	24–25 March 2014
Occurrence	Fourth edition	Third edition
Back-to-back event	Combined with G8	Combined with G7
Key stakeholders in planning and operation of security	Toronto Police Services, Royal Canadian Mounted Police, Peel Regional Police, Ontario Provincial Police, Canadian Forces, Summit Management Office	Project team Security and Safety, 17 members from different security domains and different public and private organizations, including but are not limited to: National Coordinator for Terrorism and Security, National Police, Municipality The Hague, Ministry of Infrastructure and Environment, Ministry of Defense, Ministry of Foreign Affairs, Ministry of Internal Affairs, Prorail (train network), Border Police (KMAR), hotels, etc.
Security staff employed	+/– 20,000	+/– 21,000
Number of delegations	36	58
Security zones	Inner and outer zones. Inner zone: 3–4 km^2	Five security rings: first and second up to 250m range around the conference center
High security measures in inner security zone	3m high fences, Long Range Acoustic Devices (LRAD), mobility restrictions through Regulation 233/10, Public Works Protection Act, Stop and Search	"Ring of steel": high fences, police control, CCTV systems

Source: Table Created by Authors

Table 3.3 Outcomes in terms of experienced unrest

	G20	NSS
Number of protesters	9000	+/– 800
Number of reported incidents	600	7
Number of arrests	1100	75
Number of injured security personnel	75	19

Source: Table Created by Authors

Toronto G20: Violence Met With Violence

When the Harper administration announced in June 2008 that the next G8 summit would be held on June 25 and 26, 2010, in Huntsville, Ontario, the Royal Canadian Mounted Police (RCMP) assumed general responsibility for the security of the event. They started planning for the event with Chief Superintendent Alphonse MacNeil in the lead. The Peel Regional Police (PRP, Toronto airport jurisdiction), the Ontario Provincial Police (OPP, jurisdiction travel routes of delegation) and the Canadian Forces (CF, general patrolling) all became members of the G8 steering committee and the Integrated Security Unit (ISU). The Toronto Police Service (TPS) was also part of the ISU, responsible for the media center of the G8 in Toronto. Huntsville, three hours north of Toronto, is a small town; thus, planning for the event progressed relatively smoothly between the security partners.

In December 2009, the Harper administration announced that the G8 summit would be held back-to-back with a G20 summit on June 26 and June 27, 2010. In February, they announced the venue: the Metro Toronto Convention Centre (MTCC) in the midst of the downtown financial district. This news changed everything (interview 19). Although the TPS was already part of the steering committee, they suddenly became a lead agency because the city of Toronto became the primary event location. Confusion reigned on the role of TPS, RCMP and the other partners but no formal changes were made regarding the overall responsibility for the security of the event. The prime minister's office had overall responsibility for hosting the G20. They set up a Summit Management Office (SMO), responsible for the organization of the G20 Summit and for the coordination of the federal agencies. The RCMP, as the lead law enforcement agency at the federal level, was responsible for the overall security of both the G8 and G20 Summits. Information from the prime minister's office was sent to the RCMP and then down to the other partners. This was problematic for the network because information was not shared easily among security partners. Furthermore, the fact that the summits were held back to back hindered the mobilization and deployment of staff needed in both Huntsville and Toronto.

The Harper administration's late announcement of the G20 Summit and the additional venue left the federal, provincial, and city authorities with only four months to plan for the G20. As a result, planning was rushed, information was inadequate, and time for training and preparing operational staff was limited. In terms of security within the city of Toronto, RCMP was responsible for the security of all political leaders and diplomats and took over the jurisdiction of downtown Toronto.[2] The overarching goal of the RCMP was to organize a safe and secure summit for the Internationally Protected Persons (IPPs). The RCMP closed off the summit's security zones (3–4 square miles) for the public by putting up 10-feet-high fences. This severely disrupted city life in Toronto. Businesses were temporarily closed or moved, public transport was disrupted, and major thoroughfares were closed (OIPRD 2012).

The Toronto Police Service controlled the outer zones. In these zones, public order issues unfolded resulting in violent protests and riots starting on June 26. The TPS officers in these zones received support from the OPP and RCMP officers who operated under the command of the TPS. The riots escalated to a point that the TPS chief commanders decided to "take back the streets." The use of force by both police and protestors further escalated, leading to a vicious circle of "violence to be met with violence" (OIPRD 2012). Over the course of the summit, more than 1,100 people were arrested and detained in the temporary Prisoner Processing Center. Several independent inquiries reported that these detainments resulted in severe human rights violations.

Media reports paid little attention to the content of the summit. Instead, they reported on the high security fences, massive police presence, large groups of demonstrators, protesters employing *black bloc* tactics, vandalism, and excessive violence between police and protestors. Yet most police respondents assert that, given the scope of the security operation, the number of jurisdictions involved, and the short notice, policing was carried out very well.

The Hague NSS: Dignified, Secure, and Peaceful

When the Netherlands agreed in 2012 to U.S. president Barack Obama's request to host the third global Nuclear Security Summit in March 2014, The Hague won the bid of the hosting city. The Hague, a city of half a million inhabitants, is the Dutch government residence. It likes to promote itself as a city of peace because several important international institutions are located in the city. The Dutch Ministry of Foreign Affairs (as the primary responsible government department) would organize the event in close cooperation with the city (also as its contractor) and with local and national security partners. From the start, the overarching goal of organizing the NSS was to host a "dignified, secure and peaceful" summit.

The summit, unprecedented in scope to the Dutch organizers, would bring 58 heads of state, their delegations, and the world press to the Netherlands for a three-day high security, high profile event in the heart of the densely populated country. The Netherlands is a decentralized state; thus, mayors have ultimate authority over public order and safety in their jurisdiction. Accommodating and transporting delegations from and to the World Economic Forum in The Hague would include crossing the jurisdictions of 20 different mayors/municipalities, two provinces, and four police districts. Security operations would involve the deployment of 13,000 police and 8,000 military officers. The impact on mobility, logistics, and business continuity was unparalleled.

A Ministerial Committee including the PM (chair), and the Ministers of Foreign Affairs, Security and Justice, Economic Affairs, Defence, and Infrastructure plus the National Coordinator for Counterterrorism and Security and the mayor of The Hague would be the ultimate decision unit at the highest strategic level. One level below, responsibility was divided between two committees at the Directorate-General level (one for content/diplomacy and one for security of the event). Two levels below, three project groups (Sherpa team, NSS project team and the Security Project Group – PGV) formed the administrative backbone of the event organization, coordinating the work at the operational level. At all levels, diplomacy and security formed the pillars of the event organization.

The summit was successful in the eyes of the organizers and well received by the Dutch press and international media. No major incidents occurred, and demonstrations were exercised peacefully and calmly. The Dutch government concluded that its goals were met as the summit could be characterized as dignified, secure, and peaceful.

Analysis

We will highlight the most striking differences in our analysis of fault lines and conditions that seemed to relate to the differences in outcomes between the two events.

Problem Framing: Narrow Versus Broad

For the Toronto G20 Summit, several police respondents said their overarching goal was "to get the heads of state in and out of the summit safely," which illustrates the perfect isolation of security planning in the Canadian case (interview 22). This isolation stands in stark contrast to the integrated perspective on goals of the Dutch NSS summit organization. From the start, security was but one goal of the entire network responsible for the NSS planning and operations. Security concerns in The Hague (represented by the type I organizations in the network) had to find a constant balance with the desired peaceful, undisturbed, dignified and festive character of the event (represented by type II organizations such as the Foreign Office which was in charge of hosting the Summit) as well as with the people of the city (and their local interests represented by businesses, interest groups, and residents through type III and IV organizations included in the network). Because of this compound aim, societal actors joined the decision-making tables at all governance levels. They brought in different views on how to deal with demonstrations, how to groom public opinion, and how to minimize security restrictions that hindered city life and business continuity. Their interests were constantly weighing into the security planning. The Dutch actors had experience with this inclusive approach from prior events and their constitutional setup of local autonomy ensured that local demands for a festive and peaceful event were taken into serious consideration.

Though it is unlikely that the exclusion of other interests than security in the Canadian ISU's planning efforts inspired demonstrators and violent protestors, there was clearly a "them" (summit/security, type I organizations) against "us" (demonstrators/media/spectators – type IV) atmosphere in the city. Imposed restrictions, incurred costs, and the use of law enforcement related to the summit were critically received by the press. However, the rogue nature of the protestors and the violence they displayed in the city center led 81% of the Torontonians who participated in a poll to agree that the police had done a good job during the summit (Chase 2010). Nevertheless, the escalation of violence between the police and the protesters probably did not favorably influence the public evaluations of the organization of the G20 Summit.

It seems that the integrated approach in The Hague empowered a diversity of interests. The compound motto ensured that interests that played a minor role in the Toronto G20 planning (citizen mobility and public appreciation for the event) weighed in heavily in the NSS preparations.

Single Perspectives Rule: Planners Versus Operators

The inclusive, integrated network for preparing the NSS at the strategic and tactical level in the Netherlands was mirrored by a similar network at the operational level. According to respondents, the liaisons present in both networks ensured the operability of decisions taken, regular information flows, and reality checks between the levels. Yet six months before the NSS was scheduled to take place, the PGV at the strategic level started to lose grip on the numerous expert groups created to work on specific issues. Each issue had been translated into a specific expert group which undermined the integrated approach and the number of groups had proliferated. The PGV seized the opportunity to escalate the most pressing issues to the strategic level and reduce the number (45–50) of the expert groups considerably, to regain oversight and reduce overlap. Respondents saw the lead time (1.5 years) up to the event both as a benefit and a disadvantage: it allowed both for the proliferation of network segments and for the time to "tame the beast we created" (interview 11). In any case, sufficient time existed to carefully calibrate strategic and operational plans, practices and responses before and during the event.

Such time was lacking in the Toronto case, in the four months after the Harper administration selected the MTCC venue as the G20 location. In the G8/G20 preparations phase, an operational network that mirrored the collaborative network of strategic planners (all type I organizations, but at different hierarchical levels) existed on paper but not in practice. Much of the ISU information to the operational forces was directed top-down to the chiefs of the operational services and in fact given only a few days prior to the event to the officers involved in the operation. Confusion reigned about the exact plans, strategies, and security operations, as operators were not included in the planning dialogue. As one of the lead planners of the G20 recalled in an interview: "I should have ensured that the deputy chief and chiefs of the [operational] services were involved [and] understood the plans. I did not do that." In the end, the chief was able to say

> I didn't know. I learned my lesson there, and if I ever do this again, I would definitely make sure that we were on the same page. Responsibility and accountability were on paper, but that didn't matter. Nobody took that to the chief of police to check if he understood.
>
> (interview 19)

System architecture between planners and operators in the G20 case clearly differed from the situation in The Hague, as operational actors were not involved in the G20 security planning, hindering collaborative governance and ultimately unsettling operations during the G20 Summit.

Culture Clashes: Inward Looking Versus Outreaching

In both Toronto and The Hague, the local police contacted anticipated demonstrators prior to the summit to explain the restrictions, demonstration routes, locations, and so on. In order to be able to anticipate potential demonstrations and constantly update their threat assessments, the Dutch police used international intelligence networks to stop potential protestors "from getting on the bus in Italy"' instead of just waiting for their arrival in a more reactive way. In the Toronto case, the Joint Intelligence Group (JIG) consisted mainly of key stakeholders of the ISU: the Canadian Intelligence Service (CSIS), border agencies, Transport Canada, and the Canadian Forces (type I and type II organizations). Although official inquiries indicated that "collection and dissemination of intelligence through one central theme supported the partners in working together," they found that "varying protocols and procedures for sharing and classifying information made information sharing difficult" (RCMP 2014, 10).

Diplomats from the Dutch Ministry of Foreign Affairs (type II) proactively contacted organized protestors (type III and IV) to convince them of the benefits of the NSS in terms of world peace. After all, the Nuclear Security Summit aimed to reduce the risk of criminal and terrorist use of nuclear materials worldwide. Who could be against that? This informal marketing campaign on the NSS may have contributed to the less fierce antinuclear energy protests than for instance during the Seoul NSS of 2012. In Toronto, the

Community Relations Group (CRG) of the joint police organizations (all type I) reached out to both the citizens affected by the G20 Summit and to potential protesters (type IV and III respectively) to facilitate peaceful and lawful protests. However, "For the most part, there was little positive interaction between the CRG and the more militant activists" (TPS 2011, 55; interview 18). The protestors criticized the CRG for being solely concerned about obtaining intelligence (RCMP 2012).

Demonstrators and security actors by nature have a prehistory of conflict rather than cooperation, so collaborative actors need to take positive steps to remediate low levels of trust. Though the TPS did extensive fieldwork to inform demonstrators, this was not necessarily perceived as a trust-building exercise by the protesters, and the resulting protests do not indicate any positive effects of prior bilateral communication (Ontario Ombudsman 2010). By contrast, the Dutch diplomatic approach to activists, not by the security actors in the networks but by their colleagues from the Foreign Office, to positively communicate and find agreement and support for the ultimate goals of the summit seemed to pay off in increasing mutual trust.

Both Culture Clash and Single Perspective: Mono Versus Multidisciplinary

The network in the Toronto case seemed to mainly facilitate cooperation among the police forces (all type I). Toronto police respondents characterized their cooperation as smooth, in spite of a mild historical animosity between the federal RCMP and the local TPS. In the Toronto case, elected officials representing the city, the Ontario government or the Harper administration did not assume a strong mediating role within the network of stakeholders. The homogeneity of their network (police organizations only) led to a widely shared agreement on their mission (providing security to G20 delegations). Most respondents agreed that, given the challenges, they successfully pulled off the task at hand.

In the NSS case, cooperation at the strategic level (PGV) involved the greatest possible variety of network partners, including the city (type II), cabinet departments (type II), business representatives (type III), emergency services (type I), special police forces (type I), intelligence agencies (type II), neighborhood communities (type IV), and the military (type I/II). The Chairperson of the PGV was the Deputy DG of the National Coordinator of Counterterrorism and Security in the Netherlands, a Directorate-General that by definition always plays a moderating and coordinating role among a diversity of network partners in all its regular activities. This background may have contributed to her coordinating approach and skills, allowing her to become the "honest broker" in the NSS preparations network.

The NSS network in The Hague faced an intense conflict about the integration of command centers, six months before the NSS began. The local police demanded to include the local emergency services in the operational command center *on site* (i.e., inside the secured zone). The special police forces (such as intervention squads and police intelligence groups part of the national police) in that command center, opposed vehemently against the presence of civilian actors. The special police forces argued that their information could not be shared in the presence of non-police actors. The local police escalated this issue because they valued the presence of their highly trusted local emergency counterparts for an integrated operational approach. In the end, the PGV at the strategical level intervened and included the relevant non-security actors in the command center on site. According to the local respondents, the issue harmed the overall reputation of the police in the eyes of other emergency response organizations, but the resulting integrated command center worked well before and during the summit.

Table 3.4 Overview of main findings

Fault line	G20	NSS
Culture clash	Inclusive toward protestors (managed by type I organizations – security focus) Mainly type I organizations (inward looking) Constrained information sharing through protocols and procedures	Inclusive toward protestors (managed by type II organizations – content focus) Outward looking Ability to use international information sharing and cooperation networks (EU wide)
Problem framing	"Us versus them" framing (type I versus type IV organizations) Narrow goal-setting (safe and secure)	Collective, inclusive decision making (all types of organizations) Broad goal-setting (festive, safe, peaceful)
Single perspectives	Short-term preparation seen as disadvantage Hierarchical "tension" (RCMP lead in TPS area) Clear strategic/operational division	Long-term preparation seen as both advantage and disadvantage Dispersed "tensions": who is doing what? (losing oversight) Integrated/mirrored strategic/ operational organization

Source: Table Created by Authors

Conclusions: Stay on the Slack Line

Though we cannot conclude that the observed differences of how fault lines prevailed in the cases causally relate to security outcomes of the two summits, the contrasts are insightful. The absence of scholarly research into such differences and the recurrence of summits make this exploration a valuable effort. Our cases confirm the importance of collaborative efforts between organization types to deal with crises or threats that ignore functional boundaries. Such collaborative efforts require an inclusive approach to security. Not surprisingly, taking on board societal actors (type III and IV in Dynes's typology) is imperative to meet societal security challenges.

Meanwhile, this inclusive approach can generate its own fault lines when the number of actors increases so much that a proliferation of different expert groups takes place, each embracing a single-perspective specialization. A network administrative organization that bears the responsibility to safeguard the sustainability and coherence of the network may be required to smoothen cooperation between the partners (Kenis and Provan 2009). The Dutch case study revealed the vital importance of a coordinating actor that served as an "honest broker" between the different interests involved (cf. Kuipers and Swinkels 2018).

Another finding is that smooth network cooperation can be deceptive when the network only involves the same type of organizations. When these organizations are horizontally related, such as different police organizations in the Canadian case (all type I), network collaboration can still require much effort because of disputes on tasks and responsibilities. Hierarchy within the network can help to make collaboration succeed in terms of reconciling actors involved in a single mission, as it did in Toronto (with the RCMP taking the lead in securing world leaders at all cost). The process of collaboration could even be characterized as a programmatic success (Bovens 2010). Yet, collaboration will still likely fail to cover societal interests and thus get harmed in the long run (resulting in process failure in terms of legitimacy). Including "strangers" (from a security perspective) may generate severe culture clashes within the network in the short run but may prove beneficial to the relations with other "outsiders," such as the protestors who were appeased by the diplomats in the Dutch case.

Practitioners must try to move from fault lines to slack lines. Slack lines find their origin in climbing. They are dynamic lines between two anchor points on which people can train their balance. Moving from one edge to the other is a delicate balancing act that requires cooperation of many different muscles in the body. Due to the wobbly line that moves with you as you go, long-term training to stay on the line is essential in order to cross from one point for another. As we have outlined in this chapter, preparing for secure summits can lead to dramatic outcomes when organizations fall off slack lines into fault lines. The lessons from both cases concerning problem framing, culture clashes, and single perspective rules challenge practitioners to train, prepare, and practice the balancing act from event planning and preparation to secure summit operations.

The findings of this study can guide further research on securing high profile security events through collaboration in governance networks. Collaborative networks in security and crisis management deserve more scholarly attention than they currently receive (Kuipers and Welsh 2017, 280). High profile security events will always be there, and in recent years, global summits are on the rise (Bradford, Linn, and Martin 2008). When demonstrators may become more mobile and militant against authorities in a polarized world, authorities responsible for public order cannot afford to ignore these lessons for collaborative governance in security settings.

Notes

1. Data available upon request.
2. Within the controlled access and restricted access zone.

References

Boersma, Kees. 2013. "Liminal Surveillance: An Ethnographic Control Room Study During a Local Event." *Surveillance and Society* 11 (1–2): 106–20. http://keesboersma.com/wp-content/uploads/2006/02/liminal-surveillance.pdf

Boin, Arjen and Paul 't Hart. 2012. "Aligning Executive Action in Times of Adversity: The Politics of Crisis Co-ordination." In *Executive Politics in Times of Crisis*, edited by M. Lodge and K. Wegrich, 179–96. New York, NY: Palgrave Macmillan.

Bovens, Mark. 2010. "A Comment on Marsh and McConnell: Towards a Framework for Establishing Policy Success." *Public Administration* 88 (2): 584–85. doi:10.1111/j.1467–9299.2009.01804.x

Bovens, Mark, Paul 't Hart, and B. Guy Peters. 2001. *Success and Failure in Public Governance: A Comparative Analysis*. Cheltenham: Edward Elgar.

Bradford, Colin I., Johannes F. Linn, and Paul Martin. 17 December 2008. "Global Governance Breakthrough: The G20 Summit and the Future Agenda." *Brookings Institution*. www.brookings. edu/research/global-governance-breakthrough-the-g20-summit-and-the-future-agenda/ (Accessed 1 August 2014).

Chase, Stephen. 25 May 2010. "G8/G20 Security Bill to Approach $1-Billion." *The Globe and Mail.* www.theglobeandmail.com/news/world/g8g20-security-bill-to-approach-1-billion/article1211436/ (Accessed 3 August 2016).

Dynes, Russell R. 1970. *Organized Behavior in Disaster*. Lexington, MA: D.C. Heath and Company.

George, Alexander L. and Andrew Bennett. 2005. *Case Studies and Theory Development*. Cambridge, MA: Massachusetts Institute of Technology Press.

The Globe. 28 June 2010. "A History of Summit Protest." www.theglobeandmail.com/news/world/a-history-of-summit-protest/article4084135/?from=4323163

Hansén, Dan and Ahn-Za Hagström. 2004. *I krisen prövas ordningsmakten: Sex fallstudier av extraordinära händelser där det svenska rättssamhället har satts på prov*. Stockholm: CRISMART.

KAMEDO. 2001. *KAMEDO-rapport 83: EU-toppmötet i Göteborg 2001*. www.socialstyrelsen.se/publikationer2004/2004-123-30 (Accessed 6 December 2018).

Kenis, Patrick and Keith G. Provan. 2009. "Towards an Exogenous Theory of Public Network Performance." *Public Administration* 87 (3): 440–56. doi:10.1111/j.1467–9299.2009.01775.x

Kuipers, Sanneke and Marji Swinkels. 2018. "Peak Performance: Collaborative Crisis Management Before and During International Summits." *International Journal of Emergency Management* 14 (3): 344–63.

Kuipers, Sanneke and Nicholas H. Welsh. 2017. "Taxonomy of the Crisis and Disaster Literature: Themes and Types in 34 Years of Research." *Risk, Hazards and Crisis in Public Policy* 8 (4): 272–83. doi:10.1002/rhc3.12123

Moynihan, Donald. 2012. "Extra Network Organizational Reputation and Blame Avoidance in Networks." *Governance* 25 (4): 567–88. doi:10.1111/j.1468–0491.2012.01593.x

Norris, Pippa, Stefaan Walgrave, and Peter Van Aelst. 2005. "Who Demonstrates? Antistate Rebels, Conventional Participants, or Everyone?" *Comparative Politics* 37 (2): 189–205. doi:10.2307/20072882

Office of the Parliamentary Budget Officer. 2010. "Assessment of Planned Security Costs for the 2010 G8 and G20 Summits." www.parl.gc.ca/PBO-DPB/documents/SummitSecurity.pdf (Accessed 5 May 2015).

OIPRD. 2012. "Policing the Right to Protest." www.oiprd.on.ca/EN/PDFs/G20-Systemic-Review-2012_E.pdf (Accessed 5 May 2015).

Ombudsman Ontario. 2010. "Caught in the Act: Investigation Into the Ministry of Community Safety and Correctional Services' Conduct in Relation to Ontario Regulation 233/10 Under the Public Works Protection Act." www.ombudsman.on.ca/Ombudsman/files/58/581252d9-1809-4291-831b-88e9adb480c5.pdf (Accessed 5 May 2015).

Owen, Chris, Benjamin Brooks, C. Bearman, and Steven Curnin. 2016. "Values and Complexities in Assessing Strategic Level Emergency Management Effectiveness." *Journal of Contingencies and Crisis Management* 24 (3): 181–90. doi:10.1111/1468–5973.12115

Royal Canadian Mounted Police. 2014. *2010 G8 and G20 Summits RCMP Led Horizontal Evaluation Report*. www.rcmp-grc.gc.ca/aud-ver/reports-rapports/G8-G20-eng.htm#Findings (Accessed 5 May 2015).

———. 2012. "Public Interest Investigation Into RCMP Member Conduct Related to the 2010 G8 and G20 Summits." *Civilian Review and Complaints Commission for the RCMP*. www.crcc-ccetp.gc.ca/pdf/g8g20R-eng.pdf (Accessed 5 May 2015).

The Star. 26 June 2010. "Violent Black Bloc Tactics on Display at G20 Protest." www.thestar.com/news/gta/g20/2010/06/26/violent_black_bloc_tactics_on_display_at_g20_protest.html

Statens Offentliga Utredningar (SOU). 2002. "Händelserna i samband med Europeiska rådets möte i Göteborg den 14–16 juni 2001." www.riksdagen.se/sv/dokument-lagar/?doktyp=urf,sou&riksmote=2002/03 (Accessed 6 December 2018).

Tilly, Charles and Sidney Tarrow. 2012. *Contentious Politics*. Oxford: Oxford University Press.

Toronto Police Service. 2011. "After Action Review G20 Summit Toronto, Ontario, June 2010." www.torontopolice.on.ca/publications/files/reports/g20_after_action_review.pdf (Accessed 6 December 2018).

Wallmann, F. 2006. *Ordningensdynamik-En jämförelse av demonstrationerna i Prag, Nice, Göteborg och Genua*. Stockholm: CRISMART.

Appendix 1

List of Respondents

	Position/role	Date
1	World Forum, The Hague, event manager	19 August 2015
2	The Hague Police – strategic leadership 1	10 August 2015
3	The Hague Police – strategic leadership 2	04 November 2015
4	The Hague Police – operational leadership	24 September 2015
5	National Police – strategic leadership	01 December 2015
6	Ministry of Foreign Affairs – operational leadership	07 October 2015
7	Ministry of Foreign Affairs – strategic leadership	24 September 2015
8	Ministry of Security and Justice – staff project group security (PGV)	26 August 2015
9	Ministry of Security and Justice – strategic leadership Crisis Management Unit	07 September 2015
10	Ministry of Security and Justice – strategic leadership project group security (PGV)	09 September 2015
11	Ministry of Security and Justice – strategic leadership project group security (PGV)	31 August 2015
12	Ministry of Security and Justice – staff project group security (PGV) – logistics	10 August 2015
13	Ministry of Security and Justice – staff project group security (PGV) – security heads of state	26 August 2015
14	Ministry of Infrastructure and Transportation – staff project group security (PGV)	15 September 2015
15	The Hague City – city manager	02 September 2015
16	The Hague City – NSS project leadership	23 July 2015
17	The Hague City – strategic leadership security	17 August 2015
18	Toronto Police Service – communications manager	20 August 2015
19	Toronto Police Service – strategic leadership, project leader	19 August 2015
20	Office of the Independent Police Review – lead researcher	25 August 2015
21	Royal Canadian Mounted Police – strategic leadership 1, project leader	29 August 2015
22	Royal Canadian Mounted Police – strategic leadership 2	26 August 2015
23	Peel Regional Police – strategic leadership	24 August 2015
24	Metro Toronto Convention Centre – event managers (2)	20 August 2015
25	Toronto Emergency Services – operational leadership	25 August 2015
26	Ontario Provincial Police Association – strategic leadership	19 August 2015

Chapter 4

Managing Extraordinary Influx of Migrants

The 2015 Migration Crisis in Sweden

Edward Deverell and Dan Hansén

Introduction

In later decades, Western governments have framed security issues broadly, emphasizing the need for a whole-of-society approach to crisis management (Lindberg and Sundelius 2013). When crises occur, governments and the public alike demand swift and collaborative action, especially from parties integrated in crisis management planning. But what happens when the crisis evolves outside of the traditional security sectors? More specifically, what are the effects on crisis coordination when the coordinating response calls on agencies unfamiliar with the operating procedures of the crisis response networks? Do organizations involved come to one another's rescue, or do their activities, needs, and stakes rather stifle each other's operations? In this chapter we are interested in elucidating the facilitating and hampering factors of crisis coordination, cooperation and collaboration by delving deeper into the case specifics of the Swedish response to the acute phase of the 2015 migrant crisis, which we treat as a case of crisis coordination among unaccustomed parties. In doing so, we pose the open question: How did interaction play out among stakeholders in the case of the 2015 migrant crisis?

In July 2015, migrants in large quantities from the Middle East were marching northbound in Europe. In Sweden, well over 1000 asylum seekers and others seeking refuge crossed the borders daily at the peak. Some 80,000 people more than forecasted arrived in the country in 2015. At the time, the established political parties supported a generous and open policy toward migration. Meanwhile, the policy domain had traditionally been understood as low priority and relatively unimportant by voters (see, e.g., Social Democratic Party 2015). This all changed in the fall of 2015, when the migrant situation reached crisis proportions for the local, regional, and national government agencies tasked to manage the influx.

In essence, the Migration Agency could not uphold the regulated migration policy (Swedish Migration Board 2015a). Decision makers were careful when framing the events, describing them in most cases as a challenge rather than a crisis. Nonetheless, Prime Minister Stefan Löfven acknowledged that core values such as public order, security, and even national welfare were at risk (Löfven 2016). The Cabinet's decision to reintroduce border controls on November 12 meant that the "acute" phase of the crisis was approaching termination (Strömberg 2016; Swedish Government 2017).

This chapter deals with the "cathartic" trajectory of the reception situation that unfolded during the fall of 2015, acknowledging that other aspects of the migration situation are still strenuous for public officeholders. The reception situation alone, however, involved a wide range of actors who tried to solve problems in various constellations and who were working under increasingly harsh pressure until the Cabinet's decision of November 12 that put a halt on the reception.

Crises differ from routine challenges, incidents, and accidents. Major accidents occur within predictable frames where more resources solve problems. Even if a major accident challenges organizational functions, organizations can handle them reasonably well within a framework delimited by their given presumptions. A societal crisis, much like a disaster, is not only a question of magnitude. The societal crisis cannot be solved only by adding more resources, personnel, and material (Auf der Heide 1989, 49). Most crises cross geographical and jurisdictional boundaries and require managers to take on new tasks and organizations to adapt to new structures. Coordination is one often mentioned prerequisite for coping with these challenges.

Our perspective of a crisis in a societal sense is that it threatens societal values or functions, affects more than a single organization, and thus requires coordination, cooperation, or collaboration. No single organization has sufficient resources, knowledge, or mandates to deal with the disruptive and dynamic nature of a societal crisis. Instead, a multiorganizational response is needed to come to terms with these challenges (Drabek and McEntire 2002, 206), involving multiple levels of government and various forms of assistance from outsiders.

Focus on Government Agencies

The migration crisis is an example of a complex societal challenge, involving many actors working on the local, regional, and national levels and thus requiring horizontal and vertical collaboration. Furthermore, voluntary organizations and other civil society parties also took part in the management of the situation (Swedish Government 2017, 119).

In this chapter, we focus on the roles, tasks, and decisions made by government agencies in managing the actual crisis. Experience shows that crisis overload along with uncertainty in cause requires partners, resources, and resolutions, which means that one organization is often inadequate concerning the availability of expertise and the ability to handle a crisis. A societal crisis challenges the idea of government agencies working as organizational silos and the idea of crisis ownership by one government (lead) agency. That said, a greater responsibility falls on government agencies compared to voluntary or private sector organizations in the event of a societal crisis. For instance, government agencies are obliged to invest time and resources in cross-sectoral coordinating activities during a crisis according to the principle of responsibility, which is one of the guiding principles of the Swedish national crisis management system (Andersson 2019).

Despite the importance of coordination in contemporary crisis management practices, both the precise meaning of the concept and how it relates to similar concepts of interaction (e.g., cooperation and collaboration) remain unclear. In line with Bynander and Nohrstedt (this volume), we place these concepts on a continuum of interaction ranging from cooperation and coordination to collaboration. It is of empirical interest to investigate further what depth of interaction is employed in specific crisis situations.

Why Study the Coordination of Response During the 2015 Migration Crisis?

Looking into the issue of crisis coordination in the Swedish context is appealing as the idea of crisis coordination is incorporated into the national crisis management structures. In the regulation (2006, 942), it is declared that "Authorities should cooperate and support each other in a crisis situation." What is included in such cooperation, however, is not clearly stated. The issue of adding emphasis on cooperation departs from the general Swedish national crisis management design, which strives to mirror normal operations, codified in the crisis management principles of responsibility, subsidiarity, and similarity.

Every agency is mandated to deal with its own responsibilities even during a crisis situation. There is no specific crisis law or state of emergency that alters or suspends normal executive, legislative, or judiciary powers or structures (Andersson 2019).

There are at least three additional reasons why the case of the 2015 migration crisis in Sweden is interesting to study from a coordination and cooperation perspective. First, it brings concerns of overlapping networks to the fore since both vertical and horizontal coordination and cooperation challenges are discernible in the empirical case. Second, the case illustrates the challenges associated with complex societal crisis situations when critical issues do not fall within a given actor's area of responsibility (Swedish Civil Contingencies Agency 2016, 25). Third, at the time the Migration Agency was not included in the crisis preparedness network structure, meaning that the agency lacked established routines for crisis cooperation with actors outside of their area of expertise and even previous experience in crisis management.

Method and Data

In an influential study in the field of collaborative public management, Ansell and Gash (2008, 562) stress that case studies are "particularly valuable where the interaction between variables is nonlinear" and that "intensive case study research is a successful strategy for developing greater insights into the collaborative process." In line with these ideas, we use a case study approach to shed light on relevant examples of coordination challenges that may arise when multiple agencies are involved in managing a societal crisis.

A wide range of sources is required to produce a thorough case study account of a crisis management process. Media sources, agency web sites, and official government documents compose the basis of the sources used to inform this study. In addition, we accessed transcripts of interviews with key actors. The interviews focused primarily on issues concerning voluntary organizations and public agency collaboration. They were therefore used only in a supplementary way. We used media sources to create a greater understanding of the accessible information as well as to examine how the key actors reacted to the policy issues at hand. We selected two reputable newspapers: the national Stockholm based morning paper *Dagens Nyheter*, and the biggest daily morning paper from the south of Sweden, *Sydsvenska Dagbladet*, as this part of the country was most affected by the increased migration flows. We limited our search to the most critical period of the crisis from July 1 to November 12, 2015. In addition to media sources, we trawled public investigations, such as the Swedish National Audit Office's report on the establishment of temporary border controls (Swedish National Audit Organization 2016), the government's public investigation report on the reception of refugees (Swedish Government 2017), and the Swedish Civil Contingency Agency's report on its governmental assignment during the refugee situation (Swedish Civil Contingencies Agency 2016).

In order to reveal novel takes on the issue of crisis coordination we direct our attention specifically on three within-case observations – the quest for finding housing for newcomers, the reception of unaccompanied minors, and the quest to gain control of the borders. These three aspects of the crisis management all display coordination challenges among authorities. In that sense, they do not aspire to give an exhaustive account of the entire migrant crisis but rather to highlight relevant examples that pertained to the unsustainable reception situation and that at the time demanded major attention from authorities. Selecting within-case observations for further study means that our attention was directed to a restricted number of key actors. The key agencies involved in the management of the issues of housing, unaccompanied minors, and border controls included the Swedish

The 2015 Migrant Crisis: Within-Case Observations

In June 2015, signals were ambiguous on what the effects of the deteriorating situation in the Middle East and the ongoing war in Syria could be for the EU states including Sweden. On the one hand, UNHCR claimed a steep increase of migrants into Europe; on the other, the overall number of refugees entering Sweden was decreasing. At the same time, the number of unaccompanied minors was increasing (Swedish Government 2017). On July 23, the Migration Agency lowered its prognosis on the expected numbers of people seeking asylum in Sweden from 80,000 to 74,000. Soon thereafter border controls around the Aegean Sea broke down and refugees used the route into mainland Europe via Turkey and Greece at a greater intensity. The heavily increased influx of refugees into Sweden started in August (Swedish Government 2017, 64).

Housing

Arrangements for managing the issue of housing for refugees arriving in Sweden are not entirely straightforward. Locally the issue falls under the municipal authority and nationally it is the responsibility of the Migration Agency. Local authorities are responsible for organizing housing for unaccompanied minors, while the Migration Agency is in charge of offering housing to those others who apply for asylum while their application is being assessed. The housing issue also requires public-private partnership, as the Migration Agency's accommodation facilities are mostly owned by private entrepreneurs. Private partners, in turn, operate under contracts negotiated according to the law on procurement and competitive market principles.

As pressure increased on local, regional and national authorities, the most affected organizations went into crisis mode. The need for a specific crisis arrangement to manage the events became evident when large numbers of people arrived at transportation hubs on September 7–9 (Swedish Government 2017, 280). For instance, the Migration Agency established "staff preparedness" on September 6, entailing daily briefings and centralized efforts on managing the housing situation and other critical issues (Krisinformation 2015). By mid-September, some 1000 people were arriving in Sweden daily. Media referred to the events as the "refugee crisis" (Ibid.). Around this time, a regional director at the Migration Agency told a reporter at the Swedish daily paper *Sydsvenskan* that "We reach new record levels every week, but our logistics are working. No one gets left behind at the train station."

The issue of housing required horizontal coordination as it included the local authorities, religious faith organizations, voluntary organizations and networks, and the County Boards, and hierarchical coordination as it included the Migration Agency on the local and central level and the Swedish Association of Local Authorities and Regions (SALAR) among others.

A complicating factor was that so-called transit refugees, who were not applying for asylum in Sweden, did not fall under a specific government authority responsibility. Here voluntary organizations and networks stepped in. Religious faith organizations and other voluntary organizations offered housing; however, as they were not included in the procurement processes, the government agencies could not take them up on their offer (Swedish Civil Contingencies Agency 2016, 21). High-level leaders acknowledged the issue in various ways. For instance, the Swedish Migration Agency General Director Anders Danielsson called for political leadership and for exceptions from regulations such as the law on procurement. Soon thereafter, the Migration Agency altered its standard for refugee housing, allowing for retrospective inspections, lowering the regulation regarding the number of people who may reside within a certain number of square meters, and increasing the number of people who may share a room. Nonetheless, the situation was becoming overwhelming for the authorities. The 560 vacancies at the Migration Agency's housing facilities in the larger Stockholm area filled up quickly leaving many without housing, and as a result many refugees had to spend the night at the central train station.

At the government level PM Löfven, on September 25, gave Minister of Justice and Migration Morgan Johansson the task to look into the issue of how more housing could be produced by preparing for "extraordinary measures" (Krisinformation 2015). His investigation suggested utilizing module housing and the local "evacuation sites" (such as campsites, industrial facilities, apartments, and schools) for refugee housing. These "extraordinary measures" were implemented shortly thereafter, as the Cabinet, on October 8, decided to ease the regulations on housing. In essence, the Cabinet requested that the County Boards make an inventory of all available locations within their geographic jurisdiction that could be used as temporary housing for refugees (Cabinet 2015b). In addition, the Migration Agency was permitted to construct and manage tents in order to shelter refugees (Cabinet 2015c). The tent assignment was offered to the Swedish Migration Agency and supported by Swedish Civil Contingencies Agency, the Fortification Agency, and the County Boards (Swedish Government 2017, 104). The large flows continued, and on November 5, the number of people seeking asylum in Sweden peaked to 1868 in just one day according to press reports (*Sydsvenskan* 26 December 2015). At that point the Minister of Justice and Migration Johansson stated to *Dagens Nyheter* that "The limit is reached." The system for receiving, processing, and housing refugees could not keep up with the flow (*Dagens Nyheter* 6 November 2015). On November 11, the General Director of the Migration Agency in a letter to the Ministry of Justice requested border controls. The implementation of border controls the following day along with other more restrictive migration policy measures meant that the acute crisis approached termination. On December 15, PM Löfven claimed that the acute crisis was over (*Dagens Nyheter* 18 December 2015). Although Löfven's crisis termination seemed to have been somewhat premature, the situation appeared to be returning to normalcy (Swedish Government 2017; Strömberg 2016).

Unaccompanied Minors

One of the most pressing issues for the authorities during the migration crisis concerned the reception of unaccompanied minors. Regulations applying to unaccompanied minors are rigorous and more complex than for other asylum seekers as they include specific considerations and procedures, such as the right to a legal guardian in order to maintain the rule of law during the reception of the most vulnerable migrant category.

A mix of local and central responsibilities are involved with unaccompanied minors. The Migration Agency is responsible for assessing asylum applications. The municipal administrations, and more specifically the local social services, are responsible for offering housing in two steps. First, minors are offered temporary "transit" housing in the municipality in which they first contact the authorities. Second, the Migration Agency assigns the minor to a more long-term housing solution in the municipality where he/she will reside throughout the asylum process. Further, the County Boards are required to "deliberate" and "negotiate" with the municipalities and other involved parties on the reception and availability of housing for unaccompanied minors, to "act in favor of" preparedness and capacity for the local reception of unaccompanied minors, and to develop coordination between local municipalities and other agencies in their jurisdictions (Swedish Migration Agency 2015b; National Board of Health and Welfare 2013).

The number of unaccompanied minors applying for asylum in Sweden became increasingly challenging for many municipalities in mid-August 2015. For instance, the city of Malmö began receiving as many unaccompanied minors daily as they had previously received in an entire week. This mounting pressure on the city employees caused the social secretaries' trade union to react against the stressful and unsafe environment for the newly arrived unaccompanied minors and for the local employees, as reported by *Sydsvenskan* on August 18. The Migration Agency General Director summed up the situation accordingly:

> The local administrations and agencies are short of staff, which makes the registration and distribution of children difficult. . . . Staff members have to work overtime and carry out tasks that they are not trained for. This leads to risks for the children and the staff.
>
> *(Dagens Nyheter* 19 December 2015)

The Minister of Justice and Migration Morgan Johansson, in an article in *Dagens Nyheter* on August 20, 2015, acknowledged the situation as a substantial problem, but one that "the authorities and municipalities will have to manage within the confines of their budget and operations." The pressure increased even more in mid-September as a large number of refugees arrived in Sweden by ferry from Germany. Now disturbing media reports from Stockholm Central Train Station claimed that nongovernmental representatives were greeting the unaccompanied minors and keeping them from registering with the authorities. The Migration Agency's Information Director also confirmed this phenomenon to *Sydsvenskan* on September 9, 2015. The agency's General Director described the increase in the number of unaccompanied minors as an extraordinary situation that should eventually change the migration policy system (*Dagens Nyheter* 19 December 2015). Around this time, there was also a noticeable shift in public opinion on Swedish refugee reception.

In October the chairman of the municipal board and the municipal director of Trelleborg in a letter to SALAR, the regional board, and the minister of migration described the difficulties in managing 1400 unaccompanied minors who had arrived to the municipality in the last two weeks (Trelleborg 2015). Before being able to transfer these minors to long-term housing, they first had to be registered with the Migration Agency, which was overstretched. The municipal leaders requested that Trelleborg be excluded from the national regulations forcing municipalities to accept unaccompanied minors (Swedish Migration Agency 2015b). This request was accepted.

At a press conference on October 9, PM Löfven claimed that Sweden was dealing with one of the largest humanitarian challenges ever. The PM introduced several policy initiatives including supportive housing, a new form of housing for unaccompanied minors between the ages of 16 and 20 (*Dagens Nyheter* 10 September 2015), and the request to the Swedish National Board of Institutional Care (Statens institutionsstyrelse) to investigate the conditions of establishing 1000 lodging facilities (Cabinet 2015a). The policy initiatives taken in early October aimed at facilitating the management of the increasing numbers of migrants, removing bureaucratic obstacles, and elucidating coordination roles within the agency structures. These reforms, however, did not lead to an immediate impact. Hence, on October 21, PM Löfven acknowledged that "Sweden is approaching a limit for our capacity to accept refugees" (*Sydsvenskan* 26 December 2015). Two days later the Cabinet and the center-right opposition presented a multiparty agreement on temporary residence permits, a coercive policy encouraging municipalities to accept migrants, and financial guarantee demands for family reunification (*Dagens Nyheter* 18 December 2015).

The number of unaccompanied minors entering Sweden remained the main challenge. In early November, the authorities working with asylum reception were approaching a breakdown as 23,400 unaccompanied minors had arrived in three months. The situation was especially difficult for the local administrations in reception hubs such as Malmö and Trelleborg (*Sydsvenskan* 26 December 2015). In an effort to direct upper hierarchy attention to the challenges, many municipalities were reporting their local authorities to the Health and Social Care Inspectorate for breaches of required laws and regulations. Claims of substandard housing solutions, minors disappearing upon their arrival, and personnel recruited without background checks accompanied the reports according to a *Sydsvenskan* article from October 15, 2015. The Inspectorate received 64 reports of potential transgressions in the autumn of 2015 (Swedish Civil Contingencies Agency 2016, 17; Swedish Migration Agency 2015a).

Reintroducing Border Controls

According to the Schengen Borders Code, reintroducing border controls can only be implemented in exceptional cases, limited in time to 30 days (which, if necessary, can be prolonged), and should be seen as an absolute last resort (Art. 25 of the SBC). In Sweden, the police are in charge of border security and the established chain of command stipulates that they should signal to the political leadership when they deem it necessary to reintroduce border controls (Ch. 9, §1, Aliens Act).

Already in September 2015, the Police Regions South and West reported to the Department of National Operations (NOA) that the migrant situation was getting critical and that reintroducing border controls should be considered. NOA presented three alternatives to the Police Commissioner by the end of September: to reinforce the internal control of foreigners, to reintroduce border controls, or to keep operations unaltered. On October 21, the Police Commissioner decided that the situation was not serious enough to ask the Cabinet to reintroduce border controls. However, on November 12, the Cabinet decided to do so, encouraged by above all the Migration Agency. The controls came into effect the same day at noon (Swedish National Audit Organization 2016, 8–9).

The Police Authority incorporated the Cabinet decision in an ongoing special operation, which had been set up to enforce law and order due to the large influx of migrants. The location of the border controls was not specified, but the Police Authority decided to include two harbors and the Oresund Bridge in Police Region South and two harbors in Police Region West.

In especially Police Region South, the reintroduction of border controls implied a massive effort, not least since the Oresund region has a large commuter population that lives and works on separate sides of the Oresund Strait dividing Sweden from Denmark. The existing police force was just not large enough to cope with the situation. They were in particular need of border police (who were familiar with the procedures related to asylum seekers and deporting people, among other things), and the need became heavier as time passed, and the Cabinet prolonged the border controls (Swedish National Audit Organization 2016, 27). The Police Authority had a clear and designated leadership role, and the other relevant actors involved were the Swedish Migration Agency, the Swedish Customs, and the Swedish Coast Guard, of which the latter two have received government instructions to assist the Police when necessary.

As of January 1, 2015, the Police Authority had become one single authority, instead of the previously 21 authorities. Hence, during the peak of the migration influx the Police Authority was in the midst of implementing a new organization. In the beginning, the central level in Stockholm (NOA) thought that the border controls in Region South were being carried out selectively (as in Region West), which delayed their responsiveness to the needs in the southern part of the country by four days (Swedish National Audit Organization 2016, 37 and 50). However, the unitary nature of the Police Authority facilitated regrouping of personnel, at least on paper. On the national level, it was decided how many police officers each region should send to Police Region South (Police Region West could cope with their own personnel), but the regions decided who to send. During the time studied, between 96 and 120 police officers from the rest of the country were relocated to reinforce the southern region with a biweekly rotation scheme. There was also a reinforcement rotation within Police Region South. Very few of the police reinforcements had experience of, or training in, border controls, except for the one-hour briefing that was organized for them upon arrival. This affected the quality of the border controls negatively, not least in terms of securing the legal rights of the new arrivals (Ibid, 37–38).

In terms of horizontal cooperation, the Police Authority asked the Swedish Customs and the Coast Guard on November 12 for assistance due to the migration situation, and the two authorities consented. Police Region West used both the Coast Guard and the Swedish Customs at the harbors in order to relieve the pressure on the police officers posted there. Police Region South asked the Coast Guard for assistance at the Helsingborg harbor but never asked the Swedish Customs for support. The southern region rather relied on the police reinforcements, which resulted in extra costs for travel and lodging. In contrast to police reinforcements, the support from the Coast Guard (and the Swedish Customs in the west) was given a broader education on how to conduct border controls. The Migration Agency reportedly had a preparedness to assist the police with border controls, had they been asked. The police's collaboration with the Migration Agency instead focused on handing over asylum seekers, and in that respect the authorities had differing views on where to draw the line of responsibility (Swedish National Audit Organization 2016, 41–42).

Discussion

In this section we discuss and dig further into the points of entry to this case study. We will hence return to the predicaments of overlapping networks, network adaptiveness, and issues of ownership and leadership.

Overlapping Networks

Within the field of Collaborative Public Management, challenges with cooperating and coordinating within the parameters of established networks have been widely discussed (McGuire 2006). The challenges presumably increase in crisis management efforts, where networks tend to overlap along temporal and spatial dimensions and with respect to functional task areas (Bynander and Nohrstedt, this volume). This study corroborates such assumptions. Particularly in the spatial dimension, there seems to be a function between vertical (local, regional, national) coordination and horizontal (not least within-regional) cooperation. The more unclear the vertical coordination is, the more difficult it becomes for regional actors to make use of resources outside of established networks. This in turn has to do with different layers of responsibility and accountability but also with how far from normalcy they felt comfortable to stretch. The episode with the police's implementation of the reintroduction of border controls is revealing in this regard.

The County Boards play a key role as intermediaries between the national and local levels of government. How well they managed to take on this role and support the municipalities during the migration crisis appeared to be contingent on their internal organization and the individual officials' crisis management experience. Some county boards did not modify their management structures into crisis management organizations. According to the Swedish Civil Contingencies Agency, it was easier to establish coordination in those geographical locations where contact persons shared experiences of working in emergency and crisis management structures (Swedish Civil Contingencies Agency 2016, 27).

Initially, upper hierarchies responded sluggishly to the challenges. The political level framed the problems as local issues and tasks and thus passed the buck to the local administrative level. Some of the county boards did not manage to respond vigilantly enough, leaving the local level frustrated while operating at the limit. Instead, SALAR, the Swedish Association of Local Authorities and Regions took on the "geographical regional responsibility" role that formally belongs to the County Boards (Swedish Civil Contingencies Agency 2016, 28). In the event of a crisis SALAR is not formally obliged to take specific action or coordinate its response in the way that government agencies are. In this regard, it is noteworthy that early on in the process SALAR established a crisis organization and became an important "discussion partner" for central agencies and other actors on the national level regarding the reception and transfer of unaccompanied minors (Ibid). Furthermore, SALAR also facilitated cooperation between the various local administrations, thus taking on a role that formally lies with the County Boards (Swedish Government 2017, 269). A factor contributing to SALAR taking on such a coordinating role was the fact that several County Boards took on narrow interpretations of their crisis coordinating roles (Ibid, 221; Markelius 2016). On the other hand, several County Boards noticed that civil society and government agencies did not understand the essence of the County Boards' responsibilities regarding crisis management. According to their view, expectations went beyond the tasks involved in the geographical area responsibilities (Ibid, 220). These observations clearly testify to the need for brokerage points to overcome hurdles associated with overlapping networks.

Network Adaptiveness

Collaborative learning in the aftermath of crises is a topic in need of in-depth studies, and that is true also for intra-crisis collaborative learning and adaptation (Heikkila, Weible, and Gerlak 2010; Bynander and Nohrstedt, this volume). This connotes to the temporal dimension of overlapping networks. In essence, the migration crisis in Sweden is a case of overload that cumulatively built up, and as such increasingly added demands and needs for new and alternative ways of networking. Here the needs for abiding by various laws came at odds with expectations of legitimate actions that clearly hampered collaboration and to some extent even made the involved actors competitors for resources.

At the peak of the migration influx, the Migration Agency tried, seemingly in desperation, to place mattresses in its premises, but this was not possible due to building permits. Moreover, housing facilities had to meet fire safety standards, and those who had lost a procurement often made appeals, delaying the entire process. As the operational director of the Migration Agency told the Swedish Daily *Svenska Dagbladet* on July 16, 2016, "Sometimes we felt discouraged. Society seemed to expect that everything would work as usual. The definition of a crisis is that it does not." Indeed, dealing with the paradox of operating within the boundaries of legality and managing extraordinary challenges requires intricate balancing acts from local authorities and government agencies alike.

In a similar vein, friction occurred in the coordination between the local and national levels. Local administrators in Malmö were disappointed over the perceived lack of adaptiveness provided by the Swedish Civil Contingencies Agency. According to the local authorities, the agency prioritized rule abiding rather than creative problem solving (Swedish Government 2017, 260). Moreover, the local administrations were disappointed over what they perceived as a lack of support from the County Boards assigned to facilitate coordination within the boundaries of their respective jurisdiction. For example, a local administration told the governmental inquiry commission after the events that its County Board held three telephone conferences in a short time frame and in the midst of the operational and acute crisis. Despite the mounting operational tasks and time pressure at hand, the roll call alone took an hour (Swedish Government 2017, 258–59). Such episodes demonstrate a lack of adaptive capacity during crisis conditions when flexibility is required from actors throughout the coordinating networks.

Network adaptiveness did also occur, however. As the migration policy issue approached crisis proportions, the Government Offices became increasingly involved in the coordination of the national response. Starting on October 1, the Cabinet made several decisions aimed at removing some of the bureaucratic barriers to arrange housing for newly arrived migrants. Regarding the issue of building permits for the provisional tent villages, the authorities went ahead and did not wait for the arrival of the permit (which came several months later in April 2016). Instead, regulations for temporary housing and vacation housing were utilized (Swedish Government 2017, 176).

Dealing with migrants that apply for asylum clearly falls under the Migration Agency's mandate. However, newly arrived asylum seekers who for various reasons had not registered with the Migration Agency did not fall under any specific government authority's responsibility (Save the Children 2016). This responsibility loophole created a gap in the reception system that the government and agencies failed to see. This void in the reception system, in turn, provided an opening for substantial participation in the collaborative management by voluntary organizations. This also highlights the importance of network adaptiveness in the midst of a crisis, which was visibly a challenge in this case.

The Police Authority declares that although there were dialogues on the local level, they did not initiate coordinating activities with the voluntary organizations on the national level (Wallberg 2016). On the other hand, the Swedish Civil Contingencies Agency employed a liaison officer with knowledge about voluntary organizations and who had a large network within these organizations.

When legitimacy conflicts with legality, a cooperation and coordination network could potentially facilitate steps toward legitimacy in favor of legality by way of anchoring decisions within the network. Our case study does not, however, provide conclusive evidence of this; rather, the networks heralded the legal predicaments for adaptiveness.

Issues of Ownership and Leadership

The three within-case observations, the quest for finding housing for newcomers, the reception of unaccompanied minors, and the quest to gain control of the borders, display varying degrees of designated ownership. The evidence from the Swedish experiences of the migration crisis suggests that a strong sense of ownership has a containing effect, even to the detriment of managerial effectiveness. On the other hand, when there is virtually no sense of ownership, problems fall between the cracks of responsibility. This is a challenge that perhaps does not vouch for additional coordinative responsibility but rather directs attention to leadership styles and practices within networks.

In terms of ownership, the Migration Agency was formally in charge of the core policy issue. However, the core policy issue spilled over into a number of policy areas requiring numerous networks of actors and in essence questioning the very plausibility of one government agency taking on an overarching ownership of the crisis management. Clearly, the Migration Agency was severely overstretched, and its attempts to keep up to speed with even its basic tasks in migrant reception was a challenge, often limiting its perspectives to be narrow, inward-looking, and operational rather than strategic or comprehensive. Further, vertical cooperation was another important crisis management task that was neglected. For instance, the Migration Agency did not arrange for a duty officer. Even in the midst of the crisis, the agency closed its doors for the weekend. The local municipality administrators were instructed to communicate with the migration agency by fax (Swedish Government 2017, 261).

The lack of a duty officer was one of several problems associated with the fact that the Migration Agency was not a formal part of the Swedish crisis management system. Hence, crisis preparedness issues had not been on the agency's agenda, which exacerbated the difficulties of crisis coordination (Swedish Civil Contingencies Agency 2016, 26–27). The Migration Agency staff members lacked experience of working with actors outside of their area of expertise. In an effort to clarify the crisis coordination structure, the Cabinet decided on October 1 to reiterate the Swedish Civil Contingencies Agency's coordinating mandate on the national level. Although this mandate was already included in the agency's instructions, the formal governmental agreement meant that inter-organizational interaction went from informal cooperation to formal coordination. It however remains questionable if this renewed and enforced coordinative responsibility implied an improvement for the Migration Agency and the other actors with little pre-knowledge of the national crisis management system. It remains unclear if it meant much for the authorities with a firm base in the crisis management system, such as the Police. On that end of the spectrum, familiarity with the crisis management system in combination with significant experience of managing crises and major events left little room for network expansion. These empirical findings challenge the idea of crisis ownership as pivotal for crisis mitigation and management, which in turn evokes issues of costs for networking (Hicklin et al. 2009; Agranoff and McGuire 2003) and leadership styles and behavior in cooperative crisis management (Bynander and Nohrstedt, this volume).

Conclusions

This chapter departed from an interest in finding out how interaction played out among stakeholders in the case of the 2015 migration crisis in Sweden. As we focused on the acute phase of the response, we framed the case as a cathartic crisis event with a gradual onset and sharp termination. Although the crisis management required participation from a large range of constellations drawing from civil society to the private sector and government authorities, our interest here has been in the formal government authority aspects of the crisis management. Thus, the analysis kept in line with the setup of the actual response system and drew on the local to national levels of crisis management. The response was largely institutionalized, although the ubiquity of the actual event left ample opportunity for *ad hoc* measures. In terms of joint actions taken throughout the response network, there was resource sharing on a limited scale; for instance, the Swedish Civil Contingencies Agency offered seconded workforce and expertise to overloaded agencies. Most of the joint actions, however, revolved around information sharing and establishing a common operational picture of the challenges at hand. As most agencies involved were overstretched, individual agency goals were prioritized rather than joint goals. Hardly surprising then, our within-case observations show distinct challenges that may arrive in the complex process of multiagency crisis management. The observations give us important insights into what happens when steadfast government agencies working within rigid legal structures are confronted by numerous rapidly approaching policy problems that demand their immediate attention and that require creative and flexible action.

Under crisis conditions, issues are often brought to a head. Collaboration may yield conflict (O'Leary et al. 2009). Our case demonstrates shared goals and coordination, but it also shows episodes of conflict regarding competition over resources, financial remuneration, and even downright scuffling (Mattsson 2016). The inquiry commission, for instance, reported that some municipalities saw the migration agency as a counterpart rather than a partner (Swedish Government 2017, 261). Vertical coordination between the national and local levels as well as horizontal coordination on the regional level was suboptimal at the least.

Why then did problems and conflicts arise concerning coordination between the organizations involved in the migration crisis? One obstacle referred to the legal requirements that were in need of alteration to harmonize more with crisis expectations and processes. As the legal and administrative system is constructed to deal with everyday management rather than crisis management, there are no legal ways of adapting the system in earnest to crisis management proportions, which tends to lead to frustration for the people responsible for managing the crisis. Conflicts also intensified as a result of the lack of shared experiences between the various agencies and organizations involved in managing the migration crisis. Lack of shared histories and experiences lead to difficulties in understanding the tasks, perspectives, and philosophies in use by the various actors involved, which is required in order to find common ground for cooperation and collaboration. In this regard, our case findings stress the perils of building the whole-of-society response on rhetoric rather than practice.

On a final note, it is worth mentioning that we did not find empirical evidence of such deep service integration in our empirical case to speak of collaboration. Rather coordination and cooperation are the key concepts that can be used to describe the multiorganizational responses to the 2015 migration crisis in Sweden. These limitations in the level of integration between the organizations involved in managing the crisis can also be understood as limitations to successful crisis management in the case at hand.

References

Agranoff, Robert and Michael McGuire. 2003. *Collaborative Public Management: New Strategies for Local Government*. Washington, DC: Georgetown University Press.

Andersson, Emmelie, ed. 2019. *Förutsättningar för krisberedskap och totalförsvar i Sverige [Preconditions for Crisis Preparedness and Total Defense in Sweden]*. Stockholm: Swedish Defense University.

Ansell, Chris and Alison Gash. 2008. "Collaborative Governance in Theory and in Practice." *Journal of Public Administration Research and Theory* 18 (4): 543–71.

Auf der Heide, Erik. 1989. *Disaster Response: Principles and Preparation and Coordination*. St Louis, MO: The C.V. Mosby Company.

Cabinet. 2015a. Cabinet Decision II:4 2015–10–08 S2015/06476/FST.

———. 2015b. Cabinet Decision I:2 2015–10–08 Ju2015/07537/SIM.

———. 2015c. Cabinet Decision I:1 2015–10–09 Ju2015/07557/SIM.

Drabek, Thomas and David McEntire. 2002. "Emergent Phenomena and Multiorganizational Coordination in Disasters: Lessons from the Research Literature." *International Journal of Mass Emergencies and Disasters* 20 (2): 197–224.

Heikkila, Tanya, Chris Weible, and Andrea Gerlak. 2–5 September 2010. "Upscaling from Individual to Collective Learning in Policy Process Research." Paper presented at APSA in Washington, DC.

Hicklin, Alisa, Laurence O'Toole Jr., Kenneth Meier, and Scott Robinson. 2009. "Calming the Storms: Collaborative Public Management, Hurricanes Katrina and Rita, and Disaster Response." In *The Collaborative Public Manager, New Ideas for the Twenty First Century*, edited by Rosemary O'Leary and Lisa Blomgren Bingham. Washington, DC: Georgetown University Press.

Krisinformation. 27 September 2015. "Omvärldsbevakning vecka 39." [Business Intelligence Week 39]. www.krisinformation.se/om-krisinformation.se/for-myndigheter-och-andra-aktorer/omvarldsbevakning/2015/vecka-39 (Accessed 11 February 2016).

Lindberg, Helena and Bengt Sundelius. 2013. "Whole of Society Disaster Resilience: The Swedish Way." In *McGraw Hill Homeland Security Handbook*, edited by David Kamien, 1295–319. New York, NY: McGraw Hill.

Löfven, Stefan. 2016. "KU-utfrågning Löfven." [Swedish Parliament's Standing Committee on the Constitution's Hearing with Löfven]. Video, 2 h 54 min. SVT Forum. www.svtplay.se/klipp/8192930/ku-utfragning-lofven

Markelius, Malin. 15 June 2016. Interview by Viktoria Asp with the Safety and Security Coordinator at Malmö Municipality.

Mattsson, Ola. 14 September 2016. Interview by Viktoria Asp with the Sweden Program Director, Swedish Save the Children.

McGuire, Michael. 2006. "Collaborative Public Management: Assessing What We Know and How We Know It." *Public Administration Review* 89 (2): 265–84.

National Board of Health and Welfare. 2 May 2013. *Socialtjänstens arbete med ensamkommande barn och ungdomar-en vägledning.* [The National Board of Health and Welfare's Work with Unaccompanied Children and Minors: A Guide]. Stockholm: National Board of Health and Welfare.

O'Leary, Rosemary, Beth Gazley, Michael McGuire, and Lisa Blomgren Bingham. 2009. "Public Managers in Collaboration." In *The Collaborative Public Manager, New Ideas for the Twenty First Century*, edited by Rosemary O'Leary and Lisa Blomgren Bingham, 1–12. Washington, DC: Georgetown University Press.

Save the Children. 2016. *Handbok för civilsamhällets samverkan vid kriser: En modell baserad på erfarenheter från samarbetet mellan Rädda Barnen, Röda Korset och Riksföreningen Sveriges Stadsmissioner under flyktingmottagandet hösten 2015 [Handbook for the Civil Society's Coordination During Crises: A Model Based on Experiences from Cooperation Between Save the Children, the Red Cross and the Salvation Army's City Mission During the Reception of Refugees in the Fall of 2015].* Stockholm: Taberg Media Group.

Social Democratic Party. 2015. *Valanalys 2014: Att vinna framtiden-en dubbel utmaning, Rapport från Socialdemokraternas valanalysgrupp, Valet 2014 [Election Analysis 2014: To Win the Future-A Double Challenge: Report from the Social Democratic Party's Election Analysis Group].* Stockholm 2015. www.socialdemokraterna.se/upload/Rapporter/Valanalys/Valanalys14_slutrapport.pdf (Accessed 26 January 2016).

Strömberg, Rickard. 20 September 2016. Interview by Viktoria Asp with Crisis Preparedness Expert at the Migration Agency.

Swedish Civil Contingencies Agency. 15 May 2016. *Rapportering av MSB:s uppdrag från regeringen avseende flyktingsituationen [Report from the Swedish Civil Contingencies Agency's Governmental Tasks Regarding the Refugee Situation].* dnr. 2016–2440. Stockholm: Swedish Civil Contingencies Agency.

Swedish Government. 2017. *SOU 2017:12: Att ta emot människor på flykt Sverige hösten 2015* [Receiving Refugees Sweden During the Fall of 2015]. Stockholm: Wolters Kluwer Sverige.

Swedish Migration Agency. 2015a. "Migrationsverket förordar införande av gränskontroll." [The Swedish Migration Agency Recommends the Introduction of Border Controls]. ref. 1.1.2–2015–75130, Letter from the Swedish Migration Board to the Ministry of Justice.

———. 9 October 2015b. "Trelleborgs kommun undantas anvisning av ensamkommande barn." [The Municipality of Trelleborg Exempt from Allocation of Unaccompanied Minors]. www.migrationsverket.se/Om-Migrationsverket/Nyhetsarkiv/Nyhetsarkiv-2015/2015-10-09-Trelleborgs-kommun-undantas-anvisning-av-ensamkommande-barn.html (Accessed 12 February 2016).

Swedish National Audit Organization. 2016. *Upprättande av tillfälliga gränskontroller vid inre gräns*. RIR 2016:26. Stockholm: Swedish National Audit Organization.

Trelleborg. 9 October 2015. "Trelleborg får hjälp av Migrationsverket." www.trelleborg.se/sv/aktuellt/nyheter/2015/oktober/trelleborg-far-hjalp-av-migrationsverket/ (Accessed 12 February 2016).

Wallberg, Thomas. 21 June 2016. Interview by Daniel Sandberg with the Operational Chief of Operation Alma.

Chapter 5

Overcoming Collective-Action Problems in Collaborative Crisis Management

Meta-Governance and Security Communications Systems

Oscar L. Larsson

Introduction

The emergence and presence of *collaborative crisis management networks*, in terms of close collaboration between public and private actors in managing crises and security issues, implies a major restructuring of the political field of security. This field now covers everything from external threats to national security to crises, disturbances, and accidents in society (Kapucu, Arslan, and Collins 2010; Larsson 2015, 76). As new issues as well as new actors have emerged on the crisis management scene, state authorities must be open to new ways to govern that are sensitive to various types of actors/identities, knowledge, and the decentralization of authority, while being supportive of emerging collaborative efforts (Larsson 2013). One of the key tasks for the responsible public authorities is to initiate and maintain various organizational architectures as well as technical systems in order to facilitate functional collaboration in loosely and temporarily composed networks.

The nature of crisis requires collaborating partners to communicate effectively with each other in order to make informed decisions under conditions of uncertainty and to engage and call upon the assistance of additional actors in the security network to mitigate, prepare for, respond to, and recover from crises (Sellnow and Seeger 2013). In this chapter, I will scrutinize how the Swedish state implemented and managed a new Security Communications System (SCS) called RAKEL by considering three different dimensions and core challenges: hardware, software, and economic aspects. This study concerns aspects of planning and facilitating collaborative crisis management rather than the operational phase of crisis management. The mode of governance in this regard is what the introductory chapter referred to as *system architecture* and what I elsewhere have called "the meta-governance of collaborative crisis management." Meta-governance concerns strategies and efforts to promote collaboration, among others, yet without placing explicit demands on the operative mode of collaboration and crisis management (Larsson 2017). In short, meta-governance could be seen as a way to address collective-action problems that emerge in collaborative crisis management since technical solutions and systems are to be implemented and adopted.

The benefits of a common communication system are obvious, but the management of crisis communication is a multidimensional challenge, including technical issues, knowledge, and user-friendliness, as well as financial issues, including who should pay for the communication system. In a political field where collaboration is the key mode of operation and where human lives and core values are at stake, overcoming collective-action problems is of utmost importance. The two research questions guiding this chapter are: what strategies have been used for overcoming collective-action problems in the management of Security Communications Systems (SCS), and what lessons can be learned from the Swedish case?

This chapter begins with a theoretical section discussing the role of information and communication in collaborative crisis management and the potential challenges in managing communication systems. This part also presents the methodology and the materials used in this case study. The chapter then turns to the empirical analysis and shows how the three dimensions (hardware, software, and economic aspects) have played a significant role in the Swedish case. A final section concludes the empirical analysis and specifies some core insights generated from the study.

The Role of Information and Communication in Collaborative Crisis Management

A significant factor contributing to successful crisis management in responding to both natural and human-made disasters is functional and spontaneous *communication* between all the involved actors (Manoj and Baker 2007). Difficulties or restrictions in communication are likely to create suboptimal management of a crisis, especially if there is no established high-status organization that can act as a hub for information collection and dissemination (Ansell, Boin, and Keller 2010, 199). The management of security communication is in itself a challenge that involves the overall system as well as technical development. I refer to this as the hardware. Of equal importance is the software of crisis communication, understood as the immediate knowledge of how to operate the system and how to communicate with collaborating actors (Boin and Hart 2010, 368; Gains 2004, 549f).

Whereas Boin and Hart (2010) have illustrated a conflict between hardware (technical system) and software (knowledge and user friendliness), I would suggest that we must add another element, that is, the financial aspects of managing communications systems. As we shall see, economic aspects of the crisis management infrastructure contribute to the complexity of overcoming collective-action problems in the implementation and usage of new technical infrastructure. The three dimensions of hardware, software, and financial solutions can create deadlocks and conflicts that can have a negative impact on collaborative crisis management. Let us consider these dimensions in more detail before going to the empirical analysis.

SCS are utilized in security networks to help organizations share and process information, establish communication channels, as well as reach and engage all of the necessary stakeholders in order to coordinate collaborative efforts among a large number of actors (Hu and Kapucu 2014, 2). One of the first issues is to choose between competing systems and applications using a cost-effective analysis based on needs and utility. This requires great knowledge of the existing system or the development and implementation of a new system (Kapucu 2006). In this respect, recent innovations in Information Communication Technology (ICT), if they are applied appropriately, have the potential to improve communication and help to mitigate the disturbing effects of threatening situations (Vogt, Hertweck, and Hales 2011, 1).

TETRA (Terrestrial Trunked Radio) was standardized in 1997 by the European Telecommunications Standards Institute (ETSI) and is now one of the leading digital ICTs used by many European states. The TETRA standard guarantees interoperability with unmatched versatility, efficiency, robustness, longevity, and security in respect to communications (Mikulic and Modlic 2008, 207).

All organizations involved in crisis management can benefit greatly from ICTs capable of improving their communications and coordination. Technological aspects shape how communication will take place in governance networks. New technical solutions and systems could substantially improve communication, but it requires that the end-users are willing and able to use the system. Given this background, it becomes all the more vital to understand how authorities can bridge collective-action problems while also attending to the economical dimensions of technical systems.

Despite an acknowledged commitment to deal with crisis in adequate ways, public and private actors have limited resources at hand. Most actors are often not willing to compromise their budget restraints and invest in technological systems with uncertain payoffs and utility. Technical issues, know-how, and economic concerns are interrelated (Jennings et al. 2017; Khan et al. 2017; Larsson 2015, 2017). Therefore, it is important to also attend to and give analytical weight to the management of costs in order to understand the system architecture and how technological systems are adopted in crisis management networks.

Case Selection, Methods, and Materials

The Swedish case is particularly interesting when it comes to the management of communication because the Swedish crisis management system is decentralized, collaboration among public and private actors is actively encouraged, and the new communication system was thought to be financially supported by the end-users rather than through the state. The study covers a long period, 2003–2016, which enables us to see the complexity and relational aspects of these variables rather than exploring them in isolation (George and Bennett 2005, 19f; Bennett and Checkel 2014, 20). Focusing on a single case from a specific theoretical framework is not necessarily about testing hypotheses and theories but provides foremost an excellent ground for heuristic refinement and add-ons to existing theories and understandings (George and Bennett 2005, 75). In collaborative crisis management most scholars struggle with the uniqueness of each emerging crisis. This study will, however, benefit from a systemic approach and a long time period that shows how problems emerge and are resolved by shifts in governance strategies.

In this analysis I have utilized written documents from public authorities (such as public investigations, governmental bills, annual reports, evaluations) but have also conducted interviews with key persons in order to understand the strategies and policy tools used to manage the accession and usage of the SCS by various actors. The interviews were conducted in 2012–2016 and each one lasted for approximately 60 minutes. The questions revolved around "governance in practice" and concerned the foremost strategies related to RAKEL and/or decentralized crisis management. The interviews were "semi-structured" and opened with broad questions in an attempt to stimulate the respondents to describe in their own words their work, role/functions in the system, and relations with private and public actors. Toward the end of each interview, I posed more specific questions (Kvale 2008).

The written documents were analyzed through a qualitative type of content analysis that specifically addressed the latent meanings and intersubjective understanding communicated in specific texts. This method focuses not only on overt meanings but also aims to discover the meaning within texts and analyze their communicative content. Briefly stated, qualitative content analysis emphasizes the need to interpret and contextualize the text, and its main aim is to highlight important passages and changes while eliminating more insignificant information in the presentation (Kuckartz 2014, 51).

Beyond interviews and qualitative text analysis of policy documents, I also engaged in more ethnographic participatory observations of meetings and workshops. These events enhanced my contextual understanding and provided important nuances about some of

Setting the Stage for Conflicts

On June 10, 2002, the Swedish government appointed a public investigator to prepare and present the groundwork for how a new SCS would be financed and managed. The conclusions of the public investigation were published on January 22, 2003. Besides offering a set of technical improvements in communications, the infrastructure of the new system would improve the overall robustness and secure communication during crises. One key aspect remained unresolved and that was who was to bear the costs for this new communication system; this very important unresolved issue stifled the construction and investment in a modern communication system (State Public Reports 2003). Several suggestions for cost-reductions were discussed. The most important was that end-users (such as emergency agencies and public and private organizations involved in crisis management) should finance the communication system themselves through subscription fees and payment for specific services and utility. A daunting task lay ahead for the responsible agency (KBM, a predecessor to MSB) to convince the professional emergency personnel as well as the public administrators not only to adopt the new communication system but also to financially underwrite the entire system.

A Wider Circle of Users

In 2004, the government authorized KBM to be the agency responsible for the construction, management, and development of RAKEL. One of the first initiatives proposed by KBM was that "more actors should have access to RAKEL and that many more actors must be granted permanent access" (KBM 2004, 31). KBM informed the government that it was actively looking into the possibility of increasing the circle of end-users and would provide recommendations in this direction in 2005. Consequently, KBM requested that its mission be widened and that the legal crisis management framework should be more widely defined in order to avoid restricting the circle of users (KBM 2005c). The 2005 government bill, *Collaboration in Crisis for a More Secure Society*, provided a new definition of who may be involved in the overall crisis management system effectively, widening the circle of end-users and customers to the new system (Swedish Bill [Proposition] 2005/06, 139f).

Despite the widening of the circle of end-users, KBM found it difficult to gauge the overall interest in RAKEL. Naturally, public safety agents seemed most enthusiastic. Regional authorities were also interested since they could use RAKEL in their healthcare and public safety programs. The most hesitant public organizations were the municipalities. Two key reasons for the hesitation among the municipalities can be identified as: (1) *the financial model* and the difficulties understanding the costs involved and (2) a general lack of interest based on *a different understanding of security and crisis management*. Their view followed a more traditional understanding that the military, police, and other emergency services deal with security and crises, whereas the public administrations had no role to play in the crisis management system (Högberg 2012). Thus, the municipalities and local public administrations did not identify themselves as crisis managers. These two critical approaches did supplement each other and are further explored later.

The financial model for the system suggested that all of the end-users should bear the entire cost for the communication system (Larsson 2017). In short, the security providers were responsible for buying their own equipment and paying specific subscription fees for using the system. They also needed to pay for training in and organizational adaptation to the new radio system (State Public Reports 2003, 104). The end-user fees and payment for additional services were also intended to cover the shared costs for the system, including operation, maintenance, development, and administration (State Public Reports 2003, 112). However, even if this financial model of *paying customers* solved the initial financial problem, it also generated a range of intricate problems of how to encourage accession to the communication system. On the contrary, it made actors more reluctant to join the new communication system. The majority of municipalities did not believe that RAKEL and the type of communication and functions it provided were useful for their everyday operations. The idea of a common communications system did not appeal to them, and they felt that the necessary equipment and fees would involve additional costs for them with little added value in return (Högberg 2012).

Technical Issues and Deadlocks

Another critical issue that further created unwillingness to join the system was technical problems and delays in the construction. The initial plan for building the radio system in sections was hindered by appeals and conflicts between competing contractors' companies. SAAB AB was finally granted the contract for constructing the system but was not able to meet the promised schedule. During this time, KBM also noted that operating costs would be higher than expected due to serious miscalculation on behalf of the 2003 public investigation since the system would require more maintenance than expected. Since the system should be self-financed by subscription fees and other taxes, KBM had to present the increased costs for 2006–2008 to potential end-users (KBM 2005a, 20f). This created a situation in which the rational decision for all actors was to wait and see if other actors would join, a telling case of collective-action problem causing stalemate in the entire process. KBM therefore concluded that "there must be an increased effort to inform and convince the municipalities and other potential users to join" (KBM 2005b).

In 2006 additional technical problems again increased the overall costs of the system. This included further delays with the building of new sections as the system needed more capacity to manage a larger volume of radio traffic than was previously expected. Another issue discovered at this time was that the system had difficulties with functioning in certain indoor environments, such as malls, airports, automobile and train tunnels, the subway, and various privately owned areas (KBM 2006a, 9). In addition, Sweden experienced a major storm in 2005 (Hurricane Gudrun), and this event revealed that the system was not robust enough, since it partly failed during the storm (KBM 2006a).

Software Issues – Lack of Knowledge (and Interest) Among End-Users

In the previous section we saw how technical and financial dimensions became interrelated and created coordination problems and distrust between the meta-governors and end-users. Adding to this difficult situation it was noted that different organizations and their respective end-users had widely varying knowledge of radio communications. Traditional public safety agents (e.g., the police) announced early on that they would adopt RAKEL as soon as possible. The public administrations and the municipalities were not familiar with this type of SCS, had little knowledge of radio communication, and barely knew that RAKEL existed in the first place. KBM feared that accession would be prolonged and that certain organizations would not even be capable to use the system. In a special report to the government, it was observed that many public administrations were not even interested in considering the terms or the costs for joining the system (KBM 2006b).

In 2006, KBM tried to intensify its efforts to convince crisis managers to adopt and start using the system. One way to achieve this was to provide more information about the system and its benefits (e.g., more accessible), especially to regional and local actors (KBM 2006a, 10). Another strategy that KBM used was to recruit 20 people from key crisis management organizations who would act as ambassadors for the new system within their respective organizations (KBM 2006a). These efforts could be seen as different strategies to encourage the various organizations to access the system without twisting their arms, that is, using traditional sovereign means and hierarchical implementation strategies.

Encouraging Accession and Participation

Due to the problems discussed earlier, accession to the system was much slower insofar as many security actors remained hesitant concerning the progress of the RAKEL project. RAKEL only had 400 users by the end of 2006, primarily from the police and the coast guard (KBM 2006b, 14). This is one key issue to resolve for a meta-governance approach to crisis management and communication; that is, to what extent it is possible to promote specific understandings of security and crises so that public administrations understand their role within such systems (Larsson 2015, 188)? If meta-governors are to "support activities that promote communication, coordination and collaboration across organizational boundaries" (Nohrstedt et al. 2014, 21), this also requires substantial resources, conscious strategies, and a shared agenda among the network participants. Given that both interest and knowledge were low among the potential end-users, the public authority in charge needed to take on a more active role as network manager.

One of the first actions that KBM took was to start a group for RAKEL users including the police, the local rescue services, public health services, and similar actors to pave the way for a wider adoption, in which all public administrations eventually should join. This would give KBM a better understanding of what various organizations wished to gain from the system. Hence, by getting to know and understand how different organizations viewed RAKEL, it would become possible to adjust the system, information, and marketing to make it look more attractive for each category (KBM 2006b, 23f). Yet KBM still had to take into consideration the financial model.

Changes in the Financial Model and Additional Adjustments

Another difficult year for RAKEL and KBM was 2007. The RAKEL system failed during a second hurricane (Hurricane Per) in much the same way it had during Hurricane Gudrun in 2005, which simply added to the already stressed financial situation with RAKEL (KBM 2007, 8). In 2007, the government realized that many organizations, both public and private, held a great deal of distrust toward RAKEL. Many actors were critical toward the difficulties of knowing the costs involved in joining the system. The government gave KBM the task to fix and stabilize the different fees in the system. The government also decided to provide fixed rates to those public agencies with special responsibilities in the crisis management system to ensure their commitment. The idea was that by swiftly gaining the support of public agencies on the national level it would both stimulate and accelerate

Overcoming Collective-Action Problems **63**

accession among other potential users, such as municipalities, regional authorities, and commercial and private actors. These reforms in the financial model were in many ways an acceptance that it would be impossible to reach the original goal of self-financing by 2008, and that it was not likely to reach this goal in the near future either (Budget proposal to Swedish Parliament 2008, 86).

In 2009, there was a major restructuring among the core public agencies involved in crisis management. KBM was replaced by MSB (Swedish Civil Contingencies Agency), taking over most of KBM's tasks. The first year for MSB was very much a startup year, and little happened regarding the management of the SCS. RAKEL was still being developed, but in the beginning of 2009, the first three out of six sections were finished and in full use (MSB 2009, 24).

Network Management Efforts and Communication

In the end of 2009, the Defense Department presented a new report called *RAKEL, Present and Future – Communication, Collaboration and Interoperationality* which focused on how to best proceed with RAKEL (Swedish Ministry of Defense 2010). The working group behind this report believed that RAKEL must be acknowledged and promoted as a necessary tool in the Swedish crisis management system but pointed out that there was no clear vision or overarching strategy from the government to achieve this goal (Swedish Ministry of Defense 2010, 2–4). The report revealed that RAKEL had hitherto not significantly improved communication between organizations in part due to technical knots within the system. The report concluded that even though RAKEL had resolved a range of technical problems, it continued to suffer from a bad reputation, and potential end-users remained hesitant to join the system (Swedish Ministry of Defense 2010, 6).

The report recommended that MSB come up with *a national strategy for RAKEL* that specified concrete goals and measures for the SCS. In addition, the report asserted that MSB needed to support information exchange between end-users in *different forums* and that a *strategic council* should be created (Swedish Ministry of Defense 2010, 8). The report also encouraged that the government step in and formally regulate by issuing instructions to the most important agencies in order to force them to use RAKEL. At the same time, however, the working group believed that direct instructions to the municipalities and regional authorities would be inappropriate. Such instructions would undermine the financial model that still served as the basic idea for how to finance crisis communications in Sweden. The working group believed that it would be better to advance the use of economic incentives. For instance, it was suggested that the state immediately stop its financial support for analog radios so that the actors would be strongly encouraged to switch to RAKEL (Swedish Ministry of Defense 2010, 8).

MSB presented its responses to this feedback in a report called *A National Strategy for RAKEL* (MSB 2010c). The report contained a range of strategies to strengthen participation among crisis managers. A specific communication strategy was developed to "help MSB in its efforts to create, build, cherish, and deepen the relationships with present and future RAKEL users and other important target groups" (MSB 2010c, 39). MSB also mentioned in its report the need to work closer with crisis managers in different councils and forums; in particular, the *RAKEL Council* was mentioned in this strategic document (MSB 2010c). The RAKEL Council was later launched in May 2010 with the aim to gather all of the major organizations using RAKEL twice a year to discuss general issues. The National Police, the Prison and Probation Authority, the Swedish Power Grid, SSK (the association of municipal and regional authorities), and the General Director of the Armed Forces were among the most important council members, with the Director General for MSB as the chair (MSB 2010d).

In an effort to increase the accession to RAKEL, MSB also decided to arrange physical meetings and forums with existing and potential users of RAKEL. In May 2010, MSB held the first meeting of the *User Forum* (MSB 2010a). The idea was to create an environment that allowed for open discussions and served as a meeting point for RAKEL users so that they could exchange experiences and make new connections (Gallin 2011). The *Collaboration Forum* was also started in 2010. This forum was more oriented toward technical issues, and its key aim was to develop national guidelines for collaboration between the participating organizations. This resulted in a first guideline document called *National Guidelines for Collaboration within RAKEL (Nationella riktlinjer för samverkan i RAKEL)*, which was to go into effect in January 2013 (MSB 2013c). Stefan Kvarnerås, former RAKEL operational manager, wrote that these guidelines were intended to make it easier, more effective, and more secure to cooperate across organizational borders. This was identified as a necessary measure for good preparedness and effective crisis management (MSB 2013c).

There is now a permanent group, which meets four times a year and includes all of the major organizations working with the development of national guidelines for RAKEL. MSB is the convener for this group (MSB 2013b). In the *National Strategy* from 2010, MSB also stated that additional *target-group forums* should be established if deemed necessary (MSB 2010c). In fact three such target group forums were established in 2014: one for the energy sector, one for the regional authorities (landstingen), and one for municipalities responsible for certain emergency rescue services as well as minor crises and disturbances (MSB 2013a, 2011b, 2010b).

In 2010, MSB initiated an annual *RAKEL Day*. Invitations were sent out to all organizations that currently were or potentially could be RAKEL users. The first year 700 people attended the various seminars, presentations, and exhibitions. The General Director for MSB (Helena Lindberg) and the RAKEL Operating Manager (Stefan Kvarnerås) held the opening speeches on the two RAKEL Days I attended. This clearly indicates the effort that MSB puts into this event and the importance it places on it. MSB and RAKEL representatives are quick to point out that the event is not about *selling* RAKEL but rather about showing the advantages of the system and the new products available. The discourse used is that this event should *inspire* and encourage the increased use of RAKEL (Observations 2013, 2014). For example, Helena Lindberg stated in her opening speech in 2014 that "one of the most important aims of RAKEL Day is that participants will have the opportunity to meet new collaborating partners and *create networks*" (Observations 2014). Stefan Kvarnerås also stated the same year, that "RAKEL Day is about letting narratives travel from organization to organization about the functionality and utility of RAKEL" (Observations 2014). Potentially there is strong contradiction between encouraging collaboration and the underlying logic of a self-financed system (see Larsson 2017 for further elaboration).

In Table 5.1 I have listed the number of subscriptions for each year and compared it to the goal of subscriptions that the governing public agency (KBM and MSB, respectively) hoped to achieve. One subscription is equivalent to one operational unit, which is similar to a mobile phone or communication center that can be used in crisis communication. Besides not reaching its own forecasts and desired goals for the number of subscriptions, it did not reach its goal of a self-financed system where the end-users pay accession and subscription fees and thereby cover the entire costs for the SCS. Table 5.2 shows how these subscriptions were spread among different categories of users as well as the number of organizations that have joined the SCS.

Overcoming Collective-Action Problems 65

Table 5.1 Number of subscriptions/prognosis

Year	Subscriptions	Prognosis
2006	400	
2007	8583	50000
2009	20404	50000
2010	29589	50000
2011	40151	70000
2012	45836	70000
2013	54550	70000
2014	58489	85000
2015	61717	85000
2016	66697	90000
2017	71827	90000

Source: Table Created by Author

Table 5.2 Categories of users and number of subscriptions

	Public/national authorities and the police	Regional Authorities	Municipalities	Commercial actors	Number of organizations
2007	8506	5	62	10	13
2008	13353	142	87	105	38
2009	18792	342	753	517	140
2010	25694	1467	1843	585	214
2011	31353	3256	4342	900	351
2012	32473	3530	7269	2564	391
2013	38603	3638	8738	3571	460
2014	40437	3934	9686	4432	550
2015	42608	3847	10103	5159	580
2016	46601	3857	10493	5746	582
2017	51513	4015	10634	5665	575

Source: Table Created by Author

The tables show that after the reforms in 2010 that included more interaction with potential end-users, the number of end-users rose dramatically in the subsequent years in all categories, foremost among the municipalities. After 2014, however, the increase has become less dramatic, and the number of subscriptions among commercial actors has even decreased. Yet on the other hand, public/national authorities have continued to increase rapidly.

User-Friendliness and Functionality

The construction of RAKEL was completed at the end of 2010, and thereafter the RAKEL organization at MSB was subsequently restructured (MSB 2011a). This reorganization marked a new era for how MSB works with RAKEL, and the focus has shifted from issues of construction to selling and encouraging actors to join the new system (Kvarnerås 2012). In 2013, the number of organizations using RAKEL increased to 460, and these account for 50,000 individual subscriptions. Together, they comprise a rather heterogonous group, including public agencies, regional authorities, municipalities, public and private health care providers, public transport, electrical companies, and various NGOs (MSB 2013e, 23).

Yet even the reorganization that occurred after the construction phase has been subject to criticism. The problem with the new focus is that it still pays too little attention to *how* organizations should be able to communicate with each other and how to increase the user-friendliness of RAKEL. Many end-users who are unfamiliar with radio communications are still not comfortable with RAKEL and its equipment. These factors have resulted in limited usage of the system. MSB has worked hard to increase the number of subscriptions in order to ensure the financial model underlying the system; however, it has paid less attention to how end-users actually use the system and how RAKEL contributes to the overall crisis management system. RAKEL's functionality is foremost adjusted to the needs and requirements of public safety agents, and the newer actors often find it difficult to operate the equipment. They often find that their requests for new and broader functionality better adjusted to their daily operations and potential roles in crisis management are not being prioritized. It is not uncommon that municipalities which have paid for operating licenses and bought equipment end up putting this sophisticated equipment into storage and forget about it because they find it difficult to operate (Mårtensson 2013).

The emphasis on selling equipment and increasing the number of subscriptions is evident in many interviews and reports. A staff member at MSB responsible for strategic innovation stated that MSB's key task is "selling the concept and tools of crisis management to other public agencies and organizations" (Bram 2014). The annual reports from KBM and MSB emphasize the number of subscriptions rather than the usage and functionality of the system. There are no investigations or evaluations on how RAKEL is being used and whether it has improved crisis management communications. A number of recent major accidents and crises (traffic accidents and forest fires) indicate that RAKEL neither functions as it should nor makes inter-organizational communications possible since post-incident reports reveal substantial problems with communication and in particular with RAKEL (MSB 2013d, 2014; Association of Local Authorities in Skåne 2014; Asp et al. 2015, 15, 114).

MSB, the responsible public agency, still needs to make more efforts to improve transorganizational communication in collaborative crisis management. So far, the majority of the focus has been on the technical and financial aspects of the system. Crucial aspects regarding the software in terms of user-friendliness, functionality, and how to communicate and organize information exchange in crisis situations have been given much less attention, hampering the potential usage of the improved national security communication system.

Conclusion

In this chapter I have investigated strategies for overcoming collective-action problems in collaborative crisis management by analyzing the intersection between hardware, software, and economic concerns in the management of SCS in Sweden. These efforts were guided by the following two research questions: (1) what strategies have been used for overcoming collective-action problems in the management of Security Communications Systems (SCS) and (2) what lessons could be learned from the Swedish case?

The overall finding of the study suggests that there are potential deadlocks and trade-offs as meta-governors are set out to implement and manage a new technical infrastructure that aims to assist collaborative efforts. Adding to the potential clash between hardware and software issues, as identified by Boin and Hart, the key finding in this chapter is that economic and financial aspects may have detrimental effects on crisis collaboration. The kind of self-financial models used in the Swedish case may create substantial collective-action problems and inertia, especially if end-users do not see an immediate utility with either joining or paying for a new technical system. A key insight and lesson from this case is that the financial aspects of managing technical systems in collaborative crisis management play a crucial role. In fact, the basic scheme of a self-financed system forced the meta-governor to place emphasis on selling and convincing organizations to adopt and join the national SCS while also assuming a collective responsibility for the entire system. This scheme enforced the collective-action problem, as many of the actors at least wanted to wait and see if other actors would join, thus lowering the costs for existing actors. As the system experienced delays and technical problems it was viewed with great suspicion, especially among nontraditional public safety agents. There are still some technical problems that remain to be fixed, and some of these are connected to software issues. In fact, serious incidents in Sweden have revealed that RAKEL has not functioned well and has not facilitated the necessary and requested trans-organizational communication despite the fact that the number of end-users and organizations is constantly increasing. One reason for the less than optimal usage of the system may be that too little attention has been placed on issues of software and consideration for how new crisis managers should acquire knowledge on how to use the SCS. The financial model seems to have forced the meta-governors to focus on securing the financial aspects of RAKEL and on the technical problems and construction of the communications system in order to combat the bad image of the SCS. Thus, software issues crucial for new technical advancement have not been given adequate consideration. There is still a long way to go, not the least when it comes to finding and supporting ways that end-users, who do not have any professional training in this type of communication, are able to best utilize the system.

This case study has revealed the difficulties and substantial lock-in effects that can emerge in implementing and managing a large-scale technical support system. Obviously, a comparison with similar projects in Sweden and other countries would be of great interest to see whether these problems and lock-in effects are case-specific, context/country specific, or due to some misconception on behalf of meta-governors on how collaboration could and should be encouraged and supported. The lesson from this case study is that the management of technical support systems that should facilitate collaborative crisis management must be given equal attention as hardware and software issues, and consideration should be given to how economic issues can be intertwined with these issues and create substantial deadlocks and suboptimal usage of technical improvements.

I would thus argue that meta-governors must give more attention and consideration to how to avoid collective-action problems, and at the same time they must find adequate tools to facilitate collaboration in loosely situated networks devoted to crisis management. In fact, the case study demonstrates the importance of strategies that are more attuned to the nature of networks in comparison to markets or hierarchies. In that regard, we may find that those strategies invoked in 2010 concerning more active network management (*inter alia* increased dialogue, forums, and workshops between meta-governors and end-users) have great potential to align end-users and foster the adoption of a joint system and common views. This shows the importance of *catering* networks and *facilitating* collaboration through active rather than passive meta-governance, which also requires a more fundamental understanding of the nature of networks in contrast to traditional public administration.

References

Ansell, Chris, Arjen Boin, and Ann Keller. 2010. "Managing Transboundary Crises: Identifying the Building Blocks of an Effective Response System." *Journal of Contingencies and Crisis Management* 18 (4): 195–207. doi:10.1111/j.1468–5973.2010.00620.x

Asp, Viktoria, Fredrik Bynander, Pär Daléus, and Jenny Deschamps-Berger. 2015. *Bara skog som brinner? Utvärdering av krishantering [Just Burning Trees? Evaluation of the Crisis Management of the 2014 Västmanland Wildfire]*. Stockholm: CRISMART, Swedish Defense University.

Association of Local Authorities [Kommunförbundet] in Skåne. 2014. RAKEL Skåne förvaltnings-grupp [RAKEL Skåne Executive Body] Memorandum.

Bennett, Andrew, and Jeffrey T. Checkel. 2014. *Process Tracing: From Metaphor to Analytic Tool*. Cambridge: Cambridge University Press.

Boin, Arjen, and Paul 't Hart. 2010. "Organising for Effective Emergency Management: Lessons from Research." *Australian Journal of Public Administration* 69 (4): 357–71. doi:10.1111/j.1467–8500.2010.00694.x

Bram, Kristina. 2014. Strategic Manager at MSB. Interview. Location Stockholm, Date 2014-02-14.

Budget Proposal to Swedish Parliament [Budgetpropositionen till Riksdagen]. 2008. *Utgiftsområde 6 – Försvar samt beredskap mot sårbarhet [Expenditure 6 – Defense and Preparedness Against Vulnerability]*.

Gains, Francesca. 2004. " 'Hardware, Software or Network Connection?' Theorizing Crisis in the UK Next Steps Agencies?" *Public Administration* 82 (3): 547–66.

Gallin, Anita. 2011. Coordinator for Collaboration Groups at MSB. Interview. Location Stockholm, Date 2011-10-12.

George, Alexander L. and Andrew Bennett. 2005. *Case Studies and Theory Development in the Social Sciences, BCSIA Studies in International Security*. Cambridge, MA: Massachusetts Institute of Technology Press.

Högberg, David. 2012. Firefighter/Representative for Municipalities. Telephone Interview. Date 2012-04-13.

Hu, Qian and Naim Kapucu. 2014. "Information Communication Technology Utilization for Effective Emergency Management Networks." *Public Management Review*: 1–26. doi:10.1080/1471 9037.2014.969762

Jennings, Eliot A., Sudha Arlikatti, Simon A. Andrew, and KyungWoo Kim. 2017. "Adoption of Information and Communication Technologies (ICTs) by Local Emergency Management Agencies in the United States." *International Review of Public Administration* 22 (2): 193–210. doi:1 0.1080/12294659.2017.1323481

Kapucu, Naim. 2006. "Interagency Communication Networks During Emergencies: Boundary Spanners in Multiagency Coordination." *The American Review of Public Administration* 36 (2): 207–25.

Kapucu, Naim, Tolga Arslan, and Matthew Lloyd Collins. 2010. "Examining Intergovernmental and Interorganizational Response to Catastrophic Disasters: Toward a Network-Centered Approach." *Administration & Society* 42 (2): 222–47. doi:10.1177/0095399710362517

KBM, Swedish Emergency Management Agency. 2007. *Årsapport [Annual Report]*. Stockholm

———. 2006a. *Årsapport [Annual Report]*. Stockholm

———. 2006b. *RAKEL-systemet och användarorganisationerna [The RAKEL System and the End-user Organizations]*. Stockholm

———. 2005a. *Årsapport [Annual Report]*. Stockholm

———. 2005b. *Redovisning av uppdrag nr 22 i regleringsbrevet för år 2005 [Report of Assignment No. 22 in the Government's Letter of Regulations]*. Stockholm

———. 2005c. *Utökad användarkrets för RAKEL [Increase in the Circle of Users]*. Stockholm

———. 2004. *Årsapport [Annual Report]*. Stockholm

Khan, Shabana, Jyoti L. Mishra, Kuna-hui Elaine Lin, and Emma E.H. Doyle. 2017. "Rethinking Communication in Risk Interpretation and Action." *Natural Hazards* 88 (3): 1709–26. doi:10.1007/s11069–017–2942-z www.kfsk.se/download/18.3024b87f148994f13c7d6848/1411623315387/F%C3%B6rvaltningsgrupp+anteckningar+2014–09–04.pdf

Kuckartz, Udo. 2014. *Qualitative Text Analysis: A Guide to Methods, Practice and Using Software*. Thousand Oaks, CA: Sage.

Kvarnerås, Stefan. 2012. Operational Manager for RAKEL. Interview. Location Stockholm, Date 2012-03-12.

Larsson, Oscar L. 2017. "Meta-Governance and Collaborative Crisis Management-Competing Rationalities in the Management of the Swedish Security Communications System." *Risk, Hazards & Crisis in Public Policy*. doi:10.1002/rhc3.12120

————. 2015. *The Governmentality of Meta-governance: Identifying Theoretical and Empirical Challenges of Network Governance in the Political Field of Security and Beyond*. Uppsala: Uppsala University.

————. 2013. "Sovereign Power Beyond the State: A Critical Reappraisal of Governance by Networks." *Critical Policy Studies* 7 (2): 99–114. doi:10.1080/19460171.2013.784624.

Manoj, Balakrishan S. and Alexandra Hubenko Baker. 2007. "Communication Challenges in Emergency Response." *Communications of the ACM* 50 (3): 51–53.

Mårtensson, Peråke. 2013. Adviser and expert on security communication. Former consult on RAKEL project and employee of KBM/MSB. Currently employed at the Swedish Defense University. Interview.

Mikulic, M. and B. Modlic. 10–12 September 2008. "General System Architecture of TETRA Network for Public Safety Services." *ELMAR, 2008: 50th International Symposium*. Zadar, Croatia

MSB, Swedish Civil Contingencies Agency. 2014. "Så har Rakel stärkts under branden i Västmanland." [RAKEL Strengthened During the Västmanland Fire]. (Accessed 10 December 2014).

————. 2013a. "Energibranschens Rakelforum." [Energy Sector's RAKEL Forum]. (Accessed 3 December 2014).

————. 2013b. "Förvaltningsgrupp nationella riktlinjer för samverkan i Rakel." [Executive Group's National Guidelines for RAKEL Collaboration]. Stockholm

————. 2013c. "Nationella riktlinjer för samverkan i Rakel." [National Guidelines for RAKEL Collaboration]. (Accessed 2 December 2014).

————. 2013d. "Rakels kapacitet tillräcklig vid Tranarpskrocken." [RAKEL's Capacity Sufficient for Tranarps Collision]. (Accessed 8 November 2014).

————. 2013e. *Årsapport [Annual Report]*. Stockholm, Karlstad

————. 2011a. *Årsapport [Annual Report]*. Stockholm, Karlstad

————. 2011b. "Länsstyrelseforum." [Administrative County Board Forum]. (Accessed 7 December 2014).

————. 2010a. "Användarforum." [User Forum]. (Accessed 9 December 2014).

————. 2010b. "Kommunalt Rakelforum." [Municipal RAKEL User Forum]. (Accessed 9 December 2014).

————. 2010c. "Nationell strategi för Rakel." [National Strategy for RAKEL]. (Accessed December 10 2014).

————. 2010d. "Rakelrådet." [RAKEL Council]. (Accessed 6 December 2014).

————. 2009. *Årsapport [Annual Report]*. Stockholm, Karlstad

Nohrstedt, Daniel, Fredrik Bynander, Charles F. Parker, and Paul 't Hart. 2014. "Collaborative Crisis Management: An Agenda for Research on Interorganizational Responses to Extreme Events." Washington, DC: APSA Panel.

Observations. 2014. "Kommunalt Rakelforum och Rakeldagen." [Municipal RAKEL Forum and RAKEL Day]. (2014-05-14)

————. 2013. "User Forum." (2013-06-10)

Schwartz-Shea, Peregrine and Dvora Yanow. 2012. *Interpretive Research Design: Concepts and Processes*. New York, NY: Routledge.

Sellnow, Timothy L. and Matthew W. Seeger. 2013. *Theorizing Crisis Communication*. Vol. 4. Malden, MA: John Wiley & Sons.

State Public Reports [SOU, Statens offentliga utredningar]. 2003. "Trygga medborgare-säker kommunikation." [Safe Citizens-Secure Communication]. Fritz, Stockholm

Swedish Bill [Proposition] 2005/06. 2005. "Samverkan vid kris för ett säkrare samhälle." [Collaboration for a Safer Society During a Crisis]. Parliament, Stockholm

Swedish Ministry of Defense [Försvarsdepartementet]. 2010. "Rakel, nuläge och framtid." [RAKEL, Now and in the Future]. Stockholm

Vogt, M., D. Hertweck, and K. Hales. 4–7 January 2011. "Strategic ICT Alignment in Uncertain Environments: An Empirical Study in Emergency Management Organizations." Washington, DC: 44th Hawaii International Conference on System Sciences (HICSS).

Chapter 6

Vertical Collaboration During the 2014 Swedish Wildfire

Fredrik Bynander

Introduction

The major wildfire in the province of Västmanland in central Sweden during August of 2014 was not supposed to occur in Sweden. The environmental prerequisites for a fire-storm type development is present in for example Greece, Australia, and California, but not typically in the subarctic biotope that caught fire on July 31 in Seglingsberg in Sala municipality. The mental preparedness for an event like this was nonexistent, despite reoccurring large-scale wildfires over the past 30 years, a few of which were serious enough to demand the concerted efforts of several municipal fire services. The Swedish Civil Contingencies Agencies (MSB) had excluded wildfires from their 2013 catalogue of potential serious incidents, and the legal requirement for fire services to uphold a capacity to coordinate operations in response to large-scale incidents was not in active compliance throughout most of the country. The event is not much of a "Black Swan," yet it was unanticipated and created serious problems regarding coordination and resource mobilization. Detailed fire risk assessments at the time showed uniquely high risk levels, but fire services had no procedures for systematically integrating them in their planning and readiness (they do now). As a litmus test of Swedish crisis management performance, this was fairly mild, but the local, regional, or national authorities did not pass the test. On the other hand, civil society proved to be robust and resourceful in mitigating the dangerous consequences of the event. Other troubling flaws in the system became apparent, such as the political nature of deciding on and allocating compensation to municipalities and victims, the regional authorities' inability to assume control of the crisis coordination efforts, and the poor preparedness for requesting and receiving assistance from the national and EU levels.

From a crisis management perspective, the event has several important aspects when pondering the crisis management capacity of a typical region in Sweden. It contained a major and complex challenge to first responders – the largest single emergency operation in several decades – and it involved several levels of government, including the national level (which is seldom operational in emergency management). The regional branch of the national government, the Västmanland County administrative board, assumed control of the operations in a manner that was unprepared and disorganized, but that was ultimately successful due to the appointment of an experienced and resourceful incident commander and his reorganization of the response organization. He, however, ignored parts of the legal requirements of the incident command, as they were not deemed conducive to an effective response to the incident. Operations included the evacuation of both people and animals; therefore, several private enterprises and volunteers were involved in the operations, and Sweden requested support from the European Union under the Community Mechanism for Civil Protection (ERCC).

The aim of this chapter is to assess the performance of Swedish crisis management collaboration in response to the 2014 wildfire. In order to do so, it will list some of the main challenges that were posed to the crisis response system and will detail in what way and to what degree they were met.

This study is based on evidence gathered for an evaluation report written in Swedish commissioned on the request of the Västmanland County Administrative Board (Asp et al. 2015). In preparing it, just over 200 people involved in the response were interviewed (semi-structured), and the evaluation team had access to all the staff documents compiled in the command center at Ramnäs, Västmanland. The evaluation team went through the entire media coverage of the event and talked to those government representatives who played a significant role during the event. The methods used are compliant with process tracing as described by Alexander George and Andrew Bennett (2005; see also Bennett and Checkel 2012). In addition, the evaluation team looked at the level of compliance to the applicable legal and operational frameworks.

Crisis Preparedness in Sweden

This section is a description of the legal and administrative framework that public actors abide by in the pursuit of societal security in Sweden. There is no lack of complexity in the design of the system despite the idea that normal routines should be followed in crisis situations, thus involving all the actors in crisis management who typically deal with policy and implementation in everyday operations. There are a few notable exceptions to this "principle of responsibility," which gives a municipality the right to activate a crisis management board that can bypass normal decision rules in order to act timely and effectively. For example, there is the Law on Accident Mitigation (LSO), which gives large autonomy to the incident commander of the rescue services in a dangerous and acute situation. Furthermore, the regional administrative board has the mandate to assume coordination control over the affected municipalities. The national level, primarily represented by MSB, has a supportive role, for example, in maintaining lists of professionals who can be summoned to contribute in different capacities, maintaining national reinforcement depots of crucial resources for firefighting, and handling communication with the EU Civil Protection Mechanism in the ERCC. The Swedish Government Offices have a crisis coordination secretariat that monitors ongoing situations and prepares any government decisions that may be necessary in order to deal with them.

The legal concept of geographical area responsibility requires that municipalities, county administrative boards, and the government, through their national agencies, assume responsibility for incidents within their jurisdiction. The responsibility involves upholding a functional crisis coordination on the respective level of decision making. This coordination includes information to the general public and the superior administrative level. This does not mean that sector responsibilities follow – specialized agencies and organization maintain their sector-bound mandates (MSB 2015a, 1).

After a major accident, compensation for damages is awarded municipalities according to a cost assessment model. In a so-called extraordinary event (a larger incident with wider ramifications), no such system exists. This causes an arbitrary process dominated by the national government that has on several occasions been characterized by politicization and sensitivity to the amount of media coverage and public opinion. In the case of the Västmanland wildfire, the parliamentary elections were just weeks away, which, according to many accounts, forced the government to deal with the issue (Skogö 2015; Uddholm 2015; Focus group 2015).

Initial Organization and Coordination of Information

The summer of 2014 was an exceptionally hot and dry one by Swedish standards. The temperature in the end of June hovered above 30°C, and there had not been rain in Västmanland for most of the summer. Several smaller wildfires had been managed by the local fire services. Many officials were on vacation and hard to reach during this period (Nerike Fire Department 2014, 7; MSB 2015b, 24).

On July 31, at 13:29 a wildfire was reported to the national alarm service, SOS Alarm, in Seglingsberg in Sala municipality. The call was made by the operator of a forest harvester who had accidentally started the blaze by hitting a boulder, thus creating a spark and a subsequent wildfire. At the time of the call, the wildfire was 30 x 30 meters but expanding rapidly. The fire and rescue services of the Mälaren Valley (MBR) took an hour to get to the site due to faulty GPS maps and when the first fire engines arrived, the wildfire had expanded to 400 meters x 1.5 kilometers (Västmanland County Administrative Board 2014, 5). At 18:23, five hours after the first report, the duty officer at the county received the first alert. The duty officer was inexperienced; she was the new chief legal officer of the county administrative board, it was only her fourth time on active duty, and she had no senior colleagues to confer with due to vacations (Wall 2014, 2015). In the first consultations between the rescue services and the county administrative board, the situation was not seen as acute since there were "only trees burning," and it was assumed that the wildfire would soon be under control. Operations were handed over from the MBR fire services to the Sala municipality fire services. During this time, plumes of smoke were reaching towns in the area and the local media started to take an interest.

On Friday, August 1, the wind had receded somewhat, and the fire services were optimistic that they would soon be able to control the wildfire. At that point, no buildings were at risk (Grahn Wetter 2014). The duty officer at the county administrative board had by now reached the point where she was ready to call an information coordination conference within the USAM framework, a regional coordination mechanism composed of representatives of all the municipalities in the county and the county administrative board. However, the fire chiefs she consulted were adamant that they did not want the cumbersome USAM process to distract their efforts. The duty officer backed off, which would be a recurring pattern over the coming days (Alvinge 2014; Wall 2015). By now, operations had been divided into two areas under the command of two different fire services. The wildfire was again expanding more rapidly. Three armed forces helicopters were assisting in the operations by this point.

On Saturday morning municipal leaders in Sala observed disturbing reports regarding the wildfire on social media and contacted the fire commander for a renewed assessment of the situation. The fire chief, Göran Cederholm, was self-critical after the fact: "I should have informed the mayor of Sala already on Thursday. I should have seen the societal perspective of this, but I was only thinking about firefighting" (Sala group discussion 2015). The county administrative board tried to get the fire chiefs to realize the need for a USAM conference, but they continued to decline the offer. There were ongoing discussions between officials at the county administrative board on the problems with initiating USAM without the expressed consent of the fire services (Wall 2014; Regnell 2014).

On Sunday morning, optimism had returned to the ranks of the firefighters. Additional helicopters were coming in to help, and a fire engineer with expertise in burn pace prognosis had joined the command center (Wall 2014). The duty officer at MSB called his counterpart at the county administrative board to inform that the incident commander had, via MSB, requested firefighting aircrafts through the EU mechanism. This information made the county administrative board's head of preparedness request a meeting with the incident commander to get an updated situation report. This was the first concrete step by the county to initiate coordination arrangements. The incident commander now maintained direct contact with the head of preparedness, thus bypassing the duty officer and breaking the chain of command (Wall 2014). The incident commander requested assistance with crisis communications and getting information to the public (Wall 2014). The acting county governor approved the establishment of a county-led crisis communication center. The county governor was informed of this measure and discontinued his vacation. A new incident commander rotated in and decided to relocate the command center to the parking lot of a conference center in Ramnäs. The new commander also agreed to holding the first USAM conference in the evening (Bergquist 2014).

The USAM conference was attended by the duty officer and the head of preparedness from the county administrative board, representatives of the nine municipalities of the county, representatives from local public service radio, the Swedish Armed Forces, and the Swedish National Meteorological Institute (SMHI). The rescue service representatives explained that the evacuation of three small townships might be necessary during the night. The armed forces communicated a list of resources that they could deliver on request, but they perceived no interest during that meeting. The county administrative board personnel admitted that they had no current situation report, but promised to deliver one at the 10:00 am meeting the next day (Regnell 2014; Nilsson 2015). After the USAM meeting, the incident commander expressed concern for the development of the wildfire: "It looks like it could really go to hell" (Wall 2014), and a short discussion ensued on the possibility of the county administrative board assuming control of the operations, which was rejected by everybody present. During the evening, MSB reported that offers were coming in regarding the request for planes and helicopters from Norway, France, and Italy.

"The Monday from Hell" (Monday, August 4)

Monday morning came with scorching temperatures of 30°, very low humidity, and a surging wind, which all spelled bad news for the firefighters. USAM was now fully active and convened three times during the day. However, the participants were not happy with the process. The information shared in USAM was not up-to-date, and the discussions circled around unsubstantiated issues as well as relevant ones. The command center at Ramnäs was fully installed at the conference center with most of the functions of a wider scope of operations (communications, logistics, planning, evacuation, etc.) (Nerike Fire Department 2014, 24; Västmanland County Administrative Board 2014).

After noon on this day the spread of the wildfire was extreme. The wind had picked up and the intensity of the wildfire was beyond anything the firefighters had seen previously. Throughout the afternoon, the firefighters were in full retreat not to get cornered by the fire. Forest workers active in creating fire alleys were overrun by the wildfire and had to submerge into a lake to escape the flames; they were subsequently airlifted out. Meanwhile, the incident commander was talking to the media and gave a message of "careful optimism" (Skogö 2015; Regnell 2015). He was forced to change that position only hours later. The advance of the wildfire proceeded at 80 meters per minute, and it jumped two kilometers across Lake Snyten that the commanders had consider a sure stop block. After the wildfire had died, it was concluded that three quarters of the total fire expansion took place on this day. Evacuations of several towns were now under way in several of the afflicted municipalities, now four in total (Nilsson 2014). The municipal seat of Norberg was under threat, and an evacuation was considered.

The first casualty of the wildfire was reported. A lumber truck had been caught in the flames, and the two occupants had tried to go into a patch of wetland to survive. One did not, and the other was rescued by firefighters at great risk to their own safety (Väst-manland County Administrative Board 2014). At 7:30 in the evening, representatives of the fire services and the county administrative board held a meeting at the command center. All three involved fire chiefs unanimously requested the first operation takeover by a county administrative board in Swedish history. They had a name for a new commander: Lars-Göran Uddholm, head of the Southern Stockholm Fire Services and a seasoned veteran of, among other events, the Swedish operations in Kao Lak after the Southeast Asian tsunami of 2004 (Tilly 2014).

The Takeover

On Tuesday morning the command center at Ramnäs was a chaotic place. At 6:30 there was a meeting between Uddholm and the county governor to discuss the design of a new organization. No one checked their credentials on the way in and they could gain access to any part of the command center at will (Accident investigation 2015, 25). The governor confirmed Uddholm's appointment as incident commander and signed the official decision for the county to assume control of operations (Focus group 2015). Before the decision, the county had contacted MSB to seek advice on the legal requirements that applied. The MSB legal officer had advised against the takeover, painting a bleak picture of the responsibilities that would fall onto the county. The county governor and his staff went ahead anyway (Skogö 2015).

At 10:00, Uddholm convened his first staff meeting and described the new, expanded organization to manage the community-wide crisis that the wildfire had caused. A greater pace of activities commenced, and a large number of outside experts started to fill the cells of the command center. USAM remained the only way to coordinate the municipalities, but it was sidestepped and never reached its full functionality during the event. However, the legal status of the new command center and its leader remained unclear. The takeover was unchartered territory, and the sharp tools provided in the law on accident mitigation only concerned firefighting in this case, not the far-reaching new mandates of the organization, such as logistics and evacuation (von Knorring 2015).

Over the next few days, a more wide-reaching operational pattern was consolidated. Gradually, from late Tuesday and onwards the wildfire stopped spreading and the situation became more stable, although not yet "under control." National agencies were brought into the command center and resumed control over their respective areas, such as the National Traffic Agency, MSB, the Swedish Armed Forces, and the Swedish Coast Guard. This process was not without friction, however. MSB sent lots of people, some of whom were there as observers and some as unrequested experts on firefighting. Their presence created tensions that took time to resolve, and in some cases personnel had to be rotated for cooperation to happen.

As the wildfire gradually petered out, new problems arose. Foremost among them was the dangerous work with clearing up the ravaged areas and the compensation issues that nervous municipal leaders needed to be answered in order to assess the municipal damage. Uddholm decided to keep a ban in place regarding entering the affected areas until he could consult with the forest owners on safe procedures for clearing up those areas. The national government and, in particular, the responsible ministry of defense were getting phone calls from party colleagues across the country to expedite decisions on compensation quickly in order to avoid the issue from plaguing the election campaign that by now was in full swing. A comparably generous offer was made to the affected municipalities within days after ceasing the most acute operations; the deal was made, and the issue became politically irrelevant.

Collaboration Performance Indicators

In the following, a number of common indicators of crisis management performance as they played out during the operations in the 2014 Västmanland wildfire will be scrutinized.

Situational Awareness

In the early days of the wildfire, situational awareness was nonexistent. The two, and subsequently three, fire services involved did not communicate well, and at one point they were not even aware that they were fighting the same wildfire. Spreading operational information to municipalities and the county was equally dysfunctional, partly due to the urge not to be distracted by the "civilians" in those organizations (Focus group 2015). When events consumed their organizations, there was no plan for strengthening and unifying operations which prompted the request for a county takeover.

Yet still during the first day with the takeover organization, situational awareness was equally hard to obtain. A system with senior staff meetings was introduced and contained qualitative information, but the minutes from the meetings were uninformative and the information did not travel outside that group. Eventually, and with the help of MSB and some of the municipal representatives, more accurate operational pictures were compiled and disseminated to the relevant actors (Focus group 2015). Ultimately, a number of tailor-made operational pictures were produced on a timely basis and distributed to the national level, the landowners, and the municipalities (Uddholm 2015; Åhnberg 2015).

Part of the reason for the slow development of situational awareness was the poor division of labor. The county called a national crisis coordination conference but failed to include the operative commanders. The tools used, such as the national conference, presupposed the existence of a national operational picture to be conveyed, but this was rarely the case during the Västmanland wildfire (Åhnberg 2015). Another problem was that the system assumed that information would be injected from the municipalities and expert agencies, but this never quite worked during the wildfire (von Knorring 2015).

Legal Authority Over the Command Center

The decision by the governor to assume operational responsibility created confusion as to who really had ownership of the command center. Two versions existed: (1) The county assumed control over the rescue services since the governor had appointed the incident commander, who was acting on behalf of the county's mandate and the governor was his boss. (2) The county assumed the responsibility, but the incident commander acted on his own legal mandate as specified in the Law on Accident Mitigation (LSO). Even months removed from the events, interviewees were not certain which was the more authoritative interpretation. What is more, had serious missteps been made, this would have to be resolved in court, and it would have impacted compensation and a number of other issues. Even the staff of the county administrative board was divided on this issue: did they own the command center or not (Åhnberg 2015)? The governor described his role as "a working chairman of the board" (Skogö 2015).

Uddholm demanded in the early conversations with the governor that he be appointed the only incident commander. This is unusual for Swedish standards, as a rotation process is usually imposed in order to have rested commanders in place at all times. Uddholm delegated authority for the few occasions he was not available. He became the foremost spokesperson of the organization, creating a sense of "unified command" and managing to turn the media image of the operations around. The governor upheld contacts with the Swedish Government Offices and individual ministers, as well as the Swedish Royal Court, which showed its support by having the king come to Ramnäs and speak to the operators. In sum, the legal standing of the command center was unclear but that never became an operative problem as the operations were seen as basically legitimate after the takeover. For the future of Swedish civilian command and control, however, few if any ingrained problems were solved.

Collaboration With Local Actors

The municipalities never established a presence in the command center. There were plans for a high-level "normative command" that would include mayors and the governor, but that never materialized (Åhnberg 2015). The municipalities sent liaisons to Ramnäs, but they were quickly sucked into the operations as their local knowledge immediately proved valuable; thus, their communicative function back to their employers disappeared (Uddholm 2015). The planning function of the command center was tasked with maintaining contacts with the municipalities, but they never achieved solid contact points. The Swedish crisis preparedness system has invested huge sums of money in safeguarding robust communications during crises through their national TETRA standard RAKEL radio system and the information management system WIS. Yet, these were not used widely during the event as too few had the credentials and because RAKEL masts had been destroyed by the wildfire, so mobile phones and emails became the preferred mode of communication. The local fire chiefs had access to information that others at the municipal level did not, but communications with their administrative counterparts were never very developed, and the mayors and their staffs complained throughout the event of poor coordination with Ramnäs. Of course, the core of the problem was that USAM did not function according to plan and that the command center had to be a substitute coordination mechanism (thus further undermining efforts to regenerate the USAM process).

Collaboration With National Actors

MSB was heavily involved in an advisory function throughout the incident. At the height of operations, 70 MSB employees were in Ramnäs. Exactly in which capacity they were there, however, was unclear to many of the interviewees. During the early days, MSB staff rounded up experienced operators from around the country but this was slow, and the people in Ramnäs had more success in calling their own contacts. Two MSB employees were in charge of national resource reserves. They produced seven so-called forest fire depots that could be used in the operations. They continued, however, to bring in resources, including an unauthorized extinguishing foam used in firefighting planes that later triggered a pollution legal suit against the operations. They also requested overflights by armed forces fighter jets. Their actions were not always appreciated; thus, friction between the agency and the incident command ensued. MSB's Director General traveled to Ramnäs to sort things out, and after changing individuals, cooperation worked much better. During the wildfire, MSB received a number of requests for resources and consultations that were not delivered, including support in setting up an IT system for the use of the command center. Instead, off-the-shelf products were brought in to be able to communicate and file documents within the center.

The Swedish Armed Forces was a major player in the operations and had a presence in Ramnäs. Their organization helped in firefighting, logistics, surveillance, aerial recognizance, and vehicle and equipment maintenance as well as coordination with a large number of other actors, including volunteers (Army News 2014). No other actor could conduct repairs and logistical support in the difficult terrain (Gonzalo 2015). The organizational setup was very conducive to the armed forces participating. Thirteen helicopters and 1500 military staff took part in the operations, and the officers played an important role in running the command center (Army News 2014).

The Swedish Coast Guard used their aerial surveillance resources to give incident command support overviews of the situation, using infrared cameras and other sensors to map the expansion of the wildfire. The coast guard assumed air traffic control for all the helicopter resources that were deployed in the area. The Swedish National Traffic Agency contributed with road maintenance, transportation, roadblocks, and traffic communication services throughout the event. Its contribution was in the beginning haphazard, but as the organization was incorporated in the command center and given sector responsibility, its operations were fully integrated.

Communications

The initial image of the operations in the media as the event was beginning to register nationally was one of chaotic and misdirected actions and a lack of leadership. The rotation of incident commanders created a confusing parade of faces, with different messages and descriptions of the operations. A pivot came with Uddholm. He was a national figure since the Southeast Asian tsunami; he stayed in the spotlight and was calm and systematic in telling the public about the situation. Also, he had an easier job as the wildfire started to dissipate under his command. The mayors were also front and center in the local media. They had different experiences. The mayor of Fagersta municipality called a town meeting early in the incident (on Tuesday) and arrived without much useful information to share. He received harsh criticism as a result. His colleague in neighboring Norberg had watched the meeting and had her own town hall the next day. She shared the stage with the county governor and the incident commander. Hers was a more effective meeting.

Official information distributed through public service radio and television worked well with a few exceptions. Important public announcements ("viktigt meddelande till allmänheten" in Swedish) are a mandated procedure in which agencies or municipalities submit a message to the media organizations, which in turn interrupt all broadcasting to convey a public announcement in the designated area. Several of the public announcements broadcasted during the 2014 Västmanland wildfire had factual and language flaws which made them less than effective.

Several towns and rural areas were evacuated during the wildfire. Due to the unorganized way that this was done, no one is able to say exactly how many or which areas were affected. Different methods were used: police and military personnel knocking on doors, important public announcements, and word of mouth type procedures including phone calls and mobile phone text messaging. Most of the people evacuated were not registered as they left the area. Buses took them to different locations for sheltering, but there was no coordinated system to keep track of these. As the wildfire raged and the command center began to organize for evacuations, new methods had to be invented due to the lack of planning for evacuations.

Vertical Crisis Collaboration in Sweden

As argued in the introduction to this volume, many difficulties that befall crisis collaboration include "overlapping networks" and drawing "the circle of participants" too narrowly. These highlight the tension between the meticulous and the spontaneous that both need to be part of effective emergency response (see Chapter 1). In the Västmanland wildfire, formal networks and organizations were sidelined as operative concerns bogged down the fire departments involved. As a result, there was disorganization, and the proposed solution (to hand over operations to the county level, which had no real precedent) could not be dealt with through the existing formal procedures and thus required a solution built on national networks. The disconnect that was created between a highly specialized expert command center and the key municipal partners was overcome only with great difficulty.

On the other hand, with the creation of a coherent line of communications to the public establishing Uddholm as the person "in charge," a burgeoning legitimacy was attained also vis-à-vis local managers. As operations peaked, procedures were starting to take hold that allowed for collaboration that took local concerns into account (bottom-up) as well as providing overview and a degree of regional guidance (top-down) (Boin and Bynander 2015). The inability to achieve these lines of communications and collaborative structures when local fire departments were overwhelmed is not surprising. Wildfires are often a matter of removing fuel, mustering enough locals to help out, and waiting for precipitation to do the job. As this event grew into a crisis, Swedish emergency management was at a loss to scale up operations and find the organizational solutions that could build a bridge to a structure that could match the size of the problem. This is an endemic characteristic of almost every incident management system (Boin et al. 2019). It seems that collaborative crisis management (not unlike more traditional command and control structures) has a dire need for instruments that can lubricate transition from one operative level to the next and that can expand the organizational space in ways initially planned and tested for generic scenarios.

If collaborative crisis management is to be effective, it needs to address these issues head-on to a much higher degree than is the case today. It needs to be formalized in areas where experience shows that we can expect serious challenges, but it also needs to direct organizational cultures toward common problem solving free of bureaucratic and economic friction.

References

Army News (Arménytt). 2014. "Militärregionerna med de regionala staberna – fyra över tiden insatta insatsförband till rikets försvar." [Military Regions With Regional Staff-Four Response Units Deployed for National Defense]. Nr 2.

Asp, Viktoria, Fredrik Bynander, Pär Daléus, Jenny Deschamps-Berger, Daniel Sandberg, and Erik Schyberg. 2015. *Bara skog som brinner? Utvärdering av krishanteringen under skogsbranden i Västmanland 2014 [Just Trees Burning? An Evaluation of the Crisis Management of the 2014 Västmanland Wildfires]*. Stockholm: CRISMART, Swedish Defense University.

Bennett, Andrew and Jeffrey T. Checkel. 2012. "Process Tracing: From Philosophical Roots to Best Practices." *Simons Papers in Security and Development*: 21.

Boin, Arjen, Christer Brown, and James A. Richardson. 2019. *Managing Hurricane Katrina: Lessons from a Megacrisis*. Baton Rouge, LA: LSU Press.

Boin, Arjen and Fredrik Bynander. 2015. "Explaining Success and Failure in Crisis Coordination." *Geografiska Annaler: Series A, Physical Geography* 97(1): 123–135.

George, Alexander L. and Andrew Bennett. 2005. *Case Studies and Theory Development in the Social Sciences*. Cambridge, MA: Massachusetts Institute of Technology Press.

Grahn Wetter, Karin. 1 August 2014. "Helikopter vattenbombar elden." [Helicopters Waterbomb the Fire]. http://fagersta-posten.se/nyheter/fagersta/1.2579175-helikopter-vattenbombar-elden (Accessed 5 June 2015).

MSB (Swedish Civil Contingencies Agency). 2015a. *Samverkansområde Geografiskt områdesansvar, SOGO [Geographical Collaboration Areas]*. Publ.nr. MSB842-mars 2015.

The 2014 Swedish Wildfire 79

————. 2015b. *Observatörsrapport-Skogsbranden i Västmanland 2014 [Observer Report-The 2014 Västmanland Wildfire]*.

Nerikes brandkår. 2014. *Olycksutredning-Skogsbranden Västmanland [Accident Investigation-Västmanland Wildfire]*. Dnr: 2014/336-MBR-196. Mälardalens Brand- och Räddningsförbund.

Västmanlands County Administrative Board. December 2014. *Skogsbranden i Västmanland 2014 [The 2014 Västmanland Wildfire]*. Sweden: Länsstyrelsen i Västmanlands Län.

Interviews and logs

Åhnberg, Patrik. 20 March 2015. (Chief of staff in Ramnäs during the 2014 Västmanland wildfire). Head of security, City of Stockholm (Stadsledningskontoret).

Alvinge, Kerstin. 2014. Personlig logg Kerstin Alvinge, informatör och webbansvarig på Länsstyrelsen i Västmanland. Västmanland Administrative County Board.

Bergquist, Mikael. 2014. Logg för Mikael Bergquist i samband med Skogsbranden i Västmanland. Västmanland Administrative County Board.

Gonzalo, Roberto. 28 May 2015. Major, Swedish Armed Forces.

Nilsson, Anna. 4 August 2014. Resilience officer, Norberg/Sala. Telephone log.

Nilsson, Kent. 10 April 2015. Head of the local public radio station "P4" in Västmanland.

Regnell, Ingela. 13 May 2015. Resilience officer, Västmanland Administrative County Board.

————. 2–5 August 2014. Resilience officer, Västmanland Administrative County Board. Log of the most important events during the period of 2–5 August 2014.

Tilly, Karin. 2014. Skogsbrand Västmanland-log book. Västmanland Administrative County Board.

Skogö, Ingemar. 14 April 2015. County Governor, Västmanland Administrative County Board.

Uddholm, Lars-Göran. 9 April 2015. Fire chief, Södertörns Fire Department.

von Knorring, Johan. 22 April 2015. Resilience officer, Uppsala Administrative County Board.

Wall, Caroline. 15 May 2015. Head of legal affairs/manager on call, Västmanland Administrative County Board.

Wall, Caroline. 2014. Manager on call. Log and notes taken by the duty officer during the wildfire.

Chapter 7

Collaborative Crisis Management in Turkey

Perceptions and Outcomes of Collaboration During Two Earthquakes

Helena Hermansson

Introduction

As collaboration is "still an emergent field of scholarship" within disaster and emergency management studies (Gazley 2013, 89), not every aspect of collaborative crisis management has been covered or meticulously researched. For example, "it is not at all clear what collaboration looks like (or should look like) in disaster situations" (Robinson and Gaddis 2012, 258). Indeed, a recent literature review covering "published work on collaborative public administration with a bearing on crisis management or particular hazards of public concern" (Nohrstedt et al. 2018, 3–4) notes that "there is an unmistakable geographical bias toward the US and European countries." In an effort to address some of these knowledge gaps, this chapter explores the nature and development of the political-administrative system in Turkey and the role some of its attributes played in collaboration during the response to two earthquakes in southeast Turkey in 2011. Specifically, the chapter investigates how state-society relationships, political conflicts, and intergovernmental relations influenced stakeholder collaboration during the earthquake response. The chapter will also shed light on not only whether parts of a general collaborative governance framework is applicable to a fast-burning crisis context ('t Hart and Boin 2001) but also if it is applicable in a "non-Western" and hierarchical system like the Turkish.

Scholars of collaborative governance and management often unite in the belief that the institutional context – in which actors engaging in collaboration are embedded – matter. Thus, these scholars assert that the institutional context will have a bearing on how collaborative activities turn out (Ansell and Gash 2008; Emerson and Nabatchi 2015). It is, however, rather rare that studies point to which features of the institutional context that they refer. In this chapter the "administrative" part concerns the hardware or the structural features of national/central and local administration and the nature of the public service (Kuhlmann and Wollman 2014). The "political" part of the concept concerns level of centralization, polarization, and politicization in the system and political elites' ideas concerning how to govern (Pollitt and Bouckaert 2011).

Being aware of the perspectives of those who initiate and engage in collaboration in a certain context holds the promise of improving our understanding of collaborative governance practices in various settings. The empirical part of this chapter is based on interviews, conducted in Turkey between 2013 and 2015, with state officials from varying administrative levels, municipality and NGO representatives, as well as village and neighborhood leaders. All were involved in managing the disaster in one capacity or another. How actors perceive or interpret the meaning of collaboration and how they organize collaborative activities will in all likelihood have implications for what they can achieve. This chapter therefore sheds light on perceptions of collaboration in Turkey's political-administrative system and the role it plays in collaboration during disasters.

Analyzing the system context in which collaborations operate may hold the promise of aiding us in developing "a fuller understanding of the practicality, viability, and sustainability" of collaborations (Emerson and Nabatchi 2015, 40). Especially so, I argue, when combining the analysis of such macro perspectives with an analysis of the micro-perspectives of actors that inhabit the system in question. To develop a fuller understanding of collaborations is particularly pertinent in the domain of delivering public services that often involve many actors from many different sectors (Bryson et al. 2015). The management of hazards, crises, and disasters is indeed such a domain.[1] Due to their nature, the efforts to manage and recover from them necessarily and typically involve a multitude of actors from various jurisdictions.

Collaborative Governance and System Context

Emerson and Nabatchi (2015) have developed an elaborate framework that includes many of the general complexities surrounding collaborative governance processes and outcomes. The framework sheds light on factors related to, among other things, interpersonal relationships, organization, and structure. The many parts and components are in turn constituted by a number of fruitful prerequisites that affect collaborations and their potential achievements.

This chapter will engage specifically with two components from this framework: "system context" and "drivers." The former consists of a number of influences (not causal factors) that "shape the prospects for and challenges of initiating and sustaining" collaboration (Emerson and Nabatchi 2015, 43). Among these influences are *policy and legal frameworks* that enable or constrain collaboration and *political dynamics and power relations* between participating actors that shape actors' willingness to engage in collaboration. The system context also consists of *socioeconomic and cultural characteristics*, which affect the financial, human, and informational resources available to the collaboration. The *network characteristics* also play an important role in collaborations and concern the density and connectedness in preexisting social and organizational networks that individual actors may already be part of. The last example concerns a *history of conflict* (or not) between key actors, which affects trust levels and thereby the potential of bringing actors together to collaborate.

Case Study Setting

The Political-Administrative System in Turkey

Turkey is a unitary Napoleonic state, and the political-administrative system is highly centralized, hierarchical, and rather than being horizontally coordinated at the central government level, the system is more fairly described as fragmented (Kapucu and Palabıyık 2008; Keleş 2007), which also spills over to the disaster management system (Ganapati 2008; Kapucu 2012; Hermansson 2016). Turkey has been described as a transcendental state "where bureaucrats are in the position of decision-makers, and where political parties can work as state apparatus" (Aydıner and Özgür 2016, 53), which makes the distinction between elected and appointed officials less sharp. In general, collaboration is more forthcoming in consensual systems, or at least it "fits well into political cultures built on coalitions (e.g., the Netherlands) or associated with participative democracy (e.g., Denmark)" (Dickinson and Sullivan 2014, 162). Collaboration is generally much less prevalent in Turkish political culture, which is based on several continuous tensions including those between the center and the periphery, the secular and the religious, and the Kurdish

82 Helena Hermansson

and the Turkish (Erdoğan 2018). Even though local administrations have received more responsibilities during the last two decades, they are still perceived as weak due to a lack of financial resources and expertise (Gül and Kiriş 2015). This naturally also affects the capacities to prepare for and manage disasters, which unfortunately are very low (Unlu, Kapucu, and Sahin 2010).

The state's dominance over civil society (Kapucu and Palabıyık 2008) is another trait of the political-administrative system that is also evident in the disaster management system. This is not uncommon in centralized and hierarchical disaster management systems that tend to lack voluntarism and community involvement traditions (Tierney 2012). When it comes to the relationship between state and citizen, people often refer to *devlet baba*, "father state," and the state and its central administration are expected to "serve not only as a regulator but also as a producer and provider of goods and services" (Kalaycıoğlu 2012, 174). Some however claim that this father image of the state collapsed after the poorly managed earthquakes in Turkey in 1999, and that people now rather demand an effective and highly organized state apparatus (Incıoğlu 1999). At the same time, there has been countless stories in the media reporting about how limited the state's capacity is in terms of its regulatory and distribution capacities (Kalaycıoğlu 2012). In Turkey, there is also a general "deep-seated respect for authority and state," which vacates demands for accountability (Sozen and Shaw 2002, 480).

Recent Developments in the Turkish Disaster Management System

By the time of the 2011 earthquakes, the Turkish disaster (risk) management system had recently undergone wide-ranging reforms aiming at improving collaboration and coordination (Ganapati 2008; Jacoby and Özerdem 2008). In particular, the 1999 earthquakes that shook the Marmara region in 1999 and took the lives of 17,000 individuals[2] set these collaboration reforms in motion. The new disaster legislation for example requires that actors at all levels collaborate throughout preparing for, managing, and recovering from disasters (Oktay et al. 2013). This reform also created a new agency, the Disaster and Emergency Management Presidency (AFAD), merging three previous agencies with disaster responsibilities. This move reflected an ambition to reduce fragmentation and improve coordination and collaboration.

Actors who have prescribed roles in various regulations, plans, and policies make up the "formal" disaster management system in Turkey. AFAD is the central hub in this system with headquarters in Ankara and regional and provincial offices all over Turkey. In the provinces and in the administrative level under the provinces, the districts, the respective governors (who are appointed by the central government) are responsible for managing disasters and head the crisis coordination centers (CCC), which are constituted by a host of actors including the provincial ministries, security/law enforcement agencies, and nongovernmental organizations (NGOs). The municipal representatives are elected by the populace and are responsible for the local infrastructure, fire brigade, and police, yet they do not have any particular responsibilities during disasters but rather are under the authority of governors in such circumstances. The responsibilities of the municipalities are related to prevention, preparedness, and planning (Balamir 2013). Governors do not have the power to intervene (Gülkan 2009), an arrangement that seems liable to politicization, particularly when two entities do not share the same political affiliation, as was the case in Van at the time of the earthquakes.

The informal part of the disaster management system includes the village and neighborhood leaders (muhtars), actors who are elected but have no formal role during a disaster. The muhtars are responsible for population registration, maintaining order, facilitating social welfare, and strengthening social relations (Akay 2007). The muhtars' wide community networks and local knowledge also make them potentially valuable partners during a disaster. The same can be said for NGOs. NGOs do not have any formal responsibilities during disasters either, but there is an increased appreciation for their contributions, particularly search and rescue (SAR) NGOs that are often well-trained.

Actor Perceptions of Collaboration

As mentioned earlier, Emerson and Nabatchi (2015) specify a number of "drivers" that can propel collaboration between actors. At the same time, Dickinson and Sullivan (2014) suggest that actors' motivation to engage in collaboration is also driven by the meanings and values that they associate with the concept of collaboration. The associations made will be affected by existing local beliefs and practices and how well collaboration fits with them (Acharya 2004). Such beliefs and practices are largely codified in the political-administrative system context.

One example comes from a report concerning the short-term implementation of Turkey's national earthquake strategy and action plan 2012–2023 (NESAP). The board overlooking the implementation (consisting of both AFAD managers and external advisors from various universities and agencies) noted that some organizations did not do enough to contribute to collaboration. "The first priority of all responsible organizations is to bear in mind that they have to collaborate with other involved actors" (AFAD 2014, 28). Some interviewees perceived collaboration as the equivalent of AFAD "directing" and "giving orders" and "not providing the space to let organizations do their job well." It is hardly surprising that actors who hold this view are not very interested in AFAD's initiatives to promote collaboration. Several NGOs held similar views and had developed strategies to avoid collaborating with state agencies. Yet, actors from the provincial governorate, who were also involved in responding to the 2011 earthquakes, expressed that they appreciated AFAD's clear leadership characterized as "one hand, one head" and spoke of the "messy state" that reigned when several directorates shared responsibility for disaster issues. From an AFAD official's perspective, AFAD is striving to implement the global disaster risk reduction (DRR) community's best practices regarding multi-actor partnerships and collaboration.

One NGO representative engaged in search and rescue mentioned the delicate relation between state actors' attitudes toward collaborating with them depending on the magnitude of the emergency. According to this representative, AFAD (which also engages in search and rescue) has to demonstrate its ability independently from the NGOs during smaller emergencies, which prevents collaboration. One example provided concerned a protracted search for a child that had gone missing in Istanbul. The incident put pressure on the state's (AFAD's) teams, and even though they could not find the child, they refused help from NGOs until quite late in the search. If, by contrast, the interviewee said, the emergency is of greater magnitude, it becomes obvious that the state cannot cope with it on its own, which makes it easier to engage in collaboration with NGOs. For the state, perceptions of collaboration seem related to managing public expectations and political risks. One seasoned NGO interviewee with considerable international experience of search and rescue concurred that

> Yeah, it is a slippery slope for them [the government], so that's why you have to be very careful as an NGO to not step on their toes, or you know, to try to take the leadership role in these occasions.
>
> (interview 25)

Heroism also mattered for collaboration. A number of interviewees said that heroism hindered collaborative initiatives because in collaborations it is difficult to know who did what. When many individuals want to be the sole hero, collaboration suffers and relief operations become a "one-man show," an expression used by many. It is also likely that future collaboration suffers when one party seeks credit for joint efforts. Heroism may also make agencies and organizations reluctant to work under a higher authority. "One of the most difficult things in Turkey is to coordinate the response operations because there are so many actors, so many agencies and different groups in the field, and they are not willing to work under a bigger authority" (interview 7). The same interviewee shared that

> Normally, we don't find ourselves very close to other agencies but it's not because we don't want to, but usually in Turkey, most organizations have their own way of working. I don't want to call it competition but usually, in Turkey, it is easier for organizations to work separately.

When investigating disaster and crisis management collaboration, one also has to bear in mind the extent of collaboration between various actors during normal times. One interviewee, who had been a senior advisor to AFAD, compared the extent of collaboration in Turkey and Japan, where he had lived for a long time. He meant that collaboration and collective-action exist in the Japanese nature, while these phenomena do not exist in the Turkish "genetic code" (interview 29).

Cross-Sectoral Collaboration on the Ground

The 2011 earthquakes in Turkey's southeast Van province occurred on October 23 (7.2 on the Richter scale) and November 9 (5.6 on the Richter scale). In total, 644 people lost their lives and close to 4,000 were injured (WHO 2012). Aid poured into the area from all over Turkey, and the central government officials, including the Prime Minister and AFAD staff, arrived in Van a few hours after the first quake. The relief activities had to be coordinated, and the aid, staff, and volunteers who came to the area had to be accredited, and all this action took place in the provincial and district CCCs, chaired by the provincial and district governor, respectively.

Over 2500 SAR staff from AFAD, a semi-NGO,[3] and various NGOs arrived in Van within the first 24 hours. The interviews suggest that collaboration between these actors was relatively smooth, which can be explained by preexisting relationships and interpersonal trust. Actors from the regional AFAD offices and NGOs already knew each other from regular joint trainings, and both sides mentioned the good and trusting relationships. Previous interactions also contributed to mutual understanding of role division. Representatives from SAR NGOs shared that they offered their services to AFAD and expected to be told how and where they could be of use and did not mind being under AFAD's direction (interview 2). These observations corroborate the system context in the collaborative governance framework, particularly the influences of *network characteristics* and (lack of) *history of conflict*. In this example, the preexisting ties and trusting relationships between key actors AFAD and SAR NGOs facilitated collaboration.

Not all NGOs accepted the state's preferred role division. When asked about whether they engaged in any form of collaboration with state actors during the earthquake response, an NGO representative within the health sector replied that state actors imposed many rules on them stipulating how and where they were allowed to work:

> The political color of the ones who had leadership roles affected them. They told us we could only work with certain people. We say yes yes, but then circumvent them. It is the needs of people that decide who we help, not their political affiliation.
>
> (interview 14)

This quote is an illustrative example of how decisions to collaborate or not are based on perceptions of collaboration and how they affect collaborative output in turn. These perceptions are in part shaped by influences in the system context, here perhaps most profoundly by the *political dynamics and power relations*. Accounts from other NGOs working in villages affected by the earthquakes suggest that state actors sought to steer aid to politically suitable areas. One NGO representative (interview 20) described how two villages near each other were treated very differently in terms of receiving aid due to political considerations. In fairness, interviews, reports, and media paint a picture where not only those affiliated with the governmental party, but also other factions, distributed aid based on political affiliation.

The high level of polarization in the Turkish society also affected which actors state authorities collaborated with and how long it took to initiate such collaboration. Given the state's dominance in the system, it is most often state authorities who initiate collaboration. Engaging in cross-sectoral crisis management collaboration provides access to additional resources and valuable knowledge, which has the potential to make relief operations more effective (c.f. Bae, Joo, and Won 2015; Kapucu, Arslan, and Collins 2010; Miller and Douglass 2015; Simo and Bies 2007). This is illustrative of *interdependence* as a strong motivational force for collaboration (Emerson and Nabatchi 2015; Mandell and Keast 2008). If state authorities do not take advantage of additional resources through collaboration this may pose a potential political risk of leaving the public with the impression that the state is not effective in managing the disaster. However, collaboration with actors with divergent ideas and values may also imply political risks, including ceding potential credit for successful activities to other actors or losing some of their credibility.

Despite these political considerations, state actors did engage in cross-sectoral collaboration, albeit to varying degrees, with actors from both the municipality (even, although to a very limited extent, with a pro-Kurdish municipality in Van) and civil society (Hermansson 2016). These political considerations also help explain why it took longer for state actors to initiate collaboration with actors who did not share the government's political views. In some cases, these differences were not overlooked, which effectively prevented cross-sectoral collaboration and hampered the response. One municipal interviewee (representing the pro-Kurdish party) claimed that if the municipality and the provincial governorate could have collaborated, fewer residents would have had to migrate from the city, as many of the problems that occurred could have been solved better through collaboration (interview 3).

Clearly, these two actors have had a *history of conflict* due to their political differences. The fact that the municipality represented the pro-Kurdish party aggravated collaboration not only during the response to the earthquakes but also before, which both parties acknowledged in the interviews. The assessment of houses and building stock following the 2011 earthquakes was among the activities that suffered from this political polarization (Hermansson 2016). Yet, when the living conditions for the affected population worsened, these tensions were temporarily relaxed, paving the way for collaboration during the establishment of container cities. Asking one municipality representative about how they managed to overcome conflict in this episode, the interviewee said:

> It is true, we engaged in this collaboration because of our people's safety. As a municipality, we should make it easier for our own people and the weather conditions were getting worse . . . many children froze to death in the tents. We provided them [the

provincial governorate] our own area [municipal land], and we helped them prepare the ground for the containers and the water and sewage systems.

(interview 3)

This example illustrates how disaster events can "jolt" long-term patterns of collaboration (or lack thereof) as the cost of noncollaboration becomes too high. In contrast, collaboration between the aforementioned SAR NGOs and state authorities was present from the outset of the response, and it was also pre-trained.

It was mentioned earlier that damage assessment activities suffered from poor collaboration. Damage assessment was slowed down by a lack of personnel and cadaster data and information regarding who owned and/or lived in which house. Even though the muhtars, who are responsible for population registry, had access to the information needed, it took the provincial governorate nearly three weeks to reach out to them. At an earlier stage, the municipality in Van had also offered the provincial governorate resources in the form of local damage assessors from the Union of Turkish Chambers of Engineers and Architects, but this offer was declined (interview 3). As a result, the municipality actors also stopped attending information meetings in the province's CCC. In the aftermath of the response operations, the provincial governorate received criticism for being too slow to make use of the local actors once it became obvious that there was a lack of personnel (Erkan et al. 2013; ODTÜ 2011).

Such tensions between municipality and the governorate were less evident in Erciş, the other town severely affected by the 2011 earthquakes. The explanation given to this in the interviews was that in Erciş the municipality and governor both represented the same political party (interviews 5, 38, and 41) and were used to collaborating. The *political dynamics and power relations* and *network characteristics* were therefore more favorable to collaboration here. In addition, in Erciş, there were also examples of collaboration across politically divergent actors. This was enabled by strong local *initiating leadership*. Over a stretch of five years, the district governor in Erciş at the time had made efforts to "mend" ties with those parts of the local population that he saw as his (the state's) staunchest opposition: the villages with pro-Kurdish affiliation and/or PKK affiliation, as he realized that there would be resistance due to historical and ongoing political conflicts. According to his own account, these trusting relations assisted him greatly when managing the earthquake. In this example, leadership seemed to play a decisive role for collaboration.

There were noticeable differences between how the state authorities in Van and Erciş acted toward NGOs. In Van, one interviewee involved in NGO accreditation following the earthquakes had a rather cautious and suspicious attitude and felt that since the region has "sensitive issues" one could not be too sure of the motives or agendas of the NGOs (interview 12). In Erciş, CCC officials testified that the NGOs that came to the area to assist did well and that the NGOs could choose whether they wished to work independently or in collaboration with the district governorate. These experiences suggest that there are important variations in prerequisites for collaboration even within the same system.

It was mentioned earlier that collaboration contributes to making relief operations more effective by granting access to resources and local knowledge. However, there are also a few examples where organizations acted alone, which resulted in a more effective response. For instance, several resourceful and professional NGOs decided to act fast, rather than wait for the slow, grinding bureaucracy of the highly centralized and hierarchical system. As these NGOs also made an assessment of people's needs independently from the state, the risk of aid being distributed according to political considerations (at least the state's) was also mitigated. Hence, despite that collaboration is often regarded as a necessity during disasters, it is no guarantor for more effective management of crises and disasters.

Conclusion

In highly polarized and centralized political-administrative systems like the Turkish, state actors dominate and will most often be the ones who initiate collaboration, even during crises and disasters. Such collaboration will by definition become externally mandated (Herranz 2010; Rodríguez et al. 2007) often by law or regulation. For some researchers, such constellations do not reflect "true" or "real" collaboration, as "real collaboration" entails voluntary engagement and power balance between participating actors (c.f. Lester and Krejci 2007). However, power balance in collaborations is rather unlikely in many centralized and authoritarian political-administrative systems. Studies of collaboration increasingly emphasize that collaboration does not presuppose decentralized political systems (Bryson, Crosby, and Stone 2015). One message from this chapter is that actors often engage in more than one type of collaboration and that the institutional conditions often vary even within the same system. This is in line with the various collaborative modes mentioned by Nohrstedt and Bynander in the introductory chapter, which deserves further empirical research.

The broad palette of collaboration should also be acknowledged by various practitioners and advocates of collaboration in the crisis and disaster management discourse. Otherwise, we risk upholding a skewed perception of benchmarks and progress that does not resonate well with reality. The Hyogo and Sendai frameworks for disaster risk reduction encourage states to adopt certain modes and structures of disaster management collaboration and report on their progress. One example is the National Platform for Disaster Risk Reduction, which refers to the multi-stakeholder coordination mechanism for promoting advocacy, coordination, analysis, and advice on disaster risk reduction that ideally includes key actors from the private sector and communities as well as technical experts (UNDRR 2019). Such a platform also exists in Turkey, yet some of the actors interviewed for this study are not aware of its existence – even those who are listed as participants in the platform. This suggests there needs to be a greater recognition of how prerequisites for collaboration differ and that collaboration itself may differ. In turn, it is perhaps reasonable that actors within these systems adapt or adjust the mode of collaboration to better fit their realities (Achraya 2004). As demonstrated in this chapter, collaboration did in fact occur, and in many instances it also promoted effectiveness.

This chapter has also illustrated that more general collaborative governance frameworks can be applied to cases of disaster management. Applying the framework to collaboration in a somewhat unorthodox political-administrative context, considering Turkey's strongly centralized features, further suggests that Emerson and Nabatchi's (2015) general collaborative governance framework is able to shed light on the emergence of collaboration in various political-administrative settings.

Emerson and Nabatchi (2015) call for further exploration of the interplay of the drivers in their framework (i.e., uncertainty, interdependence, initiating leadership, and consequential incentives) and "system context" to understand how these factors shape collaboration. This chapter illustrates how these factors interact. *Initiating leadership*, for example, could counter system context influences that constrain collaboration. Meanwhile, this chapter also suggests ways to improve the framework. Specifically, adding actors' perceptions of collaboration and what it means to them, or what values they attach to it, provides a more nuanced understanding of collaborations and what they realistically can be expected to achieve in different contexts. Perceptions are likely to vary between how much clout and status various actors have in the system and also on which actor/leader initiates collaboration and the relation to this leader.

One lesson of this study is that differences across political-administrative systems are evident regarding the conditions for collaboration, who is engaged in such activities, and what collaborations can realistically achieve. In return, research should pay close attention to meanings and values that actors ascribe to collaboration as well as how actors negotiate tensions between prescriptions of collaboration. Ethnographical studies and field-based research may be particularly well suited to capture these nuances. It is also worth noting that local variations often exist within the same political-administrative system, as suggested by this analysis of Van and Erciş. Hence, future work has much to gain from studying different cities or regions even within the same country.

Even though political-administrative systems and norms have a considerable influence on how collaboration is perceived and unfolds, one should avoid deterministic assertions. One type of system should not be expected to consistently lead to similar results in terms of collaboration. Moreover, political-administrative systems also change over time, even though such changes are often incremental and slow. The interviews carried out for this study suggested that the need for collaboration in relation to disasters may change perceptions of collaboration and nudge collaborative norms, procedures, and practices. These changes were noted during the disaster response but also even after returning to some kind of normalcy two years after the quakes. For example, one provincial manager elaborated how the experiences of collaboration during the earthquakes transformed working relationships and procedures in his province:

> Normally, institutions do not want to help each other but now, the relationship between us actors who dealt with the earthquake is different. We have a different relationship because of the fusion we experienced when dealing with the earthquakes. Before, we didn't get together as much as we did during this time and, even now, our relationships are still very tight. . . . The actors who worked in the CCC came together and connected and still do so. For example, if I have a problem with telecom, I now call the telecom manager and instead of approaching him as "bey" [mister] we are now "abi" [brother] and say "I have this problem, can you fix this for me?" So now, our emotions and relations are more human than institutional.

> (interview 6)

Hence, it is not only that political-administrative systems affect perceptions of collaboration, which in turn influence collaboration and collaborative outcomes. The opposite also seems possible, suggesting that outcomes of collaboration shape perceptions of collaboration, which in turn provide feedback that affects at least parts of the political-administrative system.

The polarized political system in Turkey is challenging for collaboration, and these characteristics became even more pronounced after the attempted coup in July 2016. But rather than letting this lead us to the conclusion that collaboration is not possible in this context, we should recognize that collaboration comes in different forms. Being context sensitive and recognizing the impact of actors' perceptions of collaboration *on* collaboration is one way to avoid biased analyses of collaborative arrangements in various crises and disaster contexts. Integrating the collaborative governance and crisis management literature serves us well in this endeavor.

Notes

1. This chapter sides with UNDDR (2017) in seeing "disaster management" as the organization, planning, and application of measures preparing for, responding to, and recovering from disasters.
2. Unofficial figures claim nearly twice as many died.
3. The National Medical Rescue Teams (Ulusal Medikal Kurtarma Ekipleri, UMKE) is a voluntary organization composed of professional health staff (like nurses and doctors) who work at hospitals during normal times. In times of disasters, they have the task of treating individuals whom the SAR teams have rescued from under the rubble, a task that demands medical expertise. UMKE, however, belongs to the National Ministry of Health.

References

Acharya, Amitav 2004. "How Ideas Spread: Whose Norms Matter? Norm Localization and Institutional Change in Asian Regionalism." *International Organization* 58 (2): 239–75.

AFAD, Afet ve Acil Durum Yönetimi Baskanlığı. 2014. "Ulusal Deprem Stratejisi ve Eylem Planı (UDSEP-2023): Kisa dönem (2012–2013) değerlendirme raporu."

Agranoff, Robert and Michael McGuire. 2001. "Big Questions in Public Network Management Research." *Journal of Public Administration Research and Theory* 11 (3): 295–36.

Agrawal, Arun and Maria C. Lemos. 2007. "A Greener Revolution in the Making? Environmental Governance in the 21st Century." *Environment: Science and Policy for Sustainable Development* 49 (5): 36–45.

Akay, Aslı. "Disaster Management and the Role of Local Government: Lessons Learnt from Yalova City." Paper presented at the Conference of Public Administration Theory Network, Harrisburg, PA 25–27 May 2007.

Ansell, Chris and Alison Gash. 2008. "Collaborative Governance in Theory and Practice." *Journal of Public Administration Research and Theory* 18: 543–71.

Aydıner, Tolgahan and Hüseyin Özgür. 2016. "Natural Disaster Governance: Barriers for Turkey." *European Scientific Journal* Special Edition: 47–60.

Bae, Yooil, YuMin Joo, and Soh-Yeon Won. 2015. "Decentralization and Collaborative Disaster Governance: Evidence from South Korea." *Habitat International* 52: 50–56. doi:10.1016/j.habitatint.2015.08.027

Balamir, Murat 2013. "Obstacles in the Adoption of International DRR Policies: The Case of Turkey." Draft background paper prepared for the Global Assessment Report On Disaster Risk Reduction 2013.

Bryson, John M., Barbara C. Crosby, and Melissa M. Stone. 2015. "Designing and Implementing Cross-Sector Collaborations: Needed and Challenging." *Public Administration Review* 75 (5): 647–63.

Dickinson, Helen and Helen Sullivan. 2014. "Towards a General Theory of Collaborative Performance: The Importance of Efficacy and Agency." *Public Administration* 92 (1): 161–77.

Emerson, Kirk and Tina Nabatchi. 2015. *Collaborative Governance Regimes*. Washington, DC: Georgetown University Press.

Erdoğan, Emre 2018. "Dimensions of Polarization in Turkey." www.gmfus.org/publications/dimensions-polarization-turkey

Erkan, Burcak B., Ayse N. Karanci, Sibel Kalaycıoğlu, Ali T. Özden, İdil Çalışkan, and Gamze Özakşehir. 2013. "From Emergency Response to Recovery: Multiple Impacts and Lessons Learned from 2011 Van Earthquakes." *Earthquake Spectra* 31: 527–40.

Ganapati, Nazife Emel 2008. "Disaster Management Structure in Turkey: Away from Reactive and Paternalistic Approach?" In *Disaster Management Handbook*, edited by J. Pinkowski, 281–319. Boca Raton, FL: CRC Press.

Gazley, Beth 2013. "Building Collaborative Capacity for Disaster Resiliency." In *Disaster Resiliency: Interdisciplinary Perspectives*, edited by N. Kapucu, C.V. Hawkins, and F.I. Rivera, 84–98. New York, NY: Routledge.

Gül, Hüseyin and Hakan M. Kiriş. 2015. "Democratic Governance Reforms in Turkey: Prospects and Challenges." In *Public Administration and Policy in the Middle East*, edited by A.R. Dawoody, 25–59. New York, NY: Springer Science+Business Media.

Gülkan, Polat 2009. "Disaster Management and Mitigation Systems: A (Limited) Global Picture." In *Perspectives in Disaster Management*, edited by P. Gülkan and B.B. Basbuğ Erkan, 1–37. Ankara, Turkey: Middle East Technical University Press.

Hermansson, Helena 2016. "Disaster Response in Turkey: Conditions Promoting Cross-Sectoral Collaboration and Implications for Effectiveness." *Administration and Society.* doi:10.1177/0095399716680058

Herranz Jr., Joaquín 2010. "Network Performance and Coordination: A Theoretical Review and Framework." *Public Performance and Management Review* 33 (3): 311–41.

Jacoby, Tim and Alpaslan Özerdem. 2008. "The Role of the State in the Turkish Earthquake of 1999." *Journal of International Development* 20: 297–310.

Kalaycıoğlu, Ersin 2012. "Political Culture." In *The Routledge Handbook of Modern Turkey*, edited by M. Saber and S. Sayarı, 171–93. New York, NY: Routledge.

Kapucu, Naim 2012. *The Network Governance in Response to Acts of Terrorism: Comparative Analyses.* New York, NY: Routledge.

Kapucu, Naim, Tolga Arslan, and Matthew L. Collins. 2010. "Examining Intergovernmental and Interorganizational Response to Catastrophic Disasters: Toward a Network-Centered Approach." *Administration and Society* 42: 222–47.

Kapucu, Naim and Hamit Palabıyık. 2008. *Turkish Public Administration: From Tradition to the Modern Age.* Ankara, Turkey: International Strategic Research Organization.

Keleş, Ruşen. 2007. "Administrative Culture in Turkey." In *Foundations of Administrative Culture in Europe*, edited by F. Thedieck, 146–52. University of Applied Sciences Kehl-Congress of Local and Regional Authorities of the Council of Europe. Baden-Baden: Nomos.

Kuhlmann, Sabine and Hellmut Wollman. 2014. "Introduction to Comparative Public Administration." In *Administrative Systems and Reform in Europe*, 1–8. Cheltenham: Edward Elgar.

Lester, William and Daniel Krejci. 2007. "Business 'Not' as Usual: The National Incident Management System, Federalism, and Leadership." *Public Administration Review* 67: 84–93.

Mandell, Myrna P. and Robyn Keast. 2008. "Evaluating the Effectiveness of Interorganizational Relations Through Networks." *Public Management Review* 10: 715–31.

Miller, Michelle A. and Mike Douglass. 2015. "Introduction: Decentralising Disaster Governance in Urbanising Asia." *Habitat International* 52: 1–4. doi:10.1016/j.habitatint.2015.08.028

Nohrstedt, Daniel, Fredrik Bynander, Charles Parker, and Paul 't Hart. (2018). "Managing Crises Collaboratively: Prospects and Problems-A Systematic Literature Review." *Perspectives on Public Management and Governance* 1 (4): 257–71. https://academic.oup.com/ppmg/article-abstract/1/4/257/4850664

ODTÜ (Orta Doğu Teknik Üniversetesi, Afet Yönetimi Uygulama ve Araştırma Merkezi, [Middle East Technical University, Disaster Management Implementation and Research Center]). 25–27 November 2011. *Observation Report.*

Oktay, F., C. Tetik, O. Gökçe, and G. Cebi. 2013. *New Disaster Management System in Turkey: A Case Study of the 2011 Van Earthquake.* www.witpress.com/elibrary/wit-transactions-on-ecology-and-the-environment/179/25311

Pollitt, Christopher and Geert Bouckaert. 2011. *Public Management Reform: A Comparative Analysis-New Public Management, Governance, and the Neo-Weberian State.* 3rd ed. New York, NY: Oxford University.

Robinson, Scott E. and Benjamin S. Gaddis. 2012. "Seeing Past Parallel Play: Survey Measures of Collaboration in Disaster Situations." *The Policy Studies Journal* 40 (2): 256–73.

Rodríguez, Charo, Ann Langley, François Béland, and J.L. Denis. 2007. "Governance, Power, and Mandated Collaboration in an Interorganizational Network." *Administration and Society* 39 (2): 150–93.

Simo, Gloria and Angela L. Bies. 2007. "The Role of Nonprofits in Disaster Response: An Expanded Model of Cross-Sector Collaboration." *Public Administration Review* 67: 125–42.

Sozen, Süleyman and Ian Shaw. 2002. "The International Applicability of 'New' Public Management: Lessons from Turkey." *International Journal of Public Sector Management* 15 (6): 475–86.

't Hart, Paul and Arjen Boin. 2001. "Between Crisis and Normalcy: The Long Shadow of Post-Crisis Politics." In *Managing Crises: Threats, Dilemmas, Opportunities*, edited by U. Rosenthal, A. Boin, and L.K. Comfort, 28–46. Springfield, IL: Charles C. Thomas Publisher.

Tierney, Kathleen 2012. "Disaster Governance: Social, Political, and Economic Dimensions." *The Annual Review of Environment and Resources* 37: 341–63.

UNDDR (United Nations Office for Disaster Risk Reduction). 2017. "Terminology." https://www.preventionweb.net/terminology

UNDDR (United Nations Office for Disaster Risk Reduction). 2019. "National Platforms." www.unisdr.org/we/coordinate/national-platforms

Unlu, Ali, Naim Kapucu, and Bahadir Sahin. 2010. "Disaster and Crisis Management in Turkey: A Need for a Unified Crisis Management System." *Disaster Prevention and Management* 19 (2): 155–74.

WHO (World Health Organization). 2012. "Health response to the earthquakes in Van province, Turkey, 2011." http://www.euro.who.int/__data/assets/pdf_file/0007/ 181960/e96760.pdf?ua=1

Chapter 8

Transregional Crisis Management in Africa

Simon Hollis and Eva-Karin Olsson

Introduction

Large-scale crises often require modes of collaboration between crisis management actors. As a result, it is the rule rather than the exception for crisis management to be characterized by extensive cooperation among a large set of actors. In an African context, the depth and breadth of regionalization has advanced over the last three decades to include cooperation to collectively manage transboundary crises. Just like the European Union (EU), the Caribbean Community (CARICOM), or the Association of Southeast Asian Nations (ASEAN), the African Union (AU) and its associated Regional Economic Communities (RECs) have established framework agreements and joint capacities to facilitate and provide assistance to disasters that exhaust national capacity or that affect more than one country simultaneously (Hollis 2015). While the development of collective regional response capabilities may vary from region to region, the unique process of regionalization in Africa stands out due to emerging collaboration between regional organizations.

Transregional crisis management capacity and preparedness is an important field of inquiry for those interested in the role of networks and various collaborative arrangements in managing crises that go beyond the state. As it necessarily involves a large number of actors the complexity and challenges to effectively respond across borders increases dramatically (Boin, Stern, and Sundelius 2016). The literature emphasizes, for instance, how collaboration can be difficult when there is limited planning, a lack of organizational design, conflicting interests, an upscaling of mechanisms, and an unwillingness to cooperate. On the other hand, research has also shown that collaboration can be facilitated by joint problem framings, mutual dependencies, and incentives to improve cooperation (Klijn and Koppenjan 2000, 144). In addition, it has been argued that established networks, which are already in place when a crisis happens, contribute to increased effectiveness, as repeated interactions work to reduce uncertainty leading to familiarity and trust between actors (Moynihan 2008, 356).

This exploratory study maps out and examines emerging transregional networks for crisis preparedness consisting of AU and its RECs in the period from 2014–2016. This is achieved through a two-step process. First, the networks are assessed in terms of the number of meetings between the parties involved as well as the topics of these meetings. Second, networks are categorized and discussed according to three main capacities of importance to crisis management preparedness derived from a framework developed by Ansell, Boin, and Keller (2010) and modified by the authors. A description of how these capacities are measured is provided in more detail in the following pages. Finally, the networks are evaluated and discussed in relation to their potential for transboundary crisis management.

This chapter begins with a discussion of regionalization in Africa as a case for trans-regional collaboration on crisis management. The chapter then moves to a description of the method and theoretical approach used to describe and analyze transregional crisis management networks in Africa. Next follows an analysis of the findings. The final sections review and summarize the findings, pointing toward additional research questions on transregional crisis management.

Mapping and Analyzing Transregional Crisis Management Preparedness Networks in Africa

In this chapter we draw upon the notion of transboundary crisis and boundary spanning actors in order to understand the potential transregional crisis management capacity of the AU and its RECs. In doing so we begin by applying a framework in which three key capacities are identified as crucial for crisis management preparedness: network coordination (institutional design to support cooperation), distributed sensemaking (merging conflicting problem definitions), and surge capacity (overcoming problems of supply logistics) (Ansell et al. 2010).[1] These categories are generally understood to represent some of the core foundations for responding to a crisis. Network coordination implies that like-minded practitioners share a collective understanding on the necessity to discuss and potentially solve collective-action problems that arise through existing or future trans-boundary disasters. At its most basic level this is represented through physical forums for discussion. Sense making is a central component for crisis management as it implies not only that representatives from regional organizations meet, but that they share, analyze, and communicate information to establish a general picture of a crisis event. Surge capacity implies that decisions are collectively made that result in the facilitation of a response or the mobilization of crisis response assets.

These capacities are assessed according to the range of inter-regional collaborative arrangements (see "conceptual dimensions" in the introductory chapter of this book) by analyzing whether they exhibit a high or low level of crisis response capacity. Our analysis has categorized and mapped AU and RECs transregional network meetings in the period from January 2014 to December 2016. All notifications, press releases, and descriptions of transregional activity were documented from official REC websites as well as AU websites. This produced a total of 719 meetings between two or more RECs that were coded for the type of meeting (whether it was a single or reoccurring meeting), its purpose, the type of participants, the main topic of discussion, and physical location. Once mapped and categorized, the efficiency of the networks was then analyzed by locating the existence or absence of key crisis management features that constitute the three crisis management capacities.

Network coordination refers to institutional design which we have operationalized as pre-established or self-organizing mechanisms for coordinating action in the event of a crisis. In this study we examine a range of collaborative meetings, both *ad hoc* and scheduled; an *ad hoc* meeting is a self-organized meeting similar to what sociologists identify as "emergent organizations," and a scheduled network is a pre-established meeting where members meet on a frequent pre-planned basis. The type of meeting reflects not only the motivation for collective action between regional organizations, but it also relates to the effectiveness of coordination. According to Ansell et al. (2010), formal networks will generally be more effective networks; however, there is also value in more flexible arrangements (see the introductory chapter of this book). It is also worth remembering that the focus of this study – inter-regional collaboration on crisis management – is a part of a larger collaborative network of actors that contribute to an emerging multi-sectorial and inter-organizational dimension of transboundary response efforts in Africa.

Distributed sensemaking refers to the process of forming situational awareness to reduce uncertainty. This includes gathering, sharing, communicating, and analyzing pooled information from a number of open or closed sources. The first task facing crisis managers is to make sense of the event, which includes the ability to understand what is going on and the stakes implied. Sensemaking is difficult for a number of reasons, at both individual and organizational levels. For example, past experiences play an important role in understanding the present. In organizational settings one factor influencing sensemaking is the ability for organizational members to interpret the situation based on their role and position (Weick 1995; Boin et al. 2016). Forming a shared picture of a crisis, particularly between states and regional organizations, can thus be highly challenging. Among other things, this requires trust, specified knowledge, analytical capabilities, and effective decision-making procedures to overcome hurdles produced by sequential, reciprocal, and pooled interdependence. Analyzing and gathering information for transboundary crises requires the existence or use of detection and surveillance systems, analytical capacity, real-time communication, and decision support systems (Ansell et al. 2010, 201). An initial indication on the extent to which one can observe sensemaking – in order of the weight of transaction costs – can be based on whether there is (1) basic sharing of raw information from national and/or regional sources, (2) gathering and analyzing of this information at a transregional level, and (3) provision of an analysis of the gathered information for decision making.

Surge capacity refers to the efficient mobilization of resources (Ansell et al. 2010, 198). Surge capacity relates to the network's ability to facilitate a rapid response. According to Ansell et al. (2010), surge capacity can be understood alongside components such as professional first responders, which can be deployed in crisis situations. The existence of supply chain management for the deployment of people and resources as well as organizational Standard Operating Procedures (SOPs) allows for fast-track procedures and improvisation. Finally, surge capacity in general requires an integrated command center from which resources can be mobilized. Table 8.1 summarizes the main transboundary response and preparedness capacities.

The far left column lists the three capacities that are assessed in this chapter. The center column provides indicators that express the current development of the capacity under investigation, and the far right column relates to whether the indicator represents a high or low level of capacity. To be sure, these are crude indicators that could be fine-tuned in future studies, but for the purpose of this chapter it provides a starting point to identify emerging transregional crisis management.

Table 8.1 Mapping transregional capacity

Crisis Response Capacities	Indicators	Level of Capacity
Networked Coordination	Self-organized	Low
	Pre-established	High
Distributed Sensemaking	Sharing and analysis	Low
	Decision making	High
Surge Capacity	Non-crisis meetings	Low
	Crisis meetings	High

Source: Modified classification of crisis management capacities from Ansell et al. 2010.

Material and Method

The empirical material consists of various meetings involving various RECs as well as the AU. Information used to code the meetings has been manually retrieved (no key word searches) from the official websites of Arab Maghreb Union (UMA), Common Market for Eastern and Southern Africa (COMESA), Community of Sahel-Saharan States (CEN-SAD), East African Community (EAC), Economic Community of Central African States (ECCAS), Economic Community of West African States (ECOWAS), Intergovernmental Authority on Development (IGAD), Southern African Development Community (SADC), and the AU (see Appendix).[2] In addition to these websites, we also explored their specialized sub-organizations' websites, such as the West African Health Organization (WAHO) and the Centre for Renewable Energy and Energy Efficiency (ECREEE), which are linked to ECOWAS. Note that this method is designed to provide a first-cut indication of transregional crisis management collaboration and does not provide an in-depth study on specific cases. The findings from the source material are also limited in terms of a short time series; thus, only "formal" meetings were coded since informal gatherings, and "corridor diplomacy" are outside the scope conditions for assessing transregional crisis management capacity.

The collected data thus consists of a collection of events where representatives from one or more AU institutions participated with representatives from one or more REC(s), or events where participants from two or more different RECs participated together. This aims to focus attention on the interactions between regional and subregional organizations. We began by coding observed meetings in the period from January 1, 2014–December 31, 2016, in relation to the three conceptual categories. For surge capacity we coded the data for the topics of the meetings and if the meetings related to a crisis event. For network coordination, we coded the data for whether the meetings were formal or *ad hoc*. For sensemaking, we coded for the sharing and/or analysis of information as well as decision making. These three coding schemes are elaborated upon.

Coding for Topics

The topics in meetings and events were first listed and then arranged according to their frequency. The ten most reoccurring topics consisted of the following.

Table 8.2 Description of major topics discussed in subregional meetings, 2014–2016

Topic	Description
Agriculture	Issues covering the agricultural and livestock sector. This includes policy, practices, and food production.
Democracy	Events such as elections, election observations, human rights, discussions on the current state of democracy, rule of law, and human rights in specific countries.
Economy	Monetary and fiscal policy, trade and trade barriers (e.g., customs), industrialization, business and business regulation, financial institutions, and oversight. Topics of economy often coincide with topics of regional integration and also agriculture due to the regional importance of this sector.
Environment	Climate change and climate smart practices, aquaculture, maritime protection and regulation, preservation of wildlife, nature, and biodiversity.

(Continued)

Table 8.2 (Continued)

Topic	Description
Gender	Events that relate to questions tied to equality between the sexes, including sexual violence, disparities in opportunity, and gender perspectives in specific areas (e.g., gender perspective in agriculture).
Health	Includes areas like nutrition, medicine and pharmaceutical regulation, food security, animal health, and disease surveillance and prevention.
Infrastructure	Events dealing with large transportation and construction projects, such as regional highways. Infrastructure also includes the use of water resources and digital infrastructure (like the internet and other means of communication).
Regional integration	Events and activities related to projects, frameworks, and programs with the objective to integrate and harmonize were coded as "regional integration" (e.g., establishment of multilateral free trade areas, creation of common institutions, shared migration, and border management policy).
Security	Activities dealing with the protection of human life, conflict prevention, crisis management, peacekeeping, state sovereignty and territorial/maritime defense, and terrorism and other forms of systemic violence. We chose to code urgent health issues, such as control of severe epidemics (e.g., Ebola) and other securitized health issues, as "security."
Social issues	Events dealing with matters such as labor laws, humanitarian action, human trafficking (such as child marriages), and discriminatory practices (such as racism and harmful traditional practices).

Source: Table Created by Authors

Coding for Network Coordination

A meeting was coded as scheduled if it included reoccurring planned events, such as ordinary sessions of committees, councils, and summits that include the same or similar actors on each occasion. In addition to these longstanding activities we also included inaugural meetings of newly formed committees, official expert groups, policy projects, and programs if their purpose was to meet or operate regularly in the future. High-level meetings within established collaborative frameworks, such as ministerial level meetings within a common regional integration framework, were also coded as scheduled. Meetings that were *ad hoc* include non-reoccurring events that related to a specific purpose and were often, but not necessarily, linked to an issue or event occurring within a limited timeframe. Such events consisted of workshops, sessions, conferences, or press conferences with the aim to educate, inform, facilitate discussion, gather input, and/or make decisions on a specific and/or urgent event.[3]

Coding for Sensemaking

Information exchange was coded when actors shared information regarding policies, situations, and practices. "Sharing and analysis" was coded when actors discussed issues that were officially part of the meeting agenda. For example, the statement "Ebola was discussed at the meeting (and) . . . the delegations reached a consensus on the problem" indicates that some form of analysis took place. In other cases, it was the character of the gathering (such as workshops, which include discussions among participants) that resulted in it being categorized as "sharing and analysis." Decisions were coded as "decision making" when it was clearly stated that the meeting included decision making.

Coding for Surge Capacity in Acute Crisis Events

Crises are understood as pressing events that are bound to a limited timeframe and deemed to require swift action in order to mitigate, prevent, or neutralize negative consequences and threats to certain values. In this study, an event was coded as a crisis when it clearly related to a specific current or ongoing event that posed a threat to common values (such as security and democracy) and that demanded a response from the involved actors. The meetings were categorized as "crisis" if they focused on facilitating the coordination of response efforts for a crisis and/or mobilizing resources, which are the two main indicators reflecting the general level of regional crisis response capacity.

Mapping Transregional Networks

This section maps out transregional networks and discusses their potential for crisis management in Africa. Based on the empirical data collection, 719 meetings were coded according to the criteria described in the previous section. The mapping exercise consisted of conceptualizing the empirical data into the theoretical categorization from Ansell et al. (2010); namely, surge capacity, network coordination, and sensemaking. Yet first, we will present an overview of the topics discussed in the meetings analyzed.

Table 8.3 illustrates the frequency of topics discussed in the transregional meetings included in this study. The most frequent issue discussed during the period of investigation was security followed by economic issues, health, and democracy. In the next section we will take a closer look at network coordination within the framework of these events.

Network Coordination

As already mentioned, network coordination refers to scheduled or *ad hoc* mechanisms for coordination. In this category, we looked at both the number and type of meetings. The data in Table 8.4 illustrates that the networks engaged in both formal and *ad hoc* meetings, even though the number of formal meetings were somewhat higher than the number of *ad hoc* meetings. Moreover, the number of both scheduled and *ad hoc* meetings increased in 2015, but both dropped to some extent in 2016 to their previous frequencies. Given the framework developed by Ansell et al. (2010), pre-established meetings indicate an effective network. However, as already mentioned, other scholars have stressed the strength in the network's ability to meet on an *ad hoc* basis in response to upcoming problems.

Table 8.3 Percent of topics discussed in subregional meetings and events, 2014–2016

	2014	2015	2016	Average
Security	24	27	21	24
Economy	17	16	16	16
Health	19	11	8	13
Democracy	11	11	11	11
Regional integration	13	10	8	10
Infrastructure	8	4	7	6
Agriculture	7	8	7	7
Environment	3	6	4	4
Social issues	4	3	2	3
Gender	3	4	4	4

Source: Table Created by Authors

98 Simon Hollis and Eva-Karin Olsson

Table 8.4 Number of *ad hoc* and formal transregional meetings or events, 2014–2016

	2014	2015	2016	Average
Formal	138	158	137	144
Ad hoc	108	138	125	124

Source: Table Created by Authors

Table 8.5 Number of meetings devoted to sharing, analyzing information, and decision making, 2014–2016

	2014	2015	2016	Average
Sharing	19	27	14	20
Analysis	175	180	214	190
Decision	20	38	25	28

Source: Table Created by Authors

Table 8.6 Number of subregional meetings or events used for discussing acute crisis events, 2014–2016

	2014	2015	2016	Average
Crisis	60	66	42	56
Non Crisis	291	363	464	373

Source: Table Created by Authors

Sensemaking

As previously presented, "sensemaking" refers to the process of forming situational awareness to reduce uncertainty. An initial indication on the extent to which one can observe sensemaking – in order of the weight of transaction costs – can be based on whether there is a basic sharing of raw information from national and/or regional sources or an analysis of the gathered information in the form of discussions or decision making. The crisis management literature often points to difficulties associated with the creation of joint sensemaking between actors. In Table 8.5, the number of meetings dealing with information sharing, analysis, and decisions are presented.

In Table 8.5, we can see that the majority of meetings were used for discussions and analysis. The network appeared to be strongest in terms of allowing for the creation of joint sensemaking across participants through discussion and analysis. Comparatively, it was used less for decision making although this was still a part of the network's output, which implies that the network not only has symbolic value but was also used for addressing concrete issues.

Surge Capacity

In order to explore surge capacity within the network, we examined the number of meetings dealing with acute events that included time pressure and threats to core values and that demanded the actors to take swift action. The results can be seen in Table 8.6.

Table 8.7 Acute crisis topics discussed in transregional meetings and events, 2014–2016

	2014	2015	2016	Average Facilitation
South Sudan	17	10	12	13
Ebola	13	11	2	9
Terrorism/Boko Haram	3	14	5	7
Burundi	-	10	9	6
Migration	1	4	-	2
Mali	6	4	3	4
Congo	3	5	5	4
Guinea Bissau	3	3	6	4
Central African Rep	8	2	1	4
Burkina Faso	4	5	-	3
Libya	1	3	1	2
Egypt	-	1	2	1
Somalia	2	7	6	5
Darfur	-	-	1	0
Madagascar	3	1	-	1

Source: Table Created by Authors

As can be seen from Table 8.6, the network was most frequently used for dealing with non-crisis events. However, there was a considerable number of events where the network was also used for ongoing crisis events. The distribution of crisis topics covered at these meetings can be seen in Table 8.7.

As can be seen from Table 8.7, the most frequent crisis event addressed in the network was South Sudan, followed by the Ebola pandemic and terrorism (foremost the terror organization Boko Haram). This mirrors the severe challenges confronting the region, where crisis management becomes a multifaceted and complex endeavor.

The Promise of Transregional Crisis Management

Taken together, the empirical section provides a first-cut illustration of an emerging transregional network of actors that participates in a wide range of fields relevant to crisis preparedness. In order to consolidate our findings we would need a longer time series of meetings stretching over several more years within the region and increased specificity. Keeping this in mind, the findings nevertheless point toward the possibility of a deeper interconnectedness across regional organizations in the area of crisis preparedness. We also believe that the framework can be seen as indicating future performance in the wake of crisis events.

Overall, the findings illustrate a fairly strong transregional network of actors.[4] Starting with network coordination we can see that the number of formal meetings within the network exceeded the number of *ad hoc* meetings, which, according to Ansell et al. (2010), indicates an effective response network. We could also see that the distribution of formal and *ad hoc* networks were fairly equal. In relation to this, we would like to point out that there are dividing views on the role of *ad hoc* meetings in the context of crisis management networks. Whereas Ansell et al. stress the importance of formal networks, other crisis management scholars have highlighted the creation of informal and *ad hoc* networks, which can contribute to swift responses to rapidly upcoming and new types of problems (Olsson 2015; Boin and Bynander 2015). One can also expect formal and pre-planned meetings to create the grounds for *ad hoc* meetings to take place since the former provides an environment to form working relationships, and in doing so it creates both trust between participants as well as knowledge about resources, capacities, and competences. Thus, from a crisis preparedness perspective one could argue that the high number of formal and informal meetings can contribute to making a network stronger, holding the potential for both continuity and change.

Second, distributed sensemaking indicates a network of some significance as there was not only the sharing of information, but the majority of meetings were devoted to the collective analysis of this information. However, this is mostly based on discussions and general analysis of the information shared while only a relatively small number of decisions were made, reflecting a stronger degree of response capacity. If the sharing of information is a definitional cornerstone of networks (Keck and Sikkink 1998, 2), and if the analysis of this information through transregional fora is an indication of distributed sensemaking, then the empirics demonstrate an emerging transregional crisis response and preparedness network of actors.

Finally, in terms of surge capacity, the empirics shows that the network is used for crisis related issues on average once a week per year, which must be considered quite often. We can also see that crisis-related meetings are not only about sharing and discussing responses to a crisis but also about mobilizing resources and funding. Taken together the three aspects indicate an emerging transregional network with increasing potential for both crisis management and preparedness. This is significant for at least three reasons.

First, cooperation and the potential coordination of risk management between (rather than within) regional organizations is a significant development. The types of actors participating in these networks are often below the executive level, representing a regional organization rather than a particular state. This is reminiscent of earlier studies on transgovernmental organizations (Kaiser 1971; Keohane and Nye 1974; Sundelius 1977) that represent an additional form of governance that can complement or compete with international agendas. What is particular about this type of coordination is that it has the potential to partially sidestep state sovereignty as one of the biggest obstacles to transboundary crisis management. Networks of crisis managers have the potential to influence the regionalization of crisis management by collectively establishing a semi-autonomous set of goals that aims to increase the capacity of regional organizations to prepare for and respond to crises (see, for example, Hollis 2010).

A second and interconnected reason for the significance of transregional crisis management networks is the practical outcomes of crisis meetings. If complex transboundary disasters are going to be more frequent and intense in years to come – due to climate change as well as economic, social, and cyber interdependencies – then transregional risk governance offers a viable solution to risk reduction and even collective responses to crises. A damaged power station threatened by flooding or the establishment of various terror organizations can have many knock-on effects that quickly transgress not only over national borders but also across regional borders. When member states *and* a regional organization have limited capacities to prepare for and respond to a crisis, it is imperative that transregional coordination can take place in order to manage transregional crises. The bourgeoning network of actors assessed in this chapter can provide fertile grounds for developing practical crisis management.

Third, an emerging transregional network of crisis management can contribute to pan-regionalization on the continent. Cooperating in the event of a crisis with other RECs and the AU can contribute to an increased sense of solidarity, encourage trust, and build personal relationships that are important for building a sense of community and a "we" feeling (Deutsch 1957/2006; Adler and Barnett 1998). A sense of community built through continuous exchanges between practitioners can increase the likelihood of information communication (central for situational awareness), decision-making capacities, and the interoperability of crisis coordination capacities. Moreover, social cohesion has the potential to go beyond crisis management, encouraging multidimensional pan-regionalization. A sense of community and the recognition of the value of inter-regional coordination can encourage "spill-over" into other related fields of regional activity such as health care and logistics. This point relates to institutional theories of regionalization, which would emphasize how transregional networks on crisis management can contribute to pan-regionalization by acting as an interlocutor between regional organizations and the AU. That is, as a "clearinghouse" of crisis information to enable effective and timely decision making when crises have to be managed by the AU.

An additional reflection on these tentative findings is their heuristic dimension. We believe the outcome of this chapter can be useful for thinking about crisis coordination between other regional organizations. For instance, crisis management planning and cooperation has been occurring in a number of regional organizations within Europe, such as the Council of Baltic Sea States, the Visegrad Group, the International Sava River Basin Commission, and the Disaster Preparedness and Prevention Initiative for South-Eastern Europe. However, there is little knowledge to date on whether these efforts are coordinated between these and other groups or how they might link into the Union Civil Protection Mechanism (UCPM) and other European and international response organizations.

Conclusion

Regional cooperation in crises has emerged and increased in the last few decades partly as a response to transboundary disasters. Such regional responses to regional problems are evident in most regional organizations around the world. However, just like state borders, disasters can easily transgress regional borders, increasing the demand for transregional cooperation for transregional problems. In response to this development, this chapter has outlined and made an initial assessment on transregional networks on crisis management in the African continent.

Crises, like Ebola and ongoing regional issues, such as terror attacks and abductions by Boko Haram, have seen the emergence of meetings between regional organizations that are often *ad hoc* and used for information exchange, analyses, and deliberation. According to the mode of collaboration outlined in the introduction of this book, the emerging collaborative network of actors at the inter-regional level of crisis response is mostly concerned with "fast-burning" and "long-shadow crises"; events that are often more politicized than other "slow-burning" or "cathartic crises." This indicates that the regional cooperation structure is less often used in order to address more underlying structural conditions that lead to various crisis events. Many of the arrangements have some degree of formality, as "pre-established" meetings and the actor constellations are generally regulated by public officials.

Put differently, there is much potential for trans-regional crisis management. According to the three central crisis management capacities analyzed in this chapter – sensemaking, surge capacity, and network coordination – transregional crisis response collaboration holds much potential, as it, first, provides the basis for sharing and analyzing information for sensemaking. This can reduce uncertainty in times of crisis, aiding efficient and timely decision making and communication of information. Second, the mobilization of resources and funding through network collaboration provides the grounds for surge capacity. Third, the large number of *ad hoc* and formal meetings provides favorable conditions for network coordination, which in turn can lead to familiarity and trust between actors. Even if many networks are still *ad hoc*, they establish a foundation for increasing the effectiveness of coordination in a crisis (see Moynihan 2008, 356). The existing number and type of networks and activities of sensemaking can provide an important basis for increasing the efficiency of transregional collaboration by reducing conflicting interests (through social cohesion), increasing the willingness to cooperate (by creating common objectives for reducing transboundary risks), and providing the possibility for planning (by increasing trust and information exchange). Moreover, transregional crisis management networks have the potential to act as an additional driving factor for pan-regionalization, and they have the potential to provide a realistic development for tackling transboundary crises. The limited actor constellation, crisis trajectory, and temporal perspective suggest that there is ample room for developing this important level of collaboration for securing a safer Africa in the future.

Notes

1. The framework is a modified version of Ansell et al. 2010.
2. Note that the CEN-SAD and UMA websites were both limited and "page under construction" often appeared on many webpages. This limited the amount of relevant information obtained regarding these two RECs' activities.
3. It is not always easy to distinguish between a formal and *ad hoc* meeting, such as when a non-planned meeting takes place at the sidelines of a planned summit. In other cases, the available information regarding a meeting was not sufficient to determine whether the event was pre-scheduled or part of a reoccurring series of meetings. Because of this we have chosen only to code those events that were clearly distinguishable (non-overlapping) as either "formal" or "*ad hoc*" according to our criteria.
4. While this is classified as a fairly strong level of collaboration, the level of cooperation is still at an "emerging" or low level. This is based on the following assumption. If a high level of cooperation equates to high costs in terms of human and financial resources (as well as political costs that affect state sovereignty), and if a low level of cooperation equates to low costs in terms of sharing information, then the outcome of this study is clearly related to the latter. (There is evidence of information sharing but no agreements on advanced forms of cooperation such as the pooling of permanent assets at the regional level.) The sharing of information produces important benefits such as increasing levels of trust, a common language, and shared understanding between participants, which can establish a firm foundation for further cooperation (Hollis 2015, 15).

References

Adler, E., and M. Barnett. 1998. *Security Communities*. Cambridge: Cambridge University Press.

Ansell, C., A. Boin, and A. Keller. 2010. "Managing Transboundary Crises: Identifying the Building Blocks of an Effective Response System." *Journal of Contingencies and Crisis Management* 18 (4): 195–207.

Boin, A., and F. Bynander. 2015. "Explaining Success and Failure in Crisis Coordination." *Geografiska Annaler: Series A, Physical Geography* 97 (1): 123–35.

Boin, Arjen, E. Stern, and B. Sundelius. 2016. *The Politics of Crisis Management: Public Leadership Under Pressure*. Cambridge: Cambridge University Press.

Deutsch, K.W., et al. 1957. *Political Community and the North Atlantic Area*. Princeton, NJ: Princeton University Press.

Hollis, S. 2010. "The Necessity of Protection: Transgovernmental Networks and EU Security Governance." *Cooperation and Conflict* 45 (3): 312–30

Hollis, S. 2015. *The Role of Regional Organizations in Disaster Risk Management: A strategy for global resilience*. Basingstoke: Palgrave Macmillan.

Kaiser, K. 1971. "Transnational Politics: Toward a Theory of Multinational Politics." *International Organization* 25 (4): 790–818.

Keck, M. and K. Sikkink. 1998. *Activists Beyond Borders: Advocacy Networks in International Politics*. Ithaca, NY: Cornell University Press.

Keohane, R.O. and J.S. Nye. 1974. "Transgovernmental Relations and International Organizations." *World Politics* 27 (1): 39–63.

Klijn, E.H., and J.F. Koppenjan. 2000. "Public Management and Policy Networks: Foundations of a Network Approach to Governance." *Public Management: An International Journal of Research and Theory* 2 (2): 135–58.

Moynihan, D.P. 2008. "Learning Under Uncertainty: Networks in Crisis Management." *Public Administration Review* 68 (2): 350–65.

Olsson, E.K. 2015. "Transboundary Crisis Networks: The Challenge of Coordination in the Face of Global Threats." *Risk Management* 17 (2): 91–108.

Sundelius, B.A. 1977. "Trans-Governmental Interactions in the Nordic Region." *Cooperation and Conflict* XII: 63–85.

Weick, K.E. 1995. *Sense Making in Organizations*. London: Sage.

Chapter 9

Addressing the Challenges of Transboundary Crises

The Dutch Local Response to the Global Surge in ISIS Supporters

Scott Douglas, Aline Bos and Mirko Noordegraaf

Introduction

From 2013 onwards, local governments in the Netherlands started to receive worrying reports from the national intelligence agency. Groups and individuals in their communities were developing into radical supporters of the Islamic State in Iraq and Syria (ISIS). The intelligence agency estimated that several thousand people in the Netherlands supported the extremist version of Islam propagated by ISIS and that several hundreds of them were potentially planning to join the organization in the Middle East. A very small but significant set of individuals might even be preparing attacks at home (AIVD 2014). As over 250 Dutch nationals traveled to Syria to join ISIS over the next three years, and the terrorist attacks in France, UK, and Belgium displayed the domestic danger from ISIS, the situation developed into a full-blown crisis. Although the surge of ISIS supporters had several hallmarks of a traditional crisis, the situation also transcended many of the categories typically used to slice and dice such situations.

This case description examines to what extent concepts used in the collaborative crisis management literature bear empirical relevance to transboundary collaborative crisis management initiatives such as the local response to a global terrorist threat. This crisis was not only *cross-boundary*, as it crossed the borders between nations and policy domains, but it was truly *transboundary* (Boin and Lodge 2016; Noordegraaf et al. 2017) as it transcended the normal conceptual, organizational, and geographical borders used to categorize events. This case description shows how the response to a crisis that defies a categorization based on crisis trajectories ('t Hart and Boin 2001) or crisis phases (Drennan, McConnell, and Stark 2014) requires transboundary collaborative efforts that also transcend classification by governmental level (Boin and Renaud 2013), modes of collaboration (O'Leary and Vij 2012, 508), or partner coalitions (Boin and 't Hart 2001).

The case review generates three different insights. First, transboundary crises such as the surge of ISIS supporters defy crisp distinctions between different types of crisis situations and responses. The trajectory of the ISIS surge could be framed with equal validity as a long-burning or a short-fuse crisis, just as the appropriate crisis response level was simultaneously the local, national, or global stage. Prioritizing one conceptual frame over the others leads to missing vital properties of the overall crisis. Second, the transboundary nature of a crisis does not mean that the existing categories are useless, as practitioners seeking collaboration still need conceptual frames to prevent indecision and confusion. However, these frames must be used in combination or alteration in order to get the full picture. Third, the transboundary complexity of the crisis does not necessarily make meaningful crisis responses impossible. We identify several tools that enable the partners to create a relatively targeted, legitimate, and robust collaborative response to the transboundary challenges they face.

Capturing Collaborative Crisis Management in Theoretical Constructs

The literature on crisis management has generated a wide range of concepts for categorizing and analyzing different types of crisis situations and crisis responses, which have been mirrored by equally extensive categorization of different types of collaborative responses. These frames serve an academic purpose by helping researchers to map different types of events and responses but are also used by practitioners as conceptual tools for understanding and responding to crisis situations. The conceptual categorization shapes the practical collaboration. The relevance and validity of these conceptual categories are therefore of great importance. However, as the cases of ISIS illustrates, governments may be confronted with highly complex crises that invalidate such categorizations.

Several conceptual categories can be used to identify a crisis (see Table 9.1). 't Hart and Boin (2001), for example, distinguish between four different types of crisis trajectories: *fast-burning crises* occurring suddenly, *slow-burning crises* long in the making, *cathartic crises* releasing longstanding tensions, and *long-shadow crises* generating enduring societal upheaval. Crises can also be catalogued through their different phases, from the planning and preparation phase to the implementation and evaluation phase (see, e.g., Drennan et al. 2014). Similarly, several categories can be used to map and shape of the crisis response. Boin and Renaud (2013) make an oft used distinction between crisis responses at the local, national, and international levels.

As many researchers already emphasize, crises in practice defy easy categorization. The different trajectories and phases of a crisis imagined in theory may not be so neatly observable in practice, just as many crises cross different levels of government and require an integrated response (Boin and Renaud 2013). Moreover, highly complex crises, such as climate change, the Global Financial Crisis, and the rise of ISIS, arguably transcend all definitions and categories (Noordegraaf et al. 2017). These crises are the sum of both slow- and fast-burning developments, play out simultaneously on local, national, and global scales and require responses that are both rigid and flexible at the same time. This raises the question of whether such transboundary crises are amenable at all to any categorization. The use of crisp conceptual categories may serve to obfuscate and oversimplify rather than to elucidate and structure the situation. Crisp categories may even give a false sense of manageability in the face of a fundamentally unresolvable, wicked crisis (Alford and Head 2017).

Our case description of the Dutch response to the surge in ISIS supporters serves as a case study of a particular transboundary crisis where we can test the utility and validity of the different conceptual categories generated by the crisis management literature. We examine to what extent the different categorizations in literature are useful to analyze the threat and response in the case. Drawing on the interviews with the professionals involved in the crisis response and policy evaluation documents available, we also examine to what extent practitioners were able to accept and address the transboundary complexity involved.

Categorizing a Crisis Situation to Frame the Collaborative Response

A crisis situation can be dissected by examining the crisis trajectory (e.g., slow-burning, fast-burning, cathartic, and long-shadow [Boin and Renaud 2013]) and distinguishing between the multiple phases of a crisis (e.g., planning, preparing, implementing, and

Table 9.1 Theoretical categories for understanding a crisis and observations from the case

Categories from the literature	Observations from the ISIS case
Crisis trajectories can be categorized in different pathways; e.g., slow-burning, fast-burning, cathartic, and long-shadow.	Coexisting trajectories: The rise of ISIS had the hallmarks of a fast-burning crisis but also other trajectories such as a cathartic reaction to longstanding problems. Partners had to apply multiple perspectives on the trajectory to fully understand the threat.
Crisis situations can be divided into different phases; e.g., planning, preparing, implementing, and evaluating.	Coexisting phases: Partners were both extensively prepared through the existence of detailed plans and procedures, and underprepared for this new form of threat posed by ISIS. Partners had to plan, prepare, implement, and evaluate at the same time through continuous trial-and-error loops.

Source: Table Created by Authors

evaluating (Drennan et al. 2014). These categories are intended to help academics and practitioners identify the type of crisis at hand in order to determine what type of collaborative response is appropriate (see Table 9.1). However, in the case of the ISIS surge, the crisis trajectory and phases were constantly debated by practitioners and observers alike, just as the exact phasing of the crisis was continually contentious. We argue that picking only one of the categories to "nail down" the nature of the crisis would have oversimplified the challenge and subsequently hampered the formulation of an appropriate response.

Transcending the Distinction Between Crisis Trajectories

To the local governments in the Netherlands, the ISIS crisis presented itself initially as a *"fast-burning crisis"* with a sudden onset and sharp closure ('t Hart and Boin 2001; Bynander and Nohrstedt, this volume). Just as the international community was caught off-guard with the sudden success of ISIS in the Middle East, many Dutch local officials were surprised by the rapid rise of radical elements in their communities. As the security policy advisor of a city recalled, "We got a visit from the intelligence agency in October 2013, informing us that we had been classified as a high priority radicalization city. We were completely flabbergasted" (Respondent 1). The intelligence agency was not allowed to inform the local police exactly which inhabitants were radicalizing, as the wide-ranging information gathering techniques of the intelligence services may not be used for prosecution purposes, leaving the local government with the task of quickly identifying the people involved before they could travel to Syria.

Framing this crisis as a fast-burning sequence of events helped local governments to mobilize their collaborations with sufficient rapidity. However, it was also important for the local governments to simultaneously understand and address the alternative timelines of the crisis trajectory. At an individual or local level, the crisis was also a *cathartic* reaction to longstanding problems. In most cases, the seemingly abrupt radicalization of individuals was the culmination of years of low-level crime, trouble at home, feelings of societal rejection, and/or mental health problems (Schmid 2013). An effective response required local governments to systematically identify and address the roots of this process, requiring the involvement of social workers, schools, and mental health professionals when piecing together a tailored approach to the individuals at risk of radicalization.

Similarly, also taking a *slow-burning* and *long-shadow* perspective helped local governments to confront the historical roots of the problem and anticipate the long-term consequences of this crisis. As a local official of one town stated, "We have historically been a very closed and private community. The strict Islamic groups actually resemble the closed life-style of the orthodox Christian communities living here" (Respondent 1). Furthermore, the terrorism experts cautioned from the beginning that the societal rifts caused by terrorism take years to address, pointing to the long-lasting impact of the assassination of leading political figure Pim Fortuyn by a left-wing extremist in 2001 and the Dutch filmmaker and columnist Theo van Gogh by an Al-Qaeda sympathizer in 2004. Such longitudinal perspectives encouraged policymakers to address the structural causes, such as societal divisions in the local community, rather than just respond to the crisis incidents.

Transcending the Distinction Between Crisis Response Phases

The crisis responders were also confronted with a crisis that blurred the supposed sequencing of planning, preparation, implementation, and evaluation. Framing the crisis as part of a long history would connect the response to existing plans and preparations drafted in the years prior to 2013, while an emphasis on the unique nature of this particular crisis would prioritize the production of new plans and methods. We observed a combination of recycling and innovation at both the local and national policy levels, which seemed to actually serve the response quite effectively.

There were a lot of plans and preparation routines in place already when the crisis hit in 2013, but they had to be adapted to a new situation. Following the 2004 attacks on Madrid and the 2005 attacks on London, European countries had formalized their counterterrorism systems, creating explicit laws and strategies. The Dutch national counterterrorism coordinator produced the 120 page "National Counterterrorism Strategy" in 2011, containing extensive plans for identifying and countering extremist threats (NCTV 2011). This strategy contained many elements potentially useful when dealing with ISIS, such as the focus on a comprehensive approach addressing both the causes and consequences of radicalization (see Noordegraaf et al. 2017). However, these strategies were mainly directed toward integrated international networks such as Al-Qaeda, while ISIS employed a different modus operandi by encouraging self-radicalization through social media (AIVD 2017).

Between 2007 and 2011, there was the nationwide Polarization and Deradicalization Program, which allocated subsidies to local governments for projects boosting societal and community resilience. However, this subsidy program was discontinued after 2011, leading many local governments to cut back on radicalization programs. A civil servant from the Home Office observed, "When the subsidies for Polarization and Deradicalization Program stopped in 2011, we also stopped activities in this area. Our priorities shifted to, among other things, burglaries" (Respondent 2). In almost all cities, the personnel capacity for radicalization was reduced to part-time roles or eliminated altogether. In one of the biggest Dutch cities, the issue of radicalization had to be tackled by one civil servant, who was doing it as an extra task next to his other duties. As one experienced intelligence officer wryly commented, "We keep going through this cycle, giving a lot of attention when terrorism strikes, but then gradually start neglecting the topic again until the next incident" (Respondent 3). A small set of professionals and local governments, specifically the city of Amsterdam, did maintain investment in their deradicalization programs. These select units would be the key players for bringing in capacity and experience when the crisis first became apparent in 2013. An effective response to the crisis would

108 Scott Douglas, et al.

therefore both realize that many local responses would be under-planned and underprepared but also recognize that there was some existing planning and preparation capacity available to access.

However, planning and preparing could only be useful to a limited extent, requiring any response to continuously go back and forth between planning, implementing, and learning. There is only a very limited knowledge base available from which to draw lessons for effective deradicalization programs (Schmid 2011). An extensive review by the University of Maryland of 180 hypotheses about countering violent extremism found only substantive scientific support for eight of them (National Consortium 2015). The one hypothesis with the most support ("Placing metal detectors in airports will reduce the amount of bomb attacks on planes") came with a very illustrative caveat; the introduction of metal detectors at airports was associated with the shift of bomb attacks to trains and metros. There was general scientific support for the idea that deradicalization would require both a mix of preventive and repressive, as well as security-oriented and social development-based, interventions, but the concretization of this general advice was limited (Schmid 2011; Noordegraaf et al. 2017). A local prosecutor observed, "There was not much knowledge about radicalization. Signals were often based on the gut feelings of the professionals involved. It is hard to develop policies and take actions based on gut feelings" (Respondent 4). The local governments were therefore simultaneously flooded with security officials and deradicalization consultants offering extensive policy documents or "deradicalization guidebooks" and left empty-handed when looking for concrete, evidence-based interventions.

On the whole, local governments were faced with a situation transcending the traditional categories used to classify and make sense of a crisis. The crisis was both new and old, slowly burning and quickly escalating. The government was both well-prepared through extensive planning and overwhelmed by the current manifestation of the threat. Adopting only one perspective would unduly limit the breadth of the response. Government organizations had to simultaneously plan, prepare, implement, and evaluate.

Categorizing Crisis Collaboration Forms to Shape the Response

Most crises require collaboration between different levels of government, either because the threat transcends geographic, organizational, or policy demarcations or because the responsibility for crisis management is formally transferred to a higher level of government

Table 9.2 Theoretical categories for responding to a crisis and observations from the case

Categories from the literature	Observations from the ISIS case
The crisis responses play out across different government levels and in different policy domains; e.g., local, national, and international.	Response required acting on different levels of government (from global to local) and across different policy domains (from security to mental health) to enable an effective and comprehensive response.
Partners can respond to crises through different modes of collaboration; e.g., negotiating policies or synchronizing actions.	Response required a mix of high-level negotiation between agencies to enable support for joint approach and street-level synchronization between professionals for the alignment and delivery of multiple interventions.

Source: Table Created by Authors

when the threat escalates (Boin and Renaud 2013). However, formulating the response to the ISIS surge was not about finding the appropriate level of government but to create a transboundary effort across all levels of government. Similarly, while such cross-boundary collaborations can be seen to be either about high-level negotiations about the appropriate actions or operational level synchronization of implementing actions, the response to ISIS required the involvement of high-level policy figures in street level action and vice versa.

Transcending Different Levels of Government and Sectors of Society

On a global stage, the United Nations and other international alliances sought to actively limit the reach of ISIS. At the national level, governments reasserted their control over their borders and migration flows to protect themselves. At the local level, cities such as London, Brussels, and Berlin started programs to address the causes and consequences of radicalization at the community and individual level. In the Netherlands, a total of eight cities were listed as priority deradicalization cities because of the occurrence of local networks and groups, with a further 12 joining the list in the following years (NOS 2016). This included large cities such as Amsterdam, The Hague, and Utrecht but also towns with smaller populations. Dutch municipalities are relatively strong layers of government, with extensive responsibility for policymaking and service delivery of social welfare, neighborhood development, and public order.

Moreover, the local government is also the key partner for relatively independent public organizations, such as schools and health professionals. The 2014 action program formulating the Dutch response to radicalization gave the local level "an important role in preventing social tensions and radicalization. . . . At the local level, there is knowledge about the social context, changes in teenagers and adults can be detected, and partners can collectively contribute to interventions" (Ministry for Security and Justice et al. 2014). A civil servant from the national counterterrorism coordinator explained the need for a transboundary response as follows:

> You cannot expect a small town to have all the necessary expertise on radicalization. But at the same time, the local government can have essential information that needs to be combined with data on other levels in order to create insight.
>
> (Respondent 5)

However, although the local government was given chief responsibility for deradicalization, a range of national and even international organizations would have to be involved as well in the operational execution of the initiative. At the national level, ministries ranging from security and defense to social affairs and education had to be involved, just as executive agencies in security, tax, and health. At the international level, the Dutch would cooperate with their cross-border counterparts and supranational organizations such as the EU and UN. Beyond executive government, the response also involved private businesses such as Facebook and YouTube, or societal groups such as religious communities. Ideally, all these different organizations would fall into a crisp organizational chart detailing the different hierarchies and relationships between the organizations, but in practice many of these organizations had limited formal contacts (e.g., religious groups and schools) or were intentionally separated by law in the interest of a balance of power (e.g., prosecutors versus intelligence agencies). Rather than a clear organizational chart, the constellation of different actors is better imagined as a web of actors branching out from key orchestrators of the response, such as the national counterterrorism coordinator or the local government.

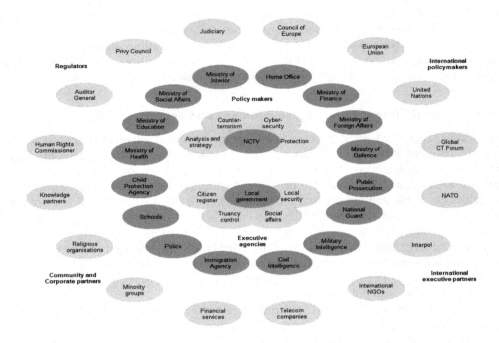

Figure 9.1 Overview of the actors involved in the crisis response

Age-old tensions between these different actors and domains would surface in this time of pressure. One local civil servant, for example, highlighted the tension between the politicians talking about counterterrorism on the national stage, and the local welfare workers offering support for the parents of teenagers recruited by ISIS. "[A] strong rhetoric around counterterrorism does not fit into our view of the issue. The prime minister stated that people going to Syria can die there as far as he is concerned, while we deal with [their] desperate parents" (Respondent 1). Moreover, the appropriate level of government or partner forum would change over time. For example, several local officials started to meet in regional groups as they noticed the radical networks they were monitoring started working on the regional level as well. An effective local response would have to be negotiated and synchronized across all these levels and domains without falling prey to fragmentation and inertia.

Transcending Different Policy Domains and Professional Perspectives

Beyond the level of government, public sector partners would also be divided by stark differences in their policy and/or professional focus. There are multiple pathways to radicalization, involving religious, economic, social, and psychiatric drivers, necessitating an integrated response of the police, health sector, schools, parents, religious groups, etc. (Schmid 2013). This broad work on all the causes and manifestations is actually the foundational belief of the "Comprehensive Approach," a Dutch policy doctrine emphasizing the combination of preventive and repressive measures against radicalization that emerged in the years just before 2013 (NCTV 2011; Noordegraaf et al. 2017). The relevance of this perspective was immediately recognized by the local officials who were confronted with radicalization. One local official reflected upon this first briefing by the intelligence agency about radicalization by saying, "By the time we got back to our own office, we had already concluded that this would require a multi-disciplinary response" (Respondent 6).

However, combining these different perspectives could be difficult to realize in practice. In the early stages of the response, mainly security agencies such as the police and the prosecution were active in the deradicalization dossier. Both at the national and local levels, several services and organizations such as schools, child services, and social workers did not immediately appreciate the scale of the problem and many did not have the personnel capacity at hand to respond. Moreover, even when sitting at the same table, these organizations would have fundamentally different professional perspectives. Where the police officers and prosecutors would look at the security threat posed to society, welfare workers and teachers would look at the social challenges of the individuals involved. Even if they did want to work together, the social workers were often hesitant to be *seen* by their clients to collaborate with "the other side." Although it would be good to align their incentives, retaining differences and diversity could in fact be beneficial and/or necessary. The intelligence agency, police force, and medical profession are limited and bound by explicit rules in their sharing of information, yet the different perspectives on the causes and consequences of radicalization could actually be one significant bonus of this approach.

Transcending Different Modes of Collaboration

The diversity of problems and actors involved meant that the actors had to combine different modes of collaborations, including operational *synchronization* and high-level *negotiation* between organizations, hinging on the strength of personal relationships and street-level operational synchronization. In very practical terms, the different local partners had to come together to formulate and implement a series of interventions targeting radicalizing individuals. For example, a radicalizing youth may be targeted with a combination of police surveillance, additional school mentoring, and social worker support for the parents.

On one hand, this was a matter of very practical, *street-level* synchronization of the delivery of multiple interventions. On the other hand, enabling street-level professionals to align their actions required high-level support and consent. The police, for example, were very willing to engage with the deradicalization program, but it was mired in a reorganization and needed top management to make frontline staff available. Many child protection agencies were at first unwilling to engage with this terrain, until the senior managers were convinced by the police and local government of the risks for children involved in radicalization. The much-needed combination of synchronization and negotiation was often dependent on a number of key individuals who were able to link both modes of collaboration. A respondent from a big city stated for example,

> The collaboration relies on specific persons. Without the energy of one of the police officers in our city, it would not have worked that well. This police officer was able to deliver input for specific cases *and* to provide relevant input at the management level.
> (Respondent 7)

Moreover, the formal relationships between the actors – the hierarchy between the police and the prosecution services, the constitutional independence of schools, the confidentiality of the medical profession – had to be accommodated within agile and flexible collaborative arrangements required for a quickly developing crisis.

Creating Transboundary Crisis Management Tools

The Dutch government organizations faced a crisis which defied categorization, with no set trajectory or distinct phases, and had to deliver a response that spanned different levels of government, policy domains, and modes of collaboration. As a consequence, the subsequent interventions could have easily been complex, vague, and fragmented as well (Alford and Head 2017). However, in practice, many local government partners were able to find through *trial-and-error* a crisis response which managed to be both transboundary and concrete. In the years that followed 2013, they managed to formulate and implement personalized, tailored interventions to target individuals in their cities at different stages of radicalization. This approach was supported by three important tools or techniques: (1) *transboundary coalitions*, (2) *transboundary interventions*, and (3) *transboundary spaces*. At times, these transboundary tools were still hampered by disruptions from the old divides, but at other times, the different partners were able to formulate and implement powerful local responses to this global crisis.

Creating Transboundary Coalitions

In most cities, one or two key officials took the lead in formulating the local response. These would usually be the civil servant coordinating the security domain or a local police officer with an affinity for the topic. All of them described their role as conveners of a coalition, rather than chiefs of a hierarchy of organizations. In some larger cities, there was already a coalition of organizations. Local government, police, social workers, and child protection services were more alert to the threat of radicalization, holding relevant expertise and community contacts. Other cities would repurpose existing coalitions which overlapped with partners required for an effective deradicalization program, such as the range of organizations involved with targeting youth crime or domestic violence. One local network coordinator described the collaborative effort as such,

> When we discuss a case, up to twenty professionals are involved who all can directly or indirectly influence the person we are talking about. Everybody at the table has his share, but in most cases, about five organizations are taking the most important actions.
> (Respondent 6)

In all cities, local key individuals had to invest heavily in mobilizing the partners and getting radicalization on the agenda. One police officer in a large city explained that he

Table 9.3 Observations from the case on responding to a transboundary crisis

Observations from the ISIS case
Response was supported by multidisciplinary, multilevel, multidomain coalitions that maintained broad support among different partners but also retained individual differences and strengths of partners.
Response was facilitated by a cross-domain perspective on the synchronized use of multiple interventions on radicalizing individuals (e.g., by police officers and social workers), while being aware of the unintended effects.
Response was facilitated by fluid, flexible, and largely informal meeting places, which provided space for partners to negotiate and synchronize their actions without too much structure and protocol.

Source: Table Created by Authors

literally got on his bicycle to shuttle between the different organizations to be involved, working overtime to get everyone connected. The budding collaboration hinged on the efforts and personal relationships of a few individuals. "I don't know what would have happened if I would have fallen ill in that period," reflected one police officer (Respondent 8). In the latter years, the national government gave extra subsidies and resources to the local government organization and national agencies to mobilize more personnel.

Beyond first contact, getting priority from the different organizations also required heavy lobbying. For example, several child protection agencies at first did not recognize the concerns. They defined problematic behavior as drinking alcohol, skipping school, and getting into trouble with the police, while radicalizing youngsters would often display the opposite of these behaviors. Sometimes the local coalition would suffer from external pressures. The national government, for example, launched a deradicalization program entitled "Action Program for a Comprehensive Approach of Jihadism" (Ministry of Security and Justice et al. 2014). Many local governments, however, avoided the term "Jihadism" and preferred the more general term "violent extremism." This latter term prevented the alienation of their local Muslim community partners that associated the term "Jihad" also with a more moderate and daily ambition to be a good Muslim (Noordegraaf et al. 2017).

Creating Transboundary Interventions

To move these coalitions from talking to acting, the convening officials and the representatives of the different partners would focus on formulating shared interventions, favoring a joint and simultaneous implementation of preventive and repressive measures. Over the months of 2013 and 2014, this was developed by the local government into a multidisciplinary, individualized approach. The focus moved beyond integrating just preventive and repressive measures, aiming to combine security and social-focused interventions, which all could help to prevent and redress radicalization (see Figure 9.2). This approach was formalized in the August 2014 Action Program. This national document stated that multidisciplinary teams would "compose individual intervention plans. The interventions to be employed are case dependent, and vary in intensity, shape, nature, and voluntariness" (Ministry of Security and Justice 2014).

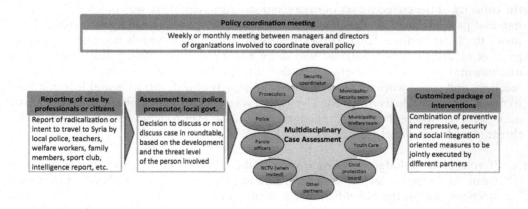

Figure 9.2 Overview of a typical local case review process

Achieving such a comprehensive joint approach could still turn out to be hard in practice. A local civil servant reported,

> Sometimes, we did a lot of social work at the local level for a particular person and then the police arrests the person. The police cannot share all their operational information with us beforehand. In such cases, the results of our deliberate actions disappeared, as social work is undermined by security measures.
>
> (Respondent 9)

Such incidents underline the need for constantly aligning actions to achieve effective interventions. As the local, multidisciplinary process developed over time, the different organizations involved were looking for more ways to combine both social and security measures. A prosecutor stated,

> Much of our information was not relevant from a legal perspective, as evidence for our case. However, information that was not helpful for us could be helpful for other partners, for prevention. We therefore started to share such information with the other organizations involved. We were not only participating to get evidence for our case, but also to share information that could help others and to be more effective together.
>
> (Respondent 4)

The extent to which these interventions were truly transboundary, combining both security and social mechanisms, relied heavily on the balanced involvement of the full spectrum of security and social affairs actors. Many local officials reflected that the absence of social partners at the beginning of the crisis in 2013, such as schools and welfare organizations, led to a domination by the police and the prosecution in the coalition, leading to more security-focused interventions. Moreover, national interventions could undermine local interventions. For example, the national government is responsible for enacting financial embargos for individuals placed on an international watch list. In the first months of the crisis response, the ministry would do this without informing the local government, leading to embarrassing situations where local professionals would have successfully gained the trust of a radicalized individual, while the national government would suddenly block his or her access to their grocery and rent money.

On the whole, the transboundary integration of interventions dramatically increased the capacity of the collective set of organizations. Although there was much debate in the national parliament about the necessity of giving more powers to the police and government, the local partners felt that they jointly possessed all the tools necessary (Noordegraaf et al. 2017). Their challenge was more about *frontline capacity* than institutional instrumental powers. The partners needed time and resources to train police officers, teachers, and social workers in recognizing the signals of radicalization and learning how to talk to the individuals involved. The local level struggled in explaining this need at the national level, where the debate remained focused on ever tougher measures to fight the threat. As a local official stated,

> If you try to dislodge someone from a [radical] network, then you should invest in them. At the higher level, this may be hard to justify, as financial embargos look much stronger. But for the individual case it creates a mess.
>
> (Respondent 6)

Creating Transboundary Spaces

The transboundary coalitions and interventions could have been formalized by creating extensive governance bodies and detailed decision protocols. However, the structure that emerged over the years was characterized instead by fluidity and flexibility. A fairly rudimentary process and partner involvement structure did emerge in all of the involved localities, but beyond the basics, there was constant change and movement. In all cities, street-level professionals and citizens were encouraged to report their concerns about radicalization to the police or the local government. An assessment team, consisting of the coordinating civil servant, local police officer, and prosecutor would then evaluate whether the case required further action. The more complex cases would be regularly discussed and assessed from different perspectives in so-called Multidisciplinary Case Assessment meetings (see Figure 9.2) by the involved partners, and together they would compose a set of interventions.

Beyond this rudimentary structure, there were very few rules or formalized procedures. This structure emerged over time, rather than being mandated by the national government, and it continued to evolve as the threats changed and as the different local governments faced slightly different challenges. The partners felt that this *fluidity* was important, as every case would require a customized process and intervention. Moreover, the inherent tensions and differences between the organizations defied formalization. It would be difficult to negotiate a high-level agreement between the different agencies involved, while it turned out to be more feasible to achieve case-by-case synchronization through discussions between the frontline staff involved. The staff involved was, for example, strict on not sharing information that they were not allowed to share (such as information in police investigations) but found informal ways to share what was legally possible.

> In the Security House [a Dutch institution: a network of partners from the criminal justice, welfare, and healthcare services as well as the municipalities] we found areas where we could work together. In this network, the police for example tried to share as much information as possible, by translating information from their investigations to information that could be shared with the other partners.
>
> (Respondent 6)

This informality did place a heavy burden on the participating partners, especially regarding sharing information. As one local official put it, "We are constantly on the edge of our seat about what information we can and cannot share" (Respondent 6). The frameworks that did emerge were mainly about information sharing protocols. Although this informal style worked well for the professionals involved, it was sometimes difficult to explain to the outside world. In Amsterdam, for example, recent criticism from the local elected council has focused on the supposedly "opaque" and "haphazard" case work methods in the city (Parool 2018). Another example of this complex situation is the child protection board that typically serves as a so-called second-line care provider (dealing with children and their families that have been referred to them by first-line organizations) but when in this transboundary space it (also) acts as a frontline worker in the first line.

Discussion

The experience of the Dutch governments in responding to the transboundary ISIS crisis highlights the limitations of the current academic categorizations of crises. If academics and practitioners would have only used one particular lens to assess and inform their perspective on the ISIS crisis (e.g., categorizing it only as a fast-burning crisis), they would only have had a fragmented understanding of the problem and thus an incomplete response strategy. The particular threat posed by ISIS defied existing categories by transcending different crisis trajectories and crisis response phases, while also going beyond the usually employed distinctions between government levels, policy domains, and modes of collaboration. Not only is an adequate understanding of the key issues at hand required when crossing boundaries between different actors and domains, but one additional – fundamental – step is also necessary; that is, the conscious elimination of practical and cultural boundaries in all legally possible ways. This in turn will facilitate a response that is just as comprehensive and integrated as the threat itself, as was the case in this study.

However, the transboundary nature of this crisis does not mean that the crisis definition and the crisis response categories lose all their utility and validity. They can be helpful, if used in a way that takes into account the transboundary nature of the issue. In order to improve the way we act and decide, we need categorization and categories, but we also must be aware and accept the fact that distinctive categories narrow our understanding of complex realities. The key lesson from this case would therefore be that scholars and practitioners must be able to apply multiple perspectives (including different categories) simultaneously to a crisis in order to best understand and tackle the transboundary challenges involved. The *interplay* of the different, distinctive perspectives (rather than meshing them into one blur) creates poignant insights that can inform concrete actions. The "slicing and dicing" categorization of crises should therefore not be disbanded altogether but complemented with an awareness of how these categories mix and interact.

This case study suggests that adequate crisis responses are still possible in the face of transboundary crises. The emergence of transboundary coalitions, interventions, and conversations demonstrates that actors can create tools and techniques to cope with very complex problems. This occurs maybe not in the shape of a grand strategy but rather through trial-and-error, piecemeal constructions of small-scale ideas and interventions. The transboundary coalitions, interventions, and conversations rely more on operational improvisation and managerial "bricolage" than planning and control.

However, accepting the improvisational nature of the response to transboundary crises still allows for strategic management action to facilitate this response. High-level policymakers and managers should shift their attention from "slicing and dicing" the problem, focusing on who is responsible and what the overall strategy should be, toward "sensing and staging," focusing instead on exploring the multiple perspectives of the issues and creating space and opportunities at all levels in their organizations for transboundary collaboration with partners from other organizations. In addition, they could offer broad but helpful concepts to enable ongoing learning and practical messiness (or ongoing managerial bricolage), such as the "Dutch Comprehensive Approach to Radicalization" in the case. They should also invest in the collaborative skills of their frontline staff (beyond their mono-disciplinary expertise) and encourage their middle managers to actively serve the operational needs of these transboundary interventions as they arise. In addition, they should serve and protect their staff in the face of political pressures that call for rigidity and clarity since an effective crisis response also calls for flexibility and learning.

Conclusion

The case we analyzed provides insight in the usefulness and limits of the traditional categories used to frame and respond to crises. Examining the various crisis categories and collaborative response modes shows how the distinct categories can help to illuminate specific parts of the crisis and distinct collaborative reactions. However, this case also shows that some crises transcend specific categories and require analytical frames that capture the challenges and responses in truly transboundary terms. Instead of "slicing and dicing" threats, and subsequently implementing targeted measures, we should be "sensing and staging"; that is, getting a grip on the multidimensional nature of the problem and creating transboundary forums for frontline action. Cases like this illustrate different collaborative tools and pathways that can be explored by actors facing transboundary crises. These lessons may therefore be relevant, not only for a new generation of radicalization and terrorist security threats but also for understanding and addressing other transboundary challenges facing the world.

List of Interviewees

Respondent 1: Local civil servant, security advisor to the mayor
Respondent 2: National civil servant, policy advisor at the Home Office
Respondent 3: National civil servant, intelligence officer
Respondent 4: Local prosecutor, active in countering violent extremism
Respondent 5: National civil servant, policy advisor to the national coordinator
Respondent 6: Local civil servant, security advisor to the mayor
Respondent 7: Local civil servant, security advisor to the mayor
Respondent 8: Local police officer, active in countering radicalization
Respondent 9: Local civil servant, security advisor to the mayor

References

Alford, J. and B.W. Head. 2017. "Wicked and Less Wicked Problems: A Typology and a Contingency Framework." *Policy and Society* 36 (3): 397–413. doi:10.1080/14494035.2017.1361634

Algemene Inlichtingen-en Veiligheidsdienst. 2017. Minderjaringen bij ISIS [Minors in ISIS]. Den Haag: AIVD.

———. 2014. *Transformatie van het jihadisme in Nederland [Transformation of Jihadism in the Netherlands]*. Den Haag: AIVD.

Boin, R.A. and M. Lodge. 2016. "Designing Resilient Institutions for Transboundary Crisis Management: A Time for Public Administration." *Public Administration* 94 (2): 289–98. doi:10.1111/padm.12264

Boin, R.A. and C. Renaud. 2013. "Orchestrating Joint Sensemaking Across Government Levels: Challenges and Requirements for Crisis Leadership." *Journal of Leadership Studies* 7 (3): 41–46. doi:10.1002/jls.21296

Drennan, L.T., A. McConnell, and A. Stark. 2014. *Risk and Crisis Management in the Public Sector.* London: Routledge.

Ministry of Justice and Security, Ministry of Social Affairs, and NCTV. 2014. *Actieprogramma Integrale Aanpak Jihadisme [Action Programme Intregral Approach Jihadism].* Den Haag: Ministry of Justice and Security.

Nationaal Coördinator Terrorismebestrijding en Veiligheid. 2011. *De Nationale Contraterrorismestrategie 2011–2015 [The National Counter-terrorism Strategy].* Den Haag: Ministry of Justice and Security.

National Consortium for the Study of Terrorism and Responses to Terrorism. 19 August 2015. "I-VEO Knowledge Matrix." *Start.* http://start.foxtrotdev.com/

Noordegraaf, M., S. Douglas, A. Bos, and W. Klem. 2017. "How to Evaluate the Governance of Transboundary Problems? Assessing a National Counterterrorism Strategy." *Evaluation* 23 (4): 389–406. doi:10.1177/1356389017733340

NOS. 1 June 2016. "Meer gemeenten krijgen geld voor aanpak radicalisering". *Hilversum*. https://nos.nl/nieuwsuur/artikel/2108570-meer-gemeenten-krijgen-geld-voor-aanpak-jihadisme.html.

O'Leary, R., & Vij, N. 2012. "Collaborative public management: Where have we been and where are we going?." *The American Review of Public Administration* 42 (5): 507–22.

Parool. 19 February 2018. "Niet regels maar snelle resultaten telden bij radicaliseringsaanpak." *Het Parool*.

Schmid, A.P. 2013. "Radicalisation, de-Radicalisation, Counter-Radicalisation: A Conceptual Discussion AND Literature Review." ICCT-The Hague Research Paper. Den Haag.

Schmid, A.P. and E. Price. 2011. "Selected Literature on Radicalization and De-Radicalization of Terrorists: Monographs, Edited Volumes, Grey Literature and Prime Articles Published Since the 1960s." *Crime, Law and Social Change* 55 (4): 337–48. doi:10.1007/s10611-011-9287-4

't Hart, P. and R.A. Boin. 2001. "Between Crisis and Normalcy: The Long Shadow of Post-Crisis Politics." In *Managing Crises: Threats, Dilemmas and Opportunities*, edited by U. Rosenthal, R.A. Boin, and L.K. Comfort, 28–46. Springfield, IL: Charles C. Thomas.

Chapter 10

Avoiding the Failures of Collaborative Crisis Management
Lessons from Research and Practice

Charles F. Parker and Bengt Sundelius

Introduction

Governments are increasingly expected to provide for the protection of their citizens and to respond effectively when disaster strikes (Boin et al. 2017; Parker, Persson, and Widmalm 2019; Ansell 2019). It is an obligation of good governance to prepare for the unthinkable and to allocate the necessary resources to minimize the impacts on people and society from catastrophic events. An array of responsible organizations must be able to collaborate across sectors, disciplines, jurisdictions, territorial boundaries, and levels of authority in order to effectively prepare and respond to complex crises, such as natural hazard events, terrorist attacks, pandemics, or other large-scale accidents and emergencies (Nohrstedt et al. 2018). Providing societal security – protecting citizens from harm, protecting critical infrastructure, and protecting the ability of the government and civil society to function under pressure – requires a holistic whole-of-government approach, and often even a whole-of-society approach, and therefore requires collaborative governance and collaborative crisis management capacities (Sundelius 2005; Sundelius 2006; Ansell and Gash 2008). This, in turn, requires collaborative political and organizational crisis leadership.

Organizations that are responsible for the protection of citizens and crisis management face special challenges (Widmalm, Parker, and Persson 2019). Just like other government institutions they are expected to engage in long-term planning and prepare for foreseeable dangers while at the same time scanning the horizon for novel threats. When a crisis hits, they are also expected to respond rapidly and to successfully coordinate multiple actors to respond correctly and resolve the situation. The occurrence of a crisis is the ultimate stress test and a poorly managed crisis can result in suboptimal outcomes and thus can have painful policy and political consequences (Boin, McConnell, and 't Hart 2008; Bovens and 't Hart 2016).

This chapter argues that leaders can improve their performance and reduce the chances of falling victim to a policy fiasco if they utilize the lessons from research and practice to help them avoid common failures of collaborative crisis management and if they better make use of scientific advice in their planning, preparedness, and response efforts (Parker and Stern 2005; 't Hart and Sundelius 2013).

Often we urge leaders of responsible governmental authorities and civil protection organizations to invest more seriously in preparedness for crisis management. Sometimes leaders listen to this advice, but often they do not find the time or energy as the seemingly urgent pushes away the truly significant. Bridging the gap between the world of research and practice is challenging, and practitioners often have little time for abstract theories or checklists of nostrums of how, in an ideal world, they might optimize performance (Eriksson and Sundelius 2005). A pedagogical approach drawn from problem-oriented research turns the abstract optimization perspective around and urges leaders and practitioners to work toward avoiding a number of well-known common failures of crisis management. If the mishaps of the past can be avoided, leaders and organizations stand a better chance to come out well when confronting a challenging crisis situation.

No leader or organization wants to be exposed to an apparent public failure, which, in the post-crisis accountability phase, may turn into a harsh blame-game contest (Boin et al. 2008). The ambition we stress here is not to reinvent the wheel but to learn from research findings and from previous experiences of known pitfalls. A number of well-known failure types and foreseeable surprises can be identified and the challenges associated with them can be better managed (Parker and Stern 2002; Posner 2004; Clarke 2006). Of course, future complex situations fraught with uncertainty may very well include novel dangers or events leading to other types of suboptimal outcomes. The yet unknown failures cannot all be foreseen, although we can point to an impressive catalogue of common mistakes to be avoided and common obstacles to be overcome.

This is a good starting point for convincing leaders and organizations to invest in preparedness long before their crisis management abilities are tested. Lessons from past experiences can point the way to a range of core capacities that need to be developed and mastered. The nexus of humans, organizations, social components, and even the political context interact in complex ways to facilitate or hinder efforts to build preparedness (Comfort, Boin, and Demchak 2010). The even more ambitious objective to think in terms of capacities for collaborative crisis management, as is done in this book, requires a holistic approach and a long-term investment strategy.

The overall failures of collaborative crisis management can be unpacked into several more specific challenges or failures. We can help leaders and organizations recognize these ahead of time, provide insights on how to avoid them when possible, and better manage particular challenges when they occur. In this way research-based knowledge and lessons from past events can guide efforts of planning, preparedness, capacity building, and training.

Based on our review of past research and the empirical record of policy failures, we have identified five failures to be avoided by leaders and their organizations (Boin et al. 2017; Bovens and 't Hart 2016; 't Hart and Sundelius 2013; Parker and Stern 2002, 2005; Parker et al. 2009): (1) Failures of imagination; (2) Failures of initiative; (3) Failures of coordination and cooperation; (4) Failures of credibility; (5) Failures of learning. In the following sections we go through each of our five failure proscriptions and give examples of how they have manifested themselves in past crises. We follow the discussion of each failure with prescriptions leaders and organizations can take to diminish their occurrence and improve their ability to cope with them.

Failures of Imagination

According to the 9/11 Commission, the September 11, 2001, terrorist attacks revealed a "failure" in "imagination" (9/11 Commission 2004, 339). The panel's final report determined that the analytical methods developed after Pearl Harbor to avoid surprise attacks had not been adapted and had fallen into disuse. As a result, the U.S. government and its intelligence community were insensitive to the warnings that were produced and were unable to "connect the dots" to prevent the attacks (Parker and Dekker 2008, 258; Parker and Stern 2002, 2005). Many similar surprises with grave consequences for people, property, and values have been noted in the rich literature on this topic. The effect of the 2004 Boxing Day Tsunami in Southeast Asia that impacted over 20,000 Swedish vacationers and took the Swedish government by surprise has been well documented. In Norway, the surprise attack by a lone wolf terrorist who bombed a government building and carried out a mass shooting in July 2011 shocked an unprepared country. More recently, in 2015, a massive influx of migrants to Europe, especially to Germany and Sweden, caught authorities off guard and caused considerable upheaval with long-term effects for society and for the political agenda.

Failures of imagination can lead to painful surprises and policy failures. These events are in some way contrary to previous expectations and often reveal faulty threat perceptions regarding acute dangers (Levite 1987). Since surprise events are to some degree unexpected, the initial cognitive framing of what is happening can be faulty as well. If the initial frame is false or incomplete, it may lock in a certain path of action with suboptimal results. Therefore, investments in robust procedures for threat assessment and quality sensemaking under conditions of uncertainty, stress, and limited time are needed to help decision makers and their organizations to avoid this frequent type of failure. Also, to be effective, sensemaking needs to be shared among all the relevant actors in order to provide a coherent framing that allows them to work in concert to achieve a shared objective.

Prescription: Institutionalize the Exercise of Imagination and Foster Shared Sensemaking

To avoid, or at least reduce, the incidents of surprise events it is vital to find ways of routinizing and institutionalizing the exercise of imagination (9/11 Commission 2004, 344). However, since all eventualities cannot be avoided, robust sensemaking capacities, which are necessary for any good warning and response system, are needed to collect and process information to help the responsible decision makers detect, properly diagnose, and correctly respond to emerging contingencies (Boin et al. 2017, 15). Therefore, as part of their risk assessment and preparedness activities, organizations and their leaders need procedures for hypothesizing possible crisis scenarios and risk mapping; procedures for assessing the likelihood and consequences of possible contingences; and capabilities to manage and respond to expected and unexpected events (Bracken 2008).

A standard recommendation for enhanced collaborative capacity is to note the value of greater information sharing across relevant actors. System integration and good collaborative practices can allow the various actors to connect the dots of vital pieces of information that in isolation would not create a meaningful picture (Bracken 2008, 23–25). Only by sharing what we know and putting the available signals together can we reduce unpleasant surprises. However, sharing information is merely an initial step toward the more ambitious objective of shared sensemaking. In order to make joint determinations and act in a coherent manner, a shared situational awareness across jurisdictional borders and diverse mental maps needs to be established.

There is a qualitative difference between simply sharing information and intelligence that may be interpreted in different ways versus taking the next step of successfully using the available knowledge to spur a shared sensemaking process that underpins collective decision making and action. This is the diagnostic task that brings the dots together and jointly solves the puzzle of what is happening and what the proper response to the situation should be. Crises are ambiguous, rich with value clashes, and riddled by uncertainties. In the midst of a crisis and facing time pressures, it can be hard to agree on a common frame of the situation that can give direction to decisions and actions (Boin et al. 2017).

Therefore, it is a collaborative crisis leadership task to force the organization and its mid-level leaders to train their mental preparedness for possible difficult contingencies. Scenario-based training exercises can help improve diagnostic performance when it matters the most ('t Hart and Sundelius 2013). Staff with operative responsibilities, mid-level leaders, and the top leadership ought to be urged to engage regularly in such training programs. Scenarios can be used to stretch the imagination beyond the obvious and into the seemingly unthinkable (Lempert 2007).

Failures of Initiative

A Failure of Initiative was the title of the House Select Committee report that documented the inadequate handling of the flooding and damage caused by Hurricane Katrina in August 2005 (SBC 2006). Hurricane Katrina and the catastrophic flooding overwhelmed all levels of government (local, state, and federal) and resulted in a suboptimal response to the crisis.

The breached levees and massive flooding wrought by Katrina disabled most communications systems and hindered first responders from reaching the scene, let alone functioning effectively. In such a situation, standing standard operating procedures (SOPs) dictated that state and local governments should make detailed requests for appropriate types of federal assistance, which proved to be an impossibility given the circumstances. The National Response Plan (NRP) and the SOPs in place at the time failed to account for a situation in which the responsible authorities lacked the capabilities to carry them out (Parker et al. 2009, 214). The limitations of the NRP, inflexible procedures, and a fear of making procedural errors delayed and hampered an effective response. Leadership failed in its sensemaking task and in its sense-giving obligations to subordinates, who instead failed to act decisively and fell prey to inertia, which, according to the House Select Committee, caused "death, injury, and suffering" (SBC 2006, 1).

Crisis leaders that fail to provide proactive guidance and organizations that are more focused on procedures than on problem solving are well-documented formulas for failures of initiative. When the after-action reports are written and the often difficult accountability processes are to be handled, these shortcomings often surface and affect the leadership. In worst-case scenarios, leaders can be removed by judicial or political procedures. Many European political leaders have lost their high positions as a result of not being able to adequately mobilize their organizations in the face of a disaster or high-stakes crisis.

Prescription: Push to Overcome Capacity Deficits

The people engaged in shared sensemaking are embedded inside social and institutional settings that influence their work. Moreover, the surrounding political context sets parameters for action and gives clues for how to solve dilemmas like value clashes. The interface of these softer elements with technological capacities, such as support tools for information collection and data sorting, should be tested in scenario-based exercises (Stern 2014). Then pitfalls can be exposed without significant cost to leadership. The endurance of organizations, equipment, and, not least, humans can also be tested without jeopardizing the enterprise. The leadership capacity of sense-giving to followers on different levels can be enhanced through such exercises as well. Sense-giving from the top is required to move the organizational machinery toward the stated objectives in times of emergency. But this leadership task can be executed in different forms and styles.

Preparedness for resilient collaborative response and recovery in different scenarios helps improve the chances to avoid future failures of initiative. Such capacity building evolves over time and clear benefits to leaders are not necessarily reaped immediately. The greatest challenge for such enduring investments is not simply funding but the ability to keep the key people motivated during the long stretches that can elapse between severe disasters and crises. There is also a risk that regular involvement in exercising becomes so routine that the players become very good exercisers but are not as well prepared as they should be for real-life contingencies. Such an effect can be self-defeating and can actually harm organizational resilience. Therefore, one should not simply exercise for success but rather to uncover hidden weaknesses and capacity deficits that may matter greatly in real emergencies. As Craig Fugate, the former head of the Federal Emergency Management Agency in the U.S., has observed, the point of training exercises is to expose problems: "People are afraid to fail. I'm seeking failure. . . . I want to break things. I want to see what's going on so we can fix it" (Ripley 2009).

Failures of Coordination and Cooperation

In the complex and interdependent modern world of today, crises that start in one place can quickly cascade across borders and sectors, increasing the risk of regional or even global harm (Galaz et al. 2011). Complex emergencies and extreme events can also exceed the capacity of any single country to manage on its own, requiring outside assistance that must be coordinated. The reality that extreme events and crises can overwhelm single actors and cross geographical, organizational, and sectoral boundaries has created the need for organizations to coordinate their efforts, horizontally and vertically, to meet these challenges (Comfort et al. 2010; Ansell, Boin, and Keller 2010; Boin and Bynander 2015).

A key objective of this book is to illuminate the obstacles to and the inducements behind fostering coordination among stakeholders in crises. As past research has shown, coordination and cooperation problems were central to the suboptimal outcomes seen when warning-response systems failed in connection with the 9/11 terrorist attacks (Parker and Stern 2002) and Hurricane Katrina (Parker et al. 2009). Communication disconnects and crisis coordination failures were also implicated in the flawed response to Hurricane Andrew in 1992 (Boin and Bynander 2015, 132).

Due to several contextual features of modern society and of contemporary demands on governing, effective crisis management requires collaboration across various boundaries. Isolated expert sectors, the public-private divide, professional corps, levels of authority, and jurisdictional mandates all offer numerous gaps to be bridged in acute and consequential situations of extreme stress ('t Hart and Sundelius 2013). These bridges are potential weak links in the "system of systems" for crisis management in Europe and maybe also on other continents.

The tight technological interconnectedness and real-time flows across Europe make for ripple effects without the traditional cushions of time and space. Also inter-organizational interdependencies may be more inter-blocking than interlocking in high stakes situations. Public services that are vital to the functionality of society and to governance are often interconnected with private businesses that own or operate these critical assets. Public service media, like the traditional BBC, drown in a sea of alternative sources of information and, more recently, by the richness of social media. The boundaries to be bridged are plentiful and the geographical borders of Europe are not necessarily the most difficult to cross (Sundelius 2006).

In addition, the notion of ill will and antagonistic actors must be added to this contextual complexity and ambiguity, even in Europe. Flow-based risks and geopolitically based threats in combination seem to define the operative setting for the national and EU officials responsible for coherently leading this continent with its many parts through its next disaster or crisis.

Prescription: Prepare for Transboundary Coordination

Past research and lessons from existing cooperative platforms, for example in the EU, provide prescriptive advice and point to the core performance attributes that are essential for building effective transboundary crisis coordination and response capacities (Ansell et al. 2010; Boin and Bynander 2015; Parker, Persson, and Widmalm 2019). Formal platforms, sensemaking and information tools, and scaling procedures for sharing and distributing resources and expertise all should be part of a transboundary crisis management system. In order to be effective, such a system must be able to provide: (1) means and practices for distributed sensemaking (the ability to overcome conflicting problem definitions in situations characterized by uncertainty); (2) the means and procedures for coordination, cooperation, and communication tasks (the ability to act in concert with the appropriate actors); and (3) the resources and procedures for supply logistics to distribute needed resources through clear decision-making structures and procedures (Ansell et al. 2010).

There are several interesting systems that attempt to facilitate the types of horizontal and vertical coordination transboundary crisis management requires. As Boin and Bynander (2015, 133) point out, in their study of success and failure in crisis coordination, the Incident Command System used in the U.S. and the U.K.'s Bronze-Silver-Gold structure are good examples of platforms that "appear to be quite successful in bringing together many actors in a semi-structured environment." However, the EU and its Union Civil Protection Mechanism (UCPM) is the system, despite some remaining shortcomings and problems, which has made the most progress in developing a true transboundary civilian collaborative crisis management capacity (Widmalm et al. 2019; Kuipers et al. 2015; Bossong and Hegemann 2015). The UCPM is the linchpin of the Union's effort to assist member states in the event of a disaster or other major crisis and is an instructive example of a collective effort to develop transboundary coordination and response capacities (Boin, Ekengren, and Rhinard 2013; Parker et al. 2019).

Since the effectiveness of transboundary coordination and response is limited by the weakest links in the chain, asymmetries must be compensated for and addressed (OECD 2018). The UCPM, for example, has mostly worked well in responding to requests for assistance to deal with disasters both inside and outside of Europe; however, there were times when it did not deliver as hoped for in specific instances. This was the case during the 2017 forest fires, which occurred when multiple member states were facing disasters simultaneously. In response, the EU has approved a new plan, rescEU, to address its weak links, namely the coordination and capacity gaps that the fires revealed. RescEU attempts to do so by boosting both national and EU level capacities (Parker et al. 2019).

Finally, if a collaborative coordination platform, such as the UCPM, is to be effective the actors and people involved in the system must trust its protocols and procedures as well as the information it produces, the utility of its communication channels, and its capacity to respond appropriately in the face of a crisis (Boin et al. 2013). Clearly, so-called hardware factors – a coherent legal framework, appropriate formal structures, and sufficient resources and technical equipment – are important for making crisis management work well. However, so-called software factors – leadership, training, networks, and trust in the people involved in the system – are equally crucial, if not more so, to the quality of coordinated action and response in the face of transboundary contingencies (Widmalm et al. 2019).

Failures of Credibility

What leaders and responsible authorities do and say before, during, and after a crisis matters greatly. Compelling communication, to all the involved actors, in the preparation stage is vital for establishing priorities, mobilizing resources, and building recognition and response capabilities. For example, years before the September 11 attacks, George

Tenet, who served as the Director of Central Intelligence (DCI) under both the Clinton and Bush administrations, declared war against Osama Bin Ladin. However, the mobilization of resources and manpower did not match the threat (Parker and Stern 2005, 319). A congressional inquiry attributed this framing failure to a "fragmented Intelligence Community that was operating without a comprehensive strategy for combating the threat posed by Bin Ladin, and a DCI without the ability to enforce consistent priorities at all levels throughout the Community" (Joint Inquiry 2002, 40). This failure to establish priorities and communicate them went all the way to the top. President Bush admitted that prior to the 9/11 attacks he "didn't feel that sense of urgency" (Woodward 2002, 39), which sheds light on his failure to establish terrorism as a top-tier security threat or back the importance of a plan to eliminate Al-Qaeda before September 11 (Parker and Stern 2005, 320).

Once a crisis strikes, what those in charge appear to do or fail to do in the face of a disaster is crucial. In the wake of the 2011 tsunami that resulted in the Fukushima nuclear disaster, Japanese Prime Minster Kan unhelpfully involved himself in the operational response to the disaster, while failing to effectively communicate and engage with the press ('t Hart 2013, 102). As a result, Kan botched the meaning-making process and suffered a loss of public support. The decision of Laila Freivalds, the Swedish Minister of Foreign Affairs, to attend the theater after being informed of the 2004 Boxing Day Tsunami, which killed over 500 of the some 20,000 vacationing Swedes caught up in the disaster, became emblematic of the Swedish government's sluggish and inadequate response (Swedish Tsunami Commission 2005). After the BP Deepwater Horizon oil disaster in the Gulf of Mexico in 2010, the Obama administration took too long to act, dramatically underestimated the amount of oil escaping into the gulf, and was slow to provide accurate information on the magnitude and nature of the spill (Witze et al. 2014, 362). By the time the administration acknowledged the existence of the oil plume from the gushing wellhead, it had undermined the trust of outside scientists and had lost public confidence in its handling of the crisis.

One core element of effective and credible crisis response involves offering a convincing and credible narrative of the situation, its consequences, and what is being done to address it. Meaning-making is a task that leaders can use to reach their audiences and to stay ahead of fake news or false rumors (Boin et al. 2017). Legitimacy is an important quality for leadership, and this element can suffer in disasters even if the actual handling on the ground and in the field is effective. Particular images may take over the media coverage, and any shortcomings in communications with the public or to concerned parties can symbolize and convey a skewed meaning of the situation that differs from the one that leadership sees or wants to promote.

The failure of meaning-making during the Hurricane Katrina response serves as a vivid case in point of what can happen when leaders at all levels of government are unable to credibly explain what is going on in a crisis and are unable to rebut widely spread misinformation and rumors (Boin et al. 2019, 137–52). As a recent reappraisal of the crisis management of Katrina shows, responsible leaders failed to counter a "mayhem narrative" that was inaccurate and instead engaged in a blame game battle that hindered the response and harmed the legitimacy of the responsible actors and institutions that sorely needed it (Boin et al. 2019, 151).

But credibility is not always lost or undermined in crises. There are examples, which we discuss later, when forward looking thinkers and proactive meaning-makers actually strengthen their credibility as political or organizational leaders as a crisis unfolds in front of them. Emergencies are both challenges to leadership as well as opportunities for leadership.

Prescription: Invest in Prompt Meaning-Making

So far we have advocated for a comprehensive management approach to the central challenges of collaborative crisis management. Such an approach is a necessary component of failure avoidance in crises, but it is not sufficient. Effective leadership also requires that due attention be given to the symbolic, emotional, and communicative dimensions of crisis response. This means investing in public information and media liaison capacities before a crisis hits ('t Hart and Sundelius 2013, 455). For it to be effective and credible it is crucial to include all important stakeholders in the communication process of meaning-making. This includes citizens, the private sector, and other concerned interest groups. The survival of leaders in and after crises is often tied to their symbolic actions and their credibility as storytellers who are able to provide the media and the public with a convincing narrative of what is happening and who provide optimism that touches the minds and hearts of followers (Boin et al. 2019, 176).

German Chancellor Gerhard Schröder's response to the 2002 flooding of the River Elbe is a good example of effective symbolic and performative leadership. By visiting the flood stricken areas and rapidly supplying emergency funding, Schröder communicated empathy and demonstrated the ability to take decisive action to ameliorate the suffering of the victims; these actions were widely credited for helping him prevail in his election victory some weeks later ('t Hart 2014, 127). Other examples of leaders that successfully provided meaning-making to the public in the immediate aftermath of devastating crises include New York Mayor Rudy Giuliani after the 9/11 attacks, Norwegian Prime Minister Jens Stoltenberg after the 2011 Breivik bombing and mass shooting, and President François Hollande after the 2015 Paris terror attack (Boin et al. 2017).

In a time of free flowing and fast-paced news stories emanating from many sources, credible meaning-making must be formulated well ahead of social media rumor mills, which, if not addressed, can undermine the legitimacy of leadership. Blame games are destructive and should be avoided as emerging blame game dynamics may have unforeseen effects on society and on governance (Brändström and Kuipers 2003; Boin et al. 2019). When blame spins out of hand, trauma can be inflicted upon the society at large and on the affected individuals. Such consequences may not be merely short-lived episodes but can linger for a long time and even turn into societal myths.

Closure needs to be constructed by leadership to avoid such a fatal projection from an emergency or disaster. Symbolic gestures, public speeches by prominent officials, and memorials can be used toward this end. Public faith in governance and in the ability of leaders to govern needs to be restored after a fatal disaster or controversial crisis. When sitting in the hot seat of crisis decision making, many leaders tend to overlook the severe consequences of ignoring the power of meaning-making. Such neglect can be fatal to their futures as leaders.

Failures of Learning

After dramatic disasters it is very common to establish blue ribbon commissions that document these events in detail, identify the turning points, assign responsibility, point to flaws and shortcomings, and offer recommendations for reform (Parker and Dekker 2008; Boin et al. 2008). For less significant disasters, so-called after-action reports by experts are generally produced and these also include suggestions for changes to avoid similar shortcomings in the future. Lessons from the past are identified, documented, and transformed into action items for leadership execution.

Considerable research has shown that post-crisis investigations and reform proposals often do not lead to organizational learning in the sense that practices in the field or inside an organization markedly improve. Implementation slippage persists within large organizations and in political systems with fairly brief election cycles. In spite of the best intentions and the good use of scholars and experts in these potential learning processes, achieving meaningful collective behavioral changes is challenging. Although there might be symbolic changes or perhaps altered mandates following a policy failure, post-crisis inquiries and the recommendations they produce rarely result in dramatic change or substantial reform (March and Olsen 1983; Zegart 2005).

Personal and organizational preparedness to avoid known failures is only built over time and not by some quick fix alteration of organizational charts, formal mandates, or even a massive infusion of funding. It is important to avoid the pathology of "fix-it-and-forget-it" approaches to crisis learning and change (Comfort et al. 2010). A major limitation to capturing and capitalizing on lessons learned is that the leader who is willing to invest in preparedness may not serve long enough to benefit from this capacity building effort. This is one factor behind the implementation shortfall that commonly occurs after the spotlight fades in the wake of reform proposals.

Prescription: Disseminating and Institutionalizing Lessons Learned

If policy-oriented learning and policy change are to result in more effective practices for collaborative crisis management, leaders and the involved organizations will need to transform lessons documented and spread them throughout the system, so they are implemented and institutionalized. To make this happen it is important to establish organizational practices and mechanisms, such as training exercises (Stern and Sundelius 2002), to ensure that the lessons learned by individuals are effectively spread within and across organizations (Nohrstedt and Parker 2014, 248). Disseminating lessons across organizations is imperative if they are going to significantly improve the capacity to collaborate in the pursuit of shared objectives (Comfort et al. 2010).

Although a range of psychological, organizational, and political hurdles need to be overcome if meaningful reform and improved performance is to be achieved (Parker et al. 2009), there are some success cases that illustrate that it is possible to successfully address key failings and problems in the wake of a crisis (Birkland 2006; Nohrstedt and Parker 2014). A good example is the revised European aviation crisis management system that emerged based on the lessons learned and the post-crisis reforms that were carried out after the 2010 Eyjafjallajökull ash cloud crisis paralyzed the European aviation transport system for an extended period (Parker 2015).

After an improvised solution ended the acute phase of the ash cloud crisis (Parker 2015; Larsson et al. 2015; Nohrstedt 2013), the lessons learned were utilized for post-crisis reform and policy change. These were carried out at the international, EU, and national levels in order to improve crisis preparedness in aviation and to better coordinate future responses for dealing with volcanic ash (Parker 2015, 102–3).

The reforms that were implemented were then followed up a with training and simulation exercise, based on an ash cloud scenario from the eruption of Iceland's most active volcano, Grímsvötn, to test the effectiveness of the new system. This exercise proved to be a beneficial dress rehearsal for the more effective management of the real eruption of Grímsvötn that occurred only a month later, in May 2011, in which the involved actors benefited from the fact that they better understood the new system and had made some adjustments based on the lessons learned from the exercise (Parker 2015, 103–5). This is a prime example that training exercises can provide useful opportunities to reflect on the strengths and weaknesses of the system as well as generate new insights that can help improve the system ('t Hart and Sundelius 2013, 456–57).

Conclusion: Improving Collaborative Crisis Management Through the Mobilization of Critical Knowledge for Strategic Purposes

Many policy areas are characterized by a high reliance on research-based knowledge as underpinnings to policy and practice. Public health, transportation, energy, and environmental issues are all policy domains that are deeply steeped in the foundations of science and science-based practices. However, in other policy spheres, such as military operations, police work, civil protection, and emergency management, the role of science has been less prominent, and instead experience-based knowledge has to a greater extent shaped practices and policies. Disasters and emergencies can be highly complex events and therefore scientific knowledge and technical expertise from multiple disciplines are needed to prepare for, respond to, and recover from the wide range of potential contingencies facing modern societies. In short, effective collaborative crisis management requires access to cutting-edge scientific and technical advice (OECD 2018).

Multidisciplinary scientific knowledge can play multiple roles in all aspects and phases of collaborative crisis management. Scientific advice can be utilized in a variety of ways, including: scanning the horizon for novel threats; mapping, understanding, and anticipating emerging risks; preparing for crises through scenario building, response planning, and training exercises; contributing to crisis response through data collection and analysis and sensemaking for decision support; and helping with recovery and post-crisis lessons learned activities that evaluate and document what did and did not work and what should be done differently in the future (OECD 2018, 31).

The U.K. government has been in the lead in its ambition to utilize science-based knowledge in building public policies, and this is also the case in the high-stakes area of emergency management. The Civil Contingencies Secretariat of the Cabinet Office has for several years relied on a Chief Science Advisor and a pool of specialized researchers to consult in acute emergency situations. This function has been helpful in providing guidance in several poorly understood and complex crisis situations, where choices among unchartered paths of action would be consequential. One example was the Pandemic Flu in 2009, when experts first investigated, compared, and assessed the potential spread of the infectious disease before any official action was taken. The UK's Scientific Advisory Group for Emergencies (SAGE) has inspired several other European governments and the EU Commission to try to build similar science-based support functions. British officials have noted that reliance on the natural sciences has proven its value, while it has been more difficult to lean on actionable scholarship in the social and behavioral sciences (OECD 2018).

Climate researchers, for example, have greatly influenced the approach taken by many governments to climate change. Numerous countries were influenced by the Intergovernmental Panel on Climate Change (IPCC) when drafting their national climate assessments, and the IPCC's scientific assessments strongly influenced the goals of the 2015 Paris Agreement, which aims to hold global warming to well below 2°C and to pursue efforts to limit it to 1.5°C. In this area, critical knowledge has, over time, successfully been mobilized for strategic purposes with concrete policy results.

In the life sciences, it has become evident that progress in the public health sector builds upon the evolving research results of many scientific groups in many nations. In the everyday safety sphere, considerable scientific work has contributed to reduced fatality rates from fires, car accidents, and the spread of disease. How can these impressive safety and health benefits, which have enhanced the lives of millions of people, inspire preparedness for handling less expected and more ambiguous contingencies and events?

Many governments invest continuously in science and technology for safety and security. The U.S. Department of Homeland Security supports a huge Science and Technology

Program. Part of the EU Horizon 2020 funding goes to a similar science program on Secure Societies. Many national programs exist, such as in Sweden, Norway, the Netherlands, Germany, and Canada. Some emphasize the science aspects, while others focus more on technological development. Some focus on the long-term usefulness of the results, while others are concerned with more immediate benefits from the scientists. In the social and behavioral fields, some have faith in research-based applications, while others tend to rely more on experience-based best practices. Still, it is agreed by many in this field of work that both research-based and experience-based knowledge should be drawn upon to enhance practices, something that has been done for centuries in the medical field.

To address the gap between the abstract world of science and the practical world of emergency management, education and training can play an important bridge-building role that "fosters familiarity and mutual understanding" (OECD 2018, 58). Future professionals should not be trained by simply teaching them about how things were done in the past in previous work contexts or by passing on old habits based on outdated findings. Science-based knowledge and novel technologies ought to infuse educational curricula, mid-career training programs, and top-level learning retreats. Even if old habits may reign among the very experienced, for good and bad, the incoming generation of professionals should have every opportunity to bring with them more recent findings, tools, and approaches to the difficult work ahead. This opportunity and even obligation goes for incoming leaders as well (Stern and Sundelius 2002).

All of the potential failures discussed in this chapter can only be fundamentally avoided by drawing on critical knowledge and on training and preparations that utilize scientific expertise from multiple disciplines. In this sense, the failure of learning is the most consequential failure, as this omission affects all of the other noted potential mishaps in critical ways. Failures of collaborative crisis management are possible, and even likely, unless those parties needed for collaboration to function effectively are open to the application of novel technologies and new knowledge to carry out their collective work. Capitalizing on this core insight is primarily a matter of shared mindsets and is crucial for transforming learning into improved preparedness for future events and better collaborative crisis management.

References

9/11 Commission (National Commission on Terrorist Attacks Upon the United States). 2004. *The 9/11 Commission Report*. New York, NY: Norton.

Ansell, Christopher. 2019. *The Protective State (Elements in Public Policy)*. Cambridge: Cambridge University Press. doi:10.1017/9781108667081

Ansell, Christopher, Arjen Boin, and Ann Keller. 2010. "Managing Transboundary Crises: Identifying the Building Blocks of an Effective Response System." *Journal of Contingencies and Crisis Management* 18 (4): 195–207.

Ansell, Christopher and Alison Gash. 2008. "Collaborative Governance in Theory and Practice." *Journal of Public Administration Research and Theory* 18 (4): 543–71.

Birkland, Thomas. 2006. *Lessons of Disaster: Policy Change After Catastrophic Events*. Washington, DC: Georgetown University Press.

Boin, Arjen, Christer Brown, and James A. Richardson. 2019. *Managing Hurricane Katrina: Lessons from a Megacrisis*. Baton Rouge, LA: LSU Press.

Boin, Arjen and Fredrik Bynander. 2015. "Explaining Success and Failure in Crisis Coordination." *Geografiska Annaler: Series A, Physical Geography* 97 (1): 123–35.

Boin, Arjen, Magnus Ekengren, and Mark Rhinard. 2013. *The European Union as Crisis Manager: Patterns and Prospects*. Cambridge: Cambridge University Press.

Boin, Arjen, Allan McConnell, and Paul 't Hart, eds. 2008. *Governing After Crisis: The Politics of Investigation, Accountability and Learning.* Cambridge: Cambridge University Press.

Boin, Arjen, Paul 't Hart, Eric Stern, and Bengt Sundelius. 2017. *The Politics of Crisis Management: Public Leadership Under Pressure.* Cambridge: Cambridge University Press.

Bossong, Raphael and Hendrik Hegemann. 2015. *European Civil Security Governance: Diversity and Cooperation in Crisis and Disaster Management.* Basingstoke: Palgrave.

Bovens, Mark and Paul 't Hart. 2016. "Revisiting the Study of Policy Failures." *Journal of European Public Policy* 23 (5): 653–66.

Bracken, Paul. 2008. "How to Build a Warning System." In *Managing Strategic Surprise: Lessons from Risk Management and Risk Assessment*, edited by P. Bracken, I. Bremmer, and D. Gordon, 255–82. Cambridge: Cambridge University Press.

Brändström, Annika and Sanneke Kuipers. 2003. "From 'Normal Incidents' to Political Crises: Understanding the Selective Politicization of Policy Failures." *Government and Opposition* 38 (3): 279–305.

Clarke, Lee. 2006. *Worst Cases.* Chicago, IL: University of Chicago Press.

Comfort, Louise, Arjen Boin, and Chris Demchak. 2010. *Designing Resilience: Preparing for Extreme Events.* Pittsburgh, PA: University of Pittsburgh Press.

Eriksson, Johan and Bengt Sundelius. 2005. "Molding Minds That Form Policy: How to Make Research Useful." *International Studies Perspectives* 6 (1): 51–71.

Galaz, Victor, Fredrik Moberg, Eva-Karin Olsson, Eric Paglia, and Charles Parker. 2011. "Institutional and Political Leadership Dimensions of Cascading Ecological Crises." *Public Administration* 89 (2): 361–80.

Joint Inquiry. 2002. *Joint Inquiry into Intelligence Community Activities Before and After the Terrorist Attacks of September 11, 2001: Report of the U.S. Senate Select Committee on Intelligence and the U.S. House Permanent Select Committee on Intelligence: With Additional Views.*

Kuipers, Sanneke, Arjen Boin, Raphael Bossong, and Hendrik Hegemann. 2015. "Building Joint Crisis Management Capacity? Comparing Civil Security Systems in 22 European Countries." *Risk, Hazards & Crisis in Public Policy* 6 (1): 1–21.

Larsson, Gerry, Fredrik Bynander, Alicia Ohlsson, Erik Schyberg, and Martin Holmberg. 2015. "Crisis Management at the Government Offices: A Swedish Case Study." *Disaster Prevention and Management* 24 (5): 542–52.

Lempert, Robert. 2007. "Can Scenarios Help Policymakers Be Both Bold and Careful?" In *Blindside*, edited by Francis Fukuyama, 109–19. Washington, DC: Brookings.

Levite, Ariel J. 1987. *Intelligence and Strategic Surprise.* New York, NY: Columbia University Press.

March, James G. and Johan P. Olsen. 1983. "Organizing Political Life: What Administrative Reorganization Tells Us About Government." *The American Political Science Review* 77 (2): 281–96.

Nohrstedt, Daniel. 2013. "Advocacy Coalitions in Crisis Resolution: Understanding Policy Dispute in the European Volcanic Ash Cloud Crisis." *Public Administration* 91 (4): 964–79.

Nohrstedt, Daniel, Fredrik Bynander, Charles Parker, and Paul 't Hart. 2018. "Managing Crises Collaboratively: Prospects and Problems – A Systematic Literature Review." *Perspectives on Public Management and Governance* 1 (4): 257–71.

Nohrstedt, Daniel and Charles Parker. 2014. "The Public Policy Dimension of Resilience in Natural Disaster Management: Sweden's Gudrun and Per Storms." In *Disasters and Development*, edited by N. Kapucu and E. Liou, 235–53. London: Springer.

OECD. 2018. *Scientific Advice During Crises: Facilitating Transnational Cooperation and Exchange of Information.* Paris: OECD.

Parker, Charles F. 2015. "Complex Negative Events and the Diffusion of Crisis: Lessons from the 2010 and 2011 Icelandic Volcanic Ash Cloud Events." *Geografiska Annaler: Series A, Physical Geography* 97 (1): 97–108.

Parker, Charles F. and Sander Dekker. 2008. "September 11 and Post Crisis Investigation: Exploring the Role and Impact of the 9/11 Commission." In *Governing After Crisis*, edited by A. Boin, A. McConnell, and P. 't Hart, 255–82. Cambridge: Cambridge University Press.

Parker, Charles F., Thomas Persson, and Sten Widmalm. 2019. "The Effectiveness of National and EU-Level Civil Protection Systems: Evidence from 17 Member States." *Journal of European Public Policy.* 26 (9): 1312–34. doi:10.1080/13501763.2018.1523219

Parker, Charles F. and Eric K. Stern. 2005. "Bolt from the Blue or Avoidable Failure? Revisiting September 11 and the Origins of Strategic Surprise." *Foreign Policy Analysis* 1 (3): 301–31.

———. 2002. "Blindsided? September 11 and the Origins of Strategic Surprise." *Political Psychology* 23 (3): 601–30.

Parker, Charles F., Eric K. Stern, Eric Paglia, and Christopher Brown. 2009. "Preventable Catastrophe? The Hurricane Katrina Disaster Revisited." *Journal of Contingencies and Crisis Management* 17 (4): 206–20.

Posner, Richard. 2004. *Catastrophe: Risk and Response*. Oxford: Oxford University Press.

Ripley, Amanda. September 2009. "In Case of Emergency." *The Atlantic*. www.theatlantic.com/magazine/archive/2009/09/in-case-of-emergency/307604/ (Accessed 23 May 2019).

SBC (Select Bipartisan Committee to Investigate the Preparation for and Response to Hurricane Katrina). 2006. "A Failure of Initiative: Final Report of the Select Bipartisan Committee to Investigate the Preparation for and Response to Hurricane Katrina." https://katrina.house.gov/full_katrina_report.htm

Stern, Eric. 2014. *Designing Crisis Management Training and Exercises for Strategic Leaders*. Stockholm: CRISMART, Swedish Defense University.

Stern, Eric and Bengt Sundelius. 2002. "Crisis Management Europe: An Integrated Regional Research and Training Program." *International Studies Perspectives* 3 (1): 171–88.

Sundelius, Bengt. 2006. "A Brief on Embedded Societal Security." *Information and Security* 17: 23–37.

———. 2005. "Disruptions: Functional Security for the EU." In *Disasters, Diseases, Disruptions: A New D-Drive for the European Union*, edited by A. Missiroli, 67–84. Chaillot Paper No. 83. Paris: Institute for Security Studies, European Union.

Swedish Tsunami Commission. 2005. "Sweden and the Tsunami: Examination and Proposals." Swedish Government Official Report No. SOU 2005:104. Stockholm.

't Hart, Paul. 2014. *Understanding Public Leadership*. Basingstoke: Palgrave.

———. 2013. "After Fukushima: Reflections on Risk and Institutional Learning in an Era of Mega-Crises." *Public Administration* 91 (1): 101–13.

't Hart, Paul and Bengt Sundelius. 2013. "Crisis Management Revisited: An Agenda for Research, Training and Capacity Building Within Europe." *Cooperation and Conflict* 48 (3): 444–61.

Widmalm, Sten, Charles F. Parker, and Thomas Persson. 2019. *Civil Protection Cooperation in the European Union: How Administrative Culture and Social Trust Matter for Crisis Management*. Basingstoke: Palgrave.

Witze, Alexandra, Lauren Morello, and Marian Turner. 2014. "Crisis Counsellors." *Nature* 512 (28): 360–63.

Woodward, Bob. 2002. *Bush at War*. New York, NY: Simon & Schuster.

Zegart, Amy B. 2005. "September 11 and the Adaptation Failure of the U.S. Intelligence Agencies." *International Security* 29 (4): 78–111.

Chapter 11

Under What Conditions Does an Extreme Event Deploy its Focal Power?

Toward Collaborative Governance in Swiss Flood Risk Management

Karin Ingold and Alexandra Gavilano

Introduction

In this chapter we study the longer-term response of a national government to natural disasters. We are interested in when and how collaborative governance arrangements spark new national flood prevention policies. Our understanding of collaborative governance not only includes public and private actors that are involved in a complex network (see Nohrstedt 2015) but also the larger institutional setting as well as regulations in the domain of flood risk management. In other words, we conceive the full range from politics and polity to policies when defining collaborative risk management (see also Driessen et al. 2012). For national flood prevention this concretely means that decision making and implementation processes are designed multilevel and cross-sectoral, that competences and responsibilities are shared between different jurisdictions and policy subsystems, and that policies and regulations reflect this horizontal and vertical integration of actors and institutions (Ingold et al. 2018; Ingold 2017).

But how does a nation-state get to such collaborative flood risk management? What conditions induce major policy or paradigm change toward collaborative governance? To answer these questions we proceed in two steps. First, we investigate the necessary conditions for a paradigm change in flood prevention. In the second step, we concentrate on the impact leading to change and the policy process factors that enhance collaborative governance (in contrast to more traditional, mono-sectoral forms of steering).

We investigate paradigm changes in Swiss flood risk management and therefore study one century of policymaking in this domain. We define paradigm change as a major shift in the approach to tackling flood risks. These approaches range from top-down policy-making and infrastructure measures to more integrative and cross-sectoral governance styles. In this context, the central focus lies on major flood events during the last century and the role they played in shaping or inducing paradigm changes in Swiss flood risk management. Can we attribute paradigm changes to major flood events and/or some other key characteristic(s) of natural disasters? Moreover, what role did the dynamics in the policy subsystem play in making a paradigm change possible? And finally, what subsystem dynamics (such as coalition structures, conflict, and brokerage) are necessary to push paradigm change in the direction of collaborative governance in flood risk management?

Theory

Since Hall's seminal work on policy paradigms (1993), one particular type of change which forms the focus of policy studies is paradigm shift. While various definitions and understandings exist about what a paradigm is and what a paradigm shift means (for an overview, see Hogan and Howlett 2015), here, we stick to what can be called "paradigmatic policy change" and thus the ideological redesign or reframing that is reflected in the political goals and measures (Cairney and Weible 2015). Such goals and measures are typically embraced by one larger political program or even by one subsystem (see Sabatier and Weible 2007). We further acknowledge that a paradigm, and thus the ideas and discourses adopted by the political community can further include institutional arrangements and actor networks. They can span more than one political field or subsystem (Baumgartner 2013).

Various policy process theories have such a paradigm shift as the focus of their attention, and several of them consider external events, shocks or natural disasters to be a decisive driving factor for such major change (Baumgartner and Jones 1993; Sabatier and Jenkins-Smith 1993). Such events are sudden and often unpredictable; they come from *outside* the policy community, political elite or policy subsystem and have their impact on different elements *within* that community, elite or subsystem (see Kingdon 1984; Laumann and Knoke 1987; Birkland 1997; Sabatier and Weible 2007). Those *"within"* mechanisms and elements are also known as *polity and politics*; and policy process theories acknowledge *shifts in polity and politics* then having a crucial impact on *shifts in policies*. For what follows, we borrow from theoretical concepts and empirical applications of Birkland's work about "focusing events" (Birkland 1997, 1998) and their impact on *politics* (e.g., elements of the policy process) in the first step and on *polity and policies* in the second. We thus ask: Under which conditions does a focusing event have the capacity to induce a paradigm shift? And what impact does a focusing event have on subsystem dynamics that spark a shift toward collaborative modes of governance?

Hypotheses

Following Birkland's seminal work, focusing events are defined as occurring suddenly, rare, very unpredictable, and affecting a large number of people (1997). The greater the magnitude of an event, the higher the focal power of it; thus, a greater impact on politics and policy is assumed. To assess the magnitude of an event, and thereby hypothesize about its public impact, some researchers have focused on certain key characteristics of the event itself (see Travis 2014) such as the number of deaths or the amount of infrastructure damage, whereas others emphasize public and media attention (Baumgartner and Jones 1993). Nevertheless, all of these point to the fact that the magnitude of an event decisively impacts focal power on politics.

> H1: The greater the magnitude of an event, the greater the tendency that this event will deploy focal power and induce a paradigm shift.

Birkland (1997, 1998) convincingly demonstrates that focusing events have agenda dynamics, but he also argues that only under certain conditions do they lead to so-called policy change. For proper change of political content and paradigm, one has to better understand the triggers within the so-called *policy communities* or subsystems (see Sabatier and Weible 2007).

Policy communities or policy subsystems might be characterized by a certain degree of coordination among like-minded actors and by one or more advocacy coalitions. Coalition members wish to see their beliefs and policy preferences translated or integrated into concrete political programs and strategies. Their activity can generate new ideas, discourse, and beliefs within one political subfield or subsystem, which ultimately has the potential to induce a paradigm shift (see also Hogan and Howlett 2015). In addition, Birkland (1998) argues that how a focusing event deploys its focal power strongly depends upon the advocacy structure available. He asserts that a subsystem or community with no clear advocacy coalition does not have a consolidation of interests or coordination for a focusing event to be absorbed and to induce policy change.

Yet a focusing event can provoke changes in the subsystem structure and Birkland asserts that there is a greater possibility for change in a situation consisting of competing coalitions. For example, the traditional majority coalition thus pushes for policy alteration in order not to lose power (Birkland 1997). On the contrary, however, the minority coalition sees their beliefs and preferences reinforced by the focusing event's impacts and it benefits from a so-called window of opportunity for reframing the issue (Kingdon 1984; Baumgartner and Jones 1993).

> Hypothesis 2: An event absorbed by a subsystem with one or several competing advocacy coalitions has the tendency to deploy focal power and thus induce a paradigm shift.

We now turn to our second research question and to factors that explain shifts toward more collaboration and cross-sectoral governance modes. Generally, in order to enhance change toward more coordination and collaboration across different sectors, interests, and beliefs, the external shock should provoke more common understanding for the problem within the subsystem and across coalitions. This in turn enhances possibilities for compromise finding. In the literature, compromise and collaborative arrangements are possible in three main situations: collaborative, unitary, and conflictive. In contrast to the latter two, actors start to coordinate actions across coalitions in collaborative subsystems (Weible, Sabatier, and Pattison 2010). Across-coalition actions in politics should then also have spill-over effects in how competences are shifted and policies redesigned. This is why we hypothesize the following:

> Hypothesis 3a: An event absorbed by a subsystem with competing coalitions has the tendency to induce change toward collaborative governance if across-coalition coordination is present.

Compromise and collaborative governance solutions can also be facilitated by key actors in the subsystem. Following the Advocacy Coalition Framework, this role is typically played by policy brokers who seek stability in the subsystem and act in a rather belief-neutral way through across-coalition action (see Ingold and Varone 2012; Sabatier and Jenkins-Smith 1993; Ingold 2011). Also other frameworks identify key actors in situations of change. Following Kingdon (1995; see also Birkland 1997; Zahariadis 2007), policy entrepreneurs exploit windows of opportunity. Yet different from brokers, these actors do not seek compromise but rather act in their own interest and want to see their own ideas translated into policies. Deduced from these insights, we formulate two hypotheses:

> Hypothesis 3b: An event absorbed by a subsystem with competing coalitions has the tendency to induce change toward collaborative governance if policy brokers are present.
>
> Hypothesis 3c: An event absorbed by a subsystem with competing coalitions has the tendency to induce change toward collaborative governance if policy entrepreneurs are present.

Case, Data, and Methods

We considered all "major" flood events as potential candidates for inducing considerable alterations in policies. In short, we compiled a list of floods, which potentially acted as focusing events and then assessed whether they did or not. The list started with events from the mid-19th century, as flood prevention policy began shortly after this period. Based on hydrological expertise, the first selection criterion consisted of the hydrological magnitude of a flood. This included the return period, hazard levels, and the runoff capacity in the respective hydrological catchment area (Flügel 2000). The Swiss Confederation has defined five hazard levels. We used the two highest levels (levels 4 and 5) for this study (SR 520.12, Art. 10) and selected those with return periods greater than 30 years. Two additional criteria helped us to identify major flood events: the floods had to be nationally significant and had to affect more than five cantons. If they did not, then they were only retained for our analysis if they caused damages over 500 million Swiss Francs (Table 11.1). This left us with 12 flood events from 1868 until today. It should be noted that in some years, more than one flood event occurred, which can be seen in the second column (dates) of Table 11.1. We considered a maximum of one event per year, and if there were two events in the same year, we considered them as one event.

In order to assess if a flood deployed focal power and thus could be linked to a paradigm shift, we applied the method of process tracing (George and Bennett 2005; for an application see Walgrave and Varone 2008). Process tracing is prominently applied in "within case" analysis, which was also done here in assessing whether a paradigm change could potentially be linked to a flood event (Collier 2011).

Here, we first systematically describe our definition of a paradigm shift, and then assess if our candidates for focusing events (see Table 11.1) can be deemed as such. Put differently, we identified whether a flood event had focal power or not. In doing so, we relied on two important steps typically applied in process tracing (Collier 2011): first *describing* all dependent and independent variables, and second *identifying sequences* for the link between one particular paradigm shift in relation to one (or several) potential focusing event(s). We based this on primary and secondary literature (Schnitter 1992; Furrer 2002; Zaugg 2006; Burger 2008; Summermatter 2012; BAFU 2013).

Conditions Driving a Flood's Focal Potential (Hypotheses Testing)

To identify under what *conditions* floods become focusing events, we do hypothesis testing with the different potential conditions driving an event's focal power (outlined in more detail here). The magnitude of the flood events was measured by the number of deaths, geographical outreach, economic damage, and coalition formation. We used a mixture of qualitative and quantitative data to assess the key systematic factors and to determine whether the identified floods could be defined as focusing events.

Table 11.1 Selected flood events

Year	Dates	Cantons affected	Spatial extent	Economic damage (million CHF)
1868	27–28 Sept 2–3 Oct	5	National	1400 (2.94 Mio value in 1868)
1910	14–15 June	16	National	584 (16 Mio value in 1910)

(Continued)

Table 11.1 (Continued)

Year	Dates	Cantons affected	Spatial extent	Economic damage (million CHF)
1978	7 Aug	4	National	513,94
1987	18 July	5	Regional (esp. UR, TI, VS, GR)	777,61
	24–25 Aug			272,04
1993	24 Sept	2	Regional (esp. Brig, VS and	2,99
	13 Oct		Locarno, TI)	662,98
1999	15–25 May	6	National	577,25
	21 June			
2000	11–17 Oct	4	Regional (esp. VS and TI)	668,546
2005	19–24 Aug	13	National	2977,598
2007	8–10 Aug	22	National	379,18
2011	10–11 Oct	7	National	84,99
2013	2 May	17	National	32,32
	31 May–11 June			60,29
2014	24 July	6	Regional	24,74
	11 Aug			1,72

Sources: Adapted from and based on WSL database 2016; Pfister 1999, 2002; BAFU 2013.

Notes pertaining to Table 11.1:
• Year – Those defined as focusing events have been shaded.
• Spatial extent – If cross-cantonal damages occurred then the event was categorized as "national."
• Economic damage – Pfister (1999, 2002) documented the economic damages of floods from 1800s until 2005. Here, economic damage is defined as the estimated amount of economic loss in relation to the nominal wages in the construction industry. Subsequently the data displayed here was adjusted by the 2005 inflation rate. The year 1868 has an adjusted value in comparison to the amount of loss in 1868 (2.94 million CHF) to the year 2005 (1400 million CHF). The more recent data on economic damage (2007–2014) is based on the data that forms the event analyses by the BAFU (2013).

The quantitative data and statistics used to determine if an event's magnitude were derived from the official databases provided by the Swiss administration (see BAFU 2012a, 2012b). Additionally, we were able to rely on a complete and systematic database categorizing and evaluating each flood event in Switzerland, which was provided to us by the Swiss Federal Institute for Forest, Snow and Landscape Research (WSL database 2016). In order to make the figures more comparable (in particular the economic damages, which depend upon various socioeconomic factors like number of deaths, inflation, or currency rate), we further considered the figures retreated by historians (Pfister 2002).

For the presence or absence of conflicting coalitions and subsystem specificities, we relied on the secondary literature presented in the next section. Additionally, we made a general appraisal of Swiss flood prevention (not only that relating to specific flood events) and systematically analyzed all parliamentary, governmental, and direct-democratic (initiatives and referenda) action over the past two centuries (see Appendix II).

Analysis: Paradigm Shift in Swiss Flood Prevention

Our analysis revealed three important paradigm shifts in Swiss flood prevention: from no regime to an infrastructural regime in 1877; then the change to a regime focusing on spatial planning in 1991; and finally in 2010, the shift toward a more integrated approach in flood risk management.

Flood prevention in the 19th century was characterized by very limited technological responses and predominantly local interventions (Schnitter 1992; Zaugg 2006). Overexploitation of forest areas increased the flood hazard, but considerably larger industrial and residential buildings in flood-prone areas also increased the pressure on the Confederation to introduce more standardized guidelines on the national level, mainly related to financial support and subsidies (Schulla 1997). With the introduction of the Hydraulic Engineering Inspectorate Act in 1877 [721.10] (and, to a lesser extent, the Forest Inspectorate Act in 1902 [921.0]), for the first time Switzerland adopted a nationwide flood risk management plan that was almost exclusively focused on *infrastructure*.

New environmental activism, fishing associations emerging in the 1970s, and the popular initiative about enhanced water protection ("zur Rettung unserer Gewässer") in the early 1980s all made clear that more space for watercourses was needed. This fact was also supported by experts and hydrological engineers, who also called for better infrastructural flood management. Fortunately, the absence of any significant flood events limited the amount of damage incurred during these decades. To further protect the population and infrastructure from potential flood events, constructions alone were not enough, and **the Spatial Planning Regime** was born and reinforced through the Hydraulic Engineering Ordinance [721.100.1] and the Water Retaining Facilities Ordinance [721.102], introduced in 1994 and 1999, respectively.

With the creation of the Extra-Parliamentary Commission for Natural Hazards (PLANAT 2015) in 1997 and general administrative strategies on the national level promoting sustainability and integrative approaches combining water protection, use, and flood prevention, a new culture was born.

Sustainability principles started to be systematically integrated in different legal revisions concerning flood prevention at the beginning of the new century (Zaugg 2006). Consequently, the Extra-Parliamentary Commission for Natural Hazards (PLANAT) designed a Natural Hazard Strategy that followed a so-called comprehensive, interlinked, and cross-sectoral approach. After 2010, Switzerland installed an **Integrated Risk Management** with the introduction of OWARNA, a consolidated management system based on multilevel decision channels.

Analysis: Identification of Floods as Focusing Events

We now systematically discuss which floods had the potential to deploy focal power. We also control if a paradigm shift could potentially have been initiated *before* the flood event had occurred (which was, for instance, partially the case with the flood event in 1987 and the paradigm shift in 1991, see Figure 11.1).

Several different sources attribute a focal power to the flood event of 1868 (Zaugg 2006; Burger 2008; Summermatter 2012). It is one of the largest in Swiss history and led to huge public attention and nationwide solidarity, demonstrated by fundraising and immediate actions to repair the flood consequences. For instance, after the 1868 flood, an institutionalized learning process and improvement of flood prevention measures was initiated (Zaugg 2006).

The first minor policy changes (such as an extension of the subsidy regime in 1871 and the constitutional baselines for the national water policy in 1874) paved the way for a larger legal innovation, the Hydraulic Engineering Inspectorate Act, drafted in 1876 and introduced in 1877 [721.10]. The **1868 flood** can therefore be classified as a focusing event, and it considerably affected the start of the infrastructural regime (Petrascheck 1989).

The major flood event in June 1910 had a severe impact on different regions of the country (see Table 11.1) and induced several changes in flood management and implementation. Nevertheless, those changes were only minor and mostly concerned adjustments to existing practices, such as financial regulation or collaboration between different administrative units (see Wanner 2016; Burger 2008; Vischer 2003). When looking at the paradigm shift toward the spatial planning regime in the early 1990s, one might intuitively

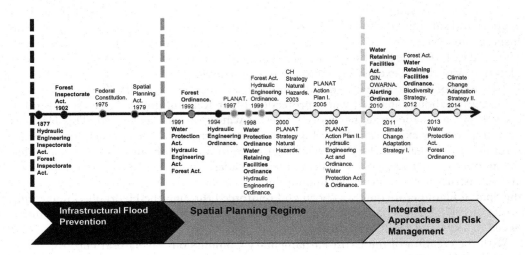

Figure 11.1 Paradigm shift in Swiss flood prevention

think that the **1987 flood event** had an impact. But this is only partially true. As mentioned earlier, in the 1970s and 1980s, various ecological movements were active and popular initiatives were launched that promoted the adoption of a spatial planning perspective, rather than a purely engineering perspective. The **flood event of 1978** considerably reinforced the environmentalists' requests (Summermatter 2012) and had considerable focal power upon the paradigm shift toward spatial planning.

While the flood event of 1993 could not be identified as a focusing event (see, for instance, Burger 2008), it may have reinforced the desire for more systematic coordination in natural hazard prevention on the national level. It may also have had an impact on the formulation of PLANAT in 1997, as well as the Water Retaining Facilities Ordinance [721.102] that came into force in 1999. However, the introduction of these strategies and their major milestones were decided long before this flood occurred.

After 1968, the **2005 event** was one of the greatest and most disastrous floods in Swiss history, even despite major flood prevention policies introduced several decades earlier. This event clearly led to an amelioration of the alarm system and more integrative and multilevel communication through the OWARNA, GIN, and PLANAT strategies, among others. Overall, the flood events between 2009 and today further justified the actions taken toward a more integrated and sustainable approach combining water engineering, water protection, climate change adaptation, sustainability, and biodiversity.

Analysis: Identifying Drivers for Change

We now answer the question, what made the floods that could be identified as focusing events so special (see floods that have been shaded in Table 11.1). What conditions and attributes made them deploy their focal power in contrast to all other floods that could not be identified as focusing events in our analysis?

We now consider the **"objective magnitude"** of the floods (number of deaths, the geographical outreach of the affected area, the amount of economic damage, and coalition formation) to see what characteristics of the focal flood events were crucial to deploy a paradigm shift.

At first glance, no clear pattern can be identified. The four floods of 1868, 1978, 1987, and 2005 that we preliminarily identified as focusing events were not constantly those with the greatest magnitude. However, some facts are still worth highlighting. For instance, the floods of 1868 and 2005 were the only ones that fulfilled all of our "flood selection criteria" (see previous section) cumulatively. Both were major, dangerous flood events, affecting five or more cantons and with damages of over 500 million Swiss francs. The 1868 flood was by far the most disastrous in terms of the number of lost lives with 50 deaths. The 2005 flood had the greatest economic consequences (2977 million CHF).

Despite the fact that severe floods also occurred in 2000, 1993, and 1999, and resulted in major human and economic losses, they did not have any focal power. Since objective magnitude and the amount of economic damages (and specifically the amount of economic damages) only partially can explain what makes a flood a focusing event, there are other indicators related to politics.

We now turn to **subsystem properties** and the presence of coalitions, policy brokers, and entrepreneurs to explain policy change in general, and paradigm shift toward more collaborative arrangements in particular. Before the first identified paradigm shift, no highly organized interests were observed. Nonetheless, after the 1868 flood some political and economic actors called for action and measures (Zaugg 2006). The pressure from the public increased and was absorbed by selected state officials and experts of that time (mainly federal engineers; see Müller 2004), who then decisively pushed for political change and gave birth to the first flood risk management regime (based on infrastructure).

From then on, and particularly from 1877 onwards, the literature emphasizes the impact of engineers and technical experts who formed a *pro-infrastructure coalition* (Summermatter 2012; Müller 2004). This coalition was also responsible for the consolidation of the infrastructure paradigm that lasted for more than one century and dominated the Swiss flood risk management. In the mid-20th century, the emergence of a second coalition can be observed: the *pro-conservation and spatial planning coalition*. It integrated three types of actors with very different core beliefs and ideologies. However, interestingly, these actors started coordinating actions because they all wanted to push the paradigm change away from pure infrastructure toward more spatial planning. The first type of actors were those in various ecological movements, generally concerned with environmental conservation, and, at first, interested in hydropower and shipping activities that caused harm to nature (Pfister 2007; Summermatter 2012). After the occurrence of the 1978 and 1983 floods, they joined this pro-conservation and spatial planning coalition. The second type of actors were the landscape protectionists: they were against further flood infrastructures, which they believed were causing harm to the natural landscape properties. The third group consisted of experts, mainly from public administration, who attributed greater economic efficiency and security performance to spatial planning rather than infrastructure (Summermatter 2012; Zaugg 2006). If the conflict between the two coalitions (pro-infrastructure versus pro-spatial planning) did not directly induce a paradigm shift, it nevertheless provoked civil-societal action and important legal revisions that then paved the way and provided a window of opportunity for the paradigm shift following the floods of 1978 and 1987. The 2005 flood was still absorbed by a subsystem characterized by the two competing coalitions, but what decisively impacted the third paradigm change toward collaborative governance in flood risk management was the fact that several administrative agencies, and in particular the three Federal Agencies for Agriculture, Spatial Planning, and Water and Geology, started to become active and induced a large integration process. Through the leading activities of those agencies, the 2005 flood decisively boosted the idea of integrated measures, and the third paradigm shift was realized.

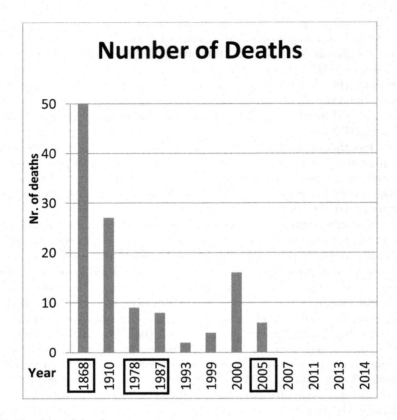

Figure 11.2A Number of deaths

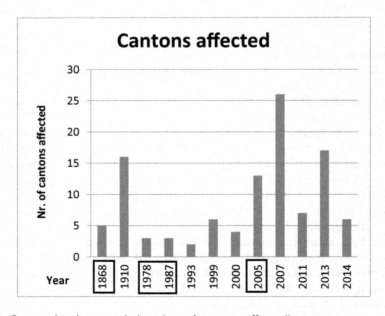

Figure 11.2B Geographical outreach (number of cantons affected)

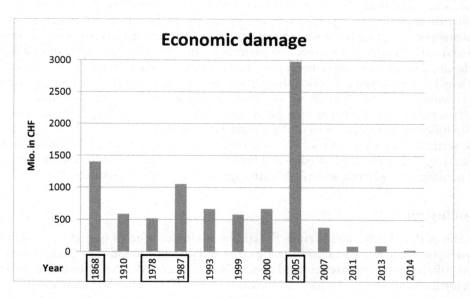

Figure 11.2C Economic damages in millions of Swiss Francs

Discussion

Looking at 12 major floods over more than one century in Swiss flood prevention, we wanted to know why some of them (1868, 1978, 1987, 2005) could deploy focal power and induce policy change in general and paradigm shifts toward new collaborative approaches in particular, while others did not. Even if the extent and magnitude of a flood seems to play an important role, it is not the unique or decisive attribute making it a focusing event. Two of the four focusing events clearly included great damage in terms of economic costs, geographical outreach, and number of deaths. However, there were also floods that we did not deem as focusing events despite the fact that they caused considerable damage to infrastructure and society. We can therefore only partly confirm our first hypothesis: we can consider "objective magnitude" and specifically the geographical extent of the disaster as one necessary, but not sufficient, condition for a flood to be defined as a focusing event.

This result brings us to the test of our second hypothesis and the claim that politics matter. But we can also here only partially confirm this. In the first period of our analysis, there was no clear advocacy coalition present but, nevertheless, a paradigm change occurred. It is thus not the presence of a larger group of well-organized, like-minded actors but the presence of *some single actors that organize actions* that seem able to initiate a paradigm shift. For example, at the beginning of the 20th century we observed the development of a pro-infrastructure coalition, but no shift occurred. The mere creation of a coalition is not sufficient to induce change, and therefore the floods occurring at the beginning of the century were not defined as focusing events.

In the set of third hypotheses, we go beyond Birkland's argument that organized interests that are at stake are significant (Birkland 1998), and therefore we investigated what exact subsystem dynamics lead to collaborative governance in flood risk management. If collaboration and governance across sectors and interests should become pioneering in flood risk management, then the external event needs to stimulate joint efforts and collaboration. Following this line of argument, this case reveals actors' coordinating actions in advocacy coalitions that coordinate actions across coalition boundaries, and when in conflict these coalitions negotiate jointly through the help of so-called policy brokers or entrepreneurs. In our case, it is the third paradigm shift that led to cross-sectoral integration and collaborative governance arrangements. This shift happened after the 2005 flood by the decisive action of three Federal agencies. These agencies did not act in a belief-neutral way but advocated for policy change very much in line with sectoral needs and with their own interests. So all in all, we can confirm Hypothesis 3a: the public administration acted as policy entrepreneurs in a subsystem with two conflicting coalitions that both finally followed the suggestions of these three key actors.

Nevertheless, as soon as two competing coalitions were present and the public administration engaged in entrepreneurship and brokerage, events could deploy their focal power, and paradigm change toward collaborative governance became possible.

Conclusion

The aim of this chapter was to study the conditions under which a special event, shock, or catastrophe becomes a so-called focusing event and manages to induce a fundamental shift in the collaborative approach toward disaster management. We were thus interested in the long-term consequences of a natural disaster that are reflected in regulation and policy but also in how actors interact and how institutions are arranged.

We investigated more than 100 years of flood risk management in Switzerland and compared floods that deployed focal power with those that did not. Process tracing, a mix of qualitative and quantitative data, and the study of primary and secondary literature helped us to first identify so-called sequences. Each sequence consisted of a paradigm shift and therefore defined a new way in which Switzerland would tackle floods by introducing policies and regulations to protect the population from natural hazards. In summary, we could identify three shifts: in 1877, the shift toward infrastructure; in 1991, toward spatial planning; and in 2010, toward integrated flood prevention. This last shift was clearly a move toward collaborative and cross-sectoral governance in flood risk management. We therefore proceeded in a two-step approach and first identified factors for change and second factors for "collaborative" governance.

Results showed that no clear indicator can be identified as the unique factor that makes a flood (or potentially any other catastrophe or shock) a focusing event. Even in the area affected, the financial and infrastructural damages or the number of deaths seemed to have a certain impact on the focal power of a flood, this "objective" magnitude could not be identified as the decisive reason for making the flood a focusing event.

We cannot confirm our second hypothesis either: the presence of advocacy coalitions in a subsystem affected by an external shock does not automatically lead to policy change. But still, politics matter. Our analysis showed that the most decisive factors for floods being defined as focusing events are (1) political activism and (2) subsystem properties. We conclude that a flood can deploy more focal power best when it is absorbed by organized action.

Furthermore, the subsystem characteristics that seem to matter are not so much related to the question of "how well interests are organized and consolidated in so-called larger advocacy coalitions." It seems that some specific organized interests and actors (such as key experts or core administrative agencies) can already take advantage of the momentum and transform a flood or external shock into a focusing event inducing a paradigm shift. What does this tell us about the potential for collaborative governance in flood risk management? Intuitively, and based on former research, collaboration should lead to collaborative solutions. More concretely, if a shock induces that actors from different coalitions to perceive a problem as severe, this fact should foster their willingness to cooperate and to start searching for collaborative, cross-sectoral, and multilevel solutions. But this logic could not be found here. Instead a few key actors, so-called entrepreneurs, were instrumental in pushing the system after the 2005 flood toward more integration and cross-sectoral flood risk management. These policy solutions will have to be implemented by actors from different sectors belonging to diverse jurisdictions and defending divergent interests. So only policy implementation will ultimately show if a collaborative policy design induced by some policy entrepreneurs can also deploy effectiveness and efficiency.

This study has shown that it is necessary to not only take objective measurements of a disaster into account but also to identify the political circumstances and subsystem conditions at the moment an event happens in order to explain fundamental changes in collaborative approaches toward disaster management. Future research should more systematically draw upon comparative evidence and thus include more robust statistical and cross-country or cross-field analysis in order to disentangle problem characteristics from politics. Finally, we have seen that the case analyzed here, and flood risk management in Switzerland, is embedded in a multilevel and federalist setting. An interesting question arises about whether the impact of focusing events and the results uncovered here would also hold true for policies designed at the regional and subnational level.

References

BAFU (Bundesamt für Umwelt) [FOEN-Federal Office for the Environment]. 2013. *Adaptation in Europe-Addressing Risks and Opportunities from Climate Change in the Context of Socio-Economic Developments*. Bern: Federal Office for the Environment.

———. 2012a. *Adaptation to Climate Change in Switzerland: Goals, Challenges and Fields of Action*. Bern: Federal Office for the Environment.

———. 2012b. *Impacts of Climate Change on Water Resources and Watercourses*. Synthesis report on the "Climate Change and Hydrology in Switzerland" (CCHydro) project. Umwelt-Wissen Nr.1217. Bern: Federal Office for the Environment.

Baumgartner, Frank. 2013. "Ideas and Policy Change." *Governance* 26 (2): 239–58.

Baumgartner, Frank and Bryan D. Jones. 1993. *Agendas and Instability in American Politics*. Chicago, IL: University of Chicago Press.

Birkland, Thomas A. 1998. "Focusing Events, Mobilization, and Agenda Setting." *Journal of Public Policy* 18: 53–74.

———. 1997. *After Disaster: Agenda Setting, Public Policy, and Focusing Events, American Governance and Public Policy*. Washington, DC: Georgetown University Press.

Burger, Lisa. 2008. *Informationsbeschaffung bei Hochwassersituationen: Dokumentation der grössten überregionalen Hochwasserkatastrophen der letzten 200 Jahre in der Schweiz [Data and Information Gathering During Flood Events: Documentation of the Most Severe Cross-Regional Flood Catastrophes in the Last 200 Years in Switzerland]*. Bern: University of Bern.

Cairney, Paul and Christopher Weible. 2015. "Comparing and Contrasting Peter Hall's Paradigms and Ideas With the Advocacy Coalition Framework." In *Policy Paradigms in Theory and Practice*, edited by Michael Howlett and John Hogan, 83–100. Basingstoke: Palgrave.

Collier, David. 2011. "Understanding Process Tracing." *Political Science and Politics* 44 (4): 823–30.

Driessen, Peter, Carel Dieperink, Frank van Laerhoven, Hens Runhaar, and Walter Vermeulen. 2012. "Towards a Conceptual Framework for the Study of Shifts in Modes of Environmental Governance: Experiences from the Netherlands." *Environmental Policy and Governance* 22 (3): 143–60.

Flügel, Wolfgang-Albert. 2000. "Systembezogene Entwicklung regionaler hydrologischer Modellsysteme." [System-Related Development of Regional Hydrological Model Systems]. *Wasser & Boden* 52 (3): 14–17.

Furrer, Christian. 2002. "Aufbruch zu neuen Ufern." [Departure Towards New Shores]. *Aquaterra* (1): 1.

George, Alexander and Andrew Bennett. 2005. *Case Studies and Theory Development in Social Sciences*. Cambridge, MA: Massachusetts Institute of Technology Press.

Hall, Peter A. 1993. "Policy Paradigms, Social Learning, and the State: The Case of Economic Policymaking in Britain." *Comparative Politics* 25 (3): 275–96.

Hogan, John and Michael Howlett. 2015. *Policy Paradigms in Theory and Practice: Discourses, Ideas and Anomalies in Public Policy Dynamics*. Basingstoke: Palgrave.

Ingold, Karin. January 2017. "How to Create and Preserve Social Capital in Climate Adaptation Policies: A Network Approach." *Ecological Economics* 131: 414–24. doi:10.1016/j.ecolecon.2016.08.033

———. 2011. "Network Structures Within Policy Processes: Coalitions, Power, and Brokerage in Swiss Climate Policy." *Policy Studies Journal* 39 (3): 435–59.

Ingold, Karin, Peter Driessen, Hens Runhaar, and Alexander Widmer. 2018. "On the Necessity of Connectivity: Linking Key Characteristics of Environmental Problems With Governance Modes." *Journal of Environmental Planning and Management*. https://doi.org/10.1080/09640568.2018.1486700

Ingold, Karin and Frédéric Varone. 2012. "Treating Policy Brokers Seriously: Evidence from the Climate Policy." *Journal of Public Administration Research and Theory* 22 (2): 319–46.

Kingdon, John. 1995. *Agenda, Alternatives and Public Policies*. 2nd ed. New York, NY: Harper Collins.

———. 1984. *Agendas, Alternatives, and Public Policies*. New York, NY: Harper Collins.

Laumann, Edward Otto and David Knoke. 1987. *The Organizational State: Social Choice in National Policy Domains*. Madison, WI: University of Wisconsin Press.

Müller, Reto. 2004. "Das wild gewordene Element. Gesellschaftliche Reaktionen auf die beiden Hochwasser im Schweizer Mittelland von 1852 und 1876." [The Unforeseeable Element: Social Reactions on Both Flood Events in the Swiss Midland in 1852 and 1876]. In *Berner Forschungen zur Regionalgeschichte [Bernese Research on the Regional History]*. Vol. 2. Nordhausen: Traugott-Bautz Verlag.

Nohrstedt, Daniel. 2015. "Paradigms and Unintended Consequences: New Public Management Reform and Emergency Planning in Swedish Local Government." In *Policy Paradigms in Theory and Practice*, edited by Michael Howlett and John Hogan, 141–63. Basingstoke: Palgrave.

Petrascheck, Armin. 1989. "Die Hochwasser 1868 und 1987. Ein Vergleich." *Wasser Energie Luft* (1): 1–6.

Pfister, Christian. 1999. Wetternachhersage. 500 Jahre Klimavariationen und Naturkatastrophen (1496–1995). [Weather after-cast. 500 years of climate variations and natural disasters (1496–1995)] Bern: Verlag Paul Haupt.

———. 2002. *Am Tag danach. Zur Bewältigung von Naturkatastrophen in der Schweiz 1500–2000. [On the day afterwards. Coping with natural disasters in Switzerland in 1500 until 2000]* Bern: Verlag Paul Haupt.

———. 2007. *Bevölkerungsgeschichte und historische Demographie 1500–1800 [The History of Society and Its Demography in 1500 until 1800]*. 2nd ed. Munich: R. Oldenbourg Verlag.

PLANAT (National Platform for Natural Hazards). 2015. www.planat.ch/de/fachleute/strategie-naturgefahren/ (Accessed 26 January 2016).

Sabatier, Paul A. and Hank C. Jenkins-Smith. 1993. *Policy Change and Learning: An Advocacy Coalition Approach*. Boulder, CO: Westview Press.

———. 2007. "The Advocacy Coalition Framework: Innovations and Clarifications." In *Theories of the Policy Process*, 2nd ed., edited by Paul A. Sabatier, 189–220. Boulder, CO: Westview Press.

Schnitter, Niklaus. 1992. "Die Geschichte des Wasserbaus in der Schweiz." [The History of Hydraulic Engineering in Switzerland]. In *Alte Forscher aktuell [Old Scientists up-to-Date]*, 2nd ed. Oberbözberg: Olynthus.

Schulla, Jörg. 1997. *Hydrologische Modellierung von Flussgebieten zur Abschätzung der Folgen von Klimaänderung [Hydraulic Modeling of River Basins to the Evaluation of Climate Change Impacts]*. Dissertation. Zurich: ETH Zurich.

Summermatter, Stephanie. 2012. *Die Prävention von Überschwemmungen durch das politische System der Schweiz von 1848 bis 1991 [Flood Prevention by the Political System of Switzerland from 1848 to 1991]*. Dissertation. Bern: University of Bern, WSU.

Travis, William R. 2014. "Weather and Climate Extremes: Pacemakers of Adaptation?" *Weather and Climate Extremes* 5–6: 29–39.

Vischer, Daniel L. 2003. *Die Geschichte des Hochwasserschutzes in der Schweiz: Von den Anfängen bis ins 19. Jahrhundert [The History of the Flood Protection in Switzerland: From the Beginning until the 19th Century]*. Berichte des BWG, Serie Wasser-Rapports de l'OFEG, Série Eaux-Rapporti dell'UFAEG, Serie Acque 5.

Walgrave, Stefaan and Frédéric Varone. 2008. "Punctuated Equilibrium and Agenda-Setting: Bringing Parties Back in: Policy Change After the Dutroux Crisis in Belgium." *Governance: An International Journal of Policy, Administration, and Institutions* 21 (3): 365–95.

Wanner, Christine. 2016. "Ein untragbares Risiko? Naturkatastrophen als Auslöser für Lernprozesse: die Entstehung der Elementarschadenversicherung in der Schweiz." [An Unacceptable Risk? Natural Disasters as Triggers for Learning Processes: The Emergence of Hazard Insurance in Switzerland]. *Traverse: Zeitschrift für Geschichte = Revue d'histoire* 10 (3): 100–14.

Weible, Christopher, Paul Sabatier, and Andrew Pattison. 2010. "Harnessing Expert-Based Information for Learning and the Sustainable Management of Complex Socio-Ecological Systems." *Environmental Science & Policy* 13: 522–34.

WSL database. 2016. *Swiss Federal Institute for Forest, Snow and Landscape Research (WSL)*. www.wsl.ch/fe/gebirgshydrologie/dossiers/hochwasser/index_DE (Accessed 26 January 2016).

Zahariadis, Nikolaos. 2007. "The Multiple Streams Framework: Structure, Limitations, Prospects." In *Theories of the Policy Process*, 2nd ed., edited by Paul Sabatier, 66–92. Boulder, CO: Westview Press.

Zaugg, Marc. 2006. *Philosophiewandel im schweizerischen Wasserbau: Zur Vollzugspraxis des nachhaltigen Hochwasserschutzes [Philosophy Change in Swiss Hydraulic Engineering: Towards the Implementation of Sustainable Flood Prevention]*. Publication Series in Human Geography. Vol. 20. Zurich: University of Zurich, GIUZ.

Appendix II

Table of Regulations and Legal Texts Taken Into Account for Paradigm Shift Identification

Decision	In Force	Policy and regulation	SR	Type	Amendment
22 June 1877	6 October 1877	Hydraulic Engineering Inspectorate Act	721.10	Act	Introduction
11 October 1902	1902 (until 1 January 1993)	Forest Inspectorate Act (new)	921.0	Act	Introduction
20 June 1975	7 December 1975	Federal Constitution	101	Constitution	Revision
22 June 1979	1 January 1980	Spatial Planning Act	700	Act	Introduction
24 January 1991	1 November 1992	Water Protection Act	814.20	Act	Introduction
21 June 1991	1 January 1993	Hydraulic Engineering Act	721.100	Act	Introduction
4 October 1991	1 January 1993	Forest Act	921.0	Act	Introduction
30 November 1992	1 January 1993	Forest Ordinance	921.01	Ordinance	Introduction
2 November 1994	1 December 1994	Hydraulic Engineering Ordinance	721.100.1	Ordinance	Introduction
1997	1997	PLANAT			Introduction
28 October 1998	1 January 1999	Water Protection Ordinance	814.201	Ordinance	Introduction
7 December 1998 (until 17 October 2012)	1 January 1999 (until 1 January 2013)	Water Retaining Facilities Ordinance	721.102	Ordinance	Introduction
28 October 1998	1 January 1999	Hydraulic Engineering Ordinance	721.100.1	Ordinance	Revision
6 December 1999	1 January 2000	Hydraulic Engineering Ordinance	721.100.1	Ordinance	Revision
18 June 1999	6 December 1999	Forest Act	921.0	Act	Revision
8 November 2000	20 August 2003	Strategy Natural Hazards PLANAT		Strategy	Introduction

(Continued)

Decision	In Force	Policy and regulation	SR	Type	Amendment
20 August 2003	18 May 2005	Strategy Natural Hazards CH		Strategy	
18 May 2005	2008	Action Plan		Strategy	
6 March 2009	2011	Action Plan II		Strategy	
11 December 2009	1 January 2011	Hydraulic Engineering Act	721.100	Act	Revision
11 December 2009	1 January 2011	Hydraulic Engineering Ordinance	721.100.1	Ordinance	Revision
11 December 2009	1 January 2011	Water Protection Act	814.20	Act	Revision
11 December 2009	1 January 2011	Water Protection Ordinance	814.201	Ordinance	Revision
18 August 2010	1 January 2011	Alerting Ordinance	520.12	Act	Introduction
26 May 2010	26 May 2010	OWARNA		Strategy	Introduction
2010	2010	GIN		Strategy	Introduction
1 October 2010	1 January 2013	Water Retaining Facilities Act (new)	721.101	Act	Introduction
2 March 2012	3 April 2012	Climate Change Adaptation Strategy I		Strategy	Introduction
16 March 2012	1 July 2013	Forest Act	921.0	Act	Revision
17 October 2012	1 January 2013	Water Retaining Facilities Ordinance	721.101.1	Ordinance	Introduction
25 April 2012	24 July 2012	Biodiversity Strategy CH		Strategy	Introduction
22 March 2013	1 August 2013	Water Protection Act	814.20	Act	Revision
14 June 2013	1 June 2013	Forest Ordinance	921.01	Ordinance	Revision
2014	2014	Climate Change Adaptation Strategy II		Strategy	Introduction

Chapter 12

Lessons and Avenues for Future Research in Collaborative Crisis Management

Daniel Nohrstedt and Fredrik Bynander

This book departs from the observation that crisis management is a policy area where there is a strong emphasis on collaborative approaches to governance. This is a field where academics and practitioners generally agree on the importance and merits of making diverse stakeholders work together toward formulating shared goals and orchestrating joint solutions, approaches to problem solving, and working methods. Commitment and engagement with collaboration are often based on the insight – sometimes gained through first-hand experience – that complex and transboundary risks and threats cannot be effectively addressed by one single actor, government, or sector.

Meanwhile, taking the step from this generic understanding to actually accomplishing viable collaboration among diverse stakeholders across organizational boundaries is no easy task. It is well known that ambitions and practices of collaboration oftentimes conflict with the everyday reality of bureaucratic fragmentation, scarce resources, uncertainty, and shortsighted, self-interested behavior among stakeholders. Social and psychological barriers to collaboration are also recognized and include divergent understandings, values, beliefs, and perspectives that are difficult to reconcile. Collaboration furthermore brings significant costs in terms of time, resources, and commitment at the expense of organizational priorities (Hicklin, O'Toole, and Meier 2007; Meier and O'Toole 2003; Nohrstedt 2018a). The available evidence and practical experience point to an interesting variation concerning the outcomes of these efforts.

This is also something that we have observed throughout this book where efforts to achieve collaboration have led to different results and varying levels of success. These differences are representative of a more general pattern; in some cases actors manage to overcome barriers and engage in meaningful collaboration that achieves desired outcomes, while in other cases these efforts are merely superficial, symbolic, or even counterproductive. In some cases hierarchical, centralized, top-down approaches would even have been more effective in achieving desired outcomes. Understanding the factors, mechanisms, and circumstances that help explain these variations within and across cases of collaboration is a legitimate concern for building theory and informing practice.

The ambition of this book, however, is not to provide a definitive answer to the question of what may explain differences across cases of collaborative crisis management. Neither do we attempt to formulate a general framework or some grand theory capturing all the conditions, considerations, drivers, and mechanisms that influence the formation, maintenance, and performance of collaborative arrangements in different cases and context.[1] Rather, by providing insight into individual cases of collaborative crisis management in different settings and contexts, we hope to contribute to broader scholarly and practical understandings concerning structures (institutional arrangements, organizational architectures, networks, etc.) and processes (formation, maintenance, performance, etc.) of collaboration in relation to different societal risks and extreme events. This task is first and foremost accomplished by the individual chapters – each which offers a unique and detailed narrative of one or several instances of collaborative crisis management.

The objective of this concluding chapter is to summarize and discuss some of the major insights and lessons that have emerged from these studies. In doing so, we will avoid as much as possible to repeat the case-specific details presented in each chapter. Instead, we aim at a comparison across cases to tease apart both localized nuances (unique observations or experiences in each individual case) and generalized patterns (similarities and recurrent observations across cases) concerning collaborative crisis management. This is an endeavor guided by a mixture of deductive and inductive ambitions; we make observations and draw inferences from the cases by returning to some of the conceptual and theoretical starting points presented in the introductory chapter but also by highlighting interesting observations emerging from the presentation of each individual case.

Localized Nuances and Generalized Patterns

We begin our summary analysis by stating the obvious: crisis management is an area where collaboration has become a strong norm and an established practice. Accordingly, collaboration is generally seen as something positive and a goal that many actors strive for, to effectively prepare for, respond to, recover from, and learn from extreme events. The contributors to this book have demonstrated that this is evident across countries, problem areas, and levels of authority. Despite these contextual differences, in most of the cases we have seen different examples of how collaboration has been the overarching organizing principle for orchestrating societal responses to threats, risks, and events at different scales. Obviously this observation is partially a product of selection bias since we began this project by looking for illustrative examples of collaborative crisis management. Nevertheless, what is striking about all of the cases is how collaboration repeatedly emerges as a managerial challenge that requires time, attention, and effort by many actors.

This observation echoes the longstanding insight in the disaster and emergency management literature that the effort to respond to unscheduled events itself creates a series of demands besides the problems brought by the event as such (Quarantelli 1997). That is, organized efforts to collectively respond to any type of crisis, disaster, or emergency are likely to generate problems that stem from the process of establishing and maintaining a collaborative response, including, for example, swift mobilization and coordination of personnel and resources, delegation of tasks, division of labor, communication, and joint decision making.

Breadth of Arrangements and Relationships

Although collaboration emerges as an important feature of crisis management, the level or intensity of collaboration varies considerably across cases and contexts. This variation applies across episodes of crisis management but also within cases through time. Returning briefly to collaboration as a theoretical concept, some scholars define it as interactions that go deeper than just doing things together. In this view, collaboration entails efforts to solve or address problems that no single organization can solve alone, which in turn requires purposive relationships and joint actions that go beyond cooperation (Agranoff 2012). The turbulent environment of crisis – including the simultaneous occurrence of threat, uncertainty, and urgency to take action – brings considerable challenges to establishing and maintaining such relationships.

The cases investigated in this book showcase a variety of different types of collaborative arrangements that have been put in place to facilitate and enhance collaboration during crisis preparedness, recovery, and response. As we suggested in the introduction, these arrangements range from relatively informal and fluid forums for stakeholder interaction to more formalized inter-organizational structures. Yet, we have also seen examples of collaboration (or efforts to achieve collaboration) unfolding without any clear institutional structures in place to support interaction. This is perhaps a recurrent challenge in crisis management more generally, when actors are confronted with unprecedented or unforeseen events for which there is limited or no institutional preparedness. One example includes the Swedish response to the 2015 migration crisis (Hansén and Deverell, this volume), which was handled largely within established bureaucratic structures with some organizations taking the role as intermediaries. For instance, whereas there was some uncertainty about the County Administrative Board's role, SALAR (Swedish Association of Local Authorities and Regions) – which lacked formal responsibility in times of crisis – took on a coordinating role. Meanwhile, although the collective response involved multiple actors from different levels of government and sectors, there were no evident institutional forms for fostering deeper collaboration. Scott, Bos, and Noordegraaf (this volume) similarly observed that the Dutch response to the ISIS threat was orchestrated by a relatively fluid and informal process where collaboration initially largely hinged on personal relationships. In that case though, local level coalitions of different stakeholders gradually emerged as the result of trial-and-error and were eventually formalized as hubs for coordinating shared interventions. In contrast, Kuipers and Swinkels (this volume) provide an illustration of more pre-planned collaborative structures, both at strategic and operational levels in preparation for the summits in the Hague and Toronto. In both cases, these included strategic level committees with representatives from different government organizations as well as operational level coordination.

In their chapter on transregional networks in Africa, Hollis and Olsson (this volume) present an overview of the range of institutional arrangements that have evolved to facilitate cross-boundary collaboration in crisis preparedness. Their investigation of 719 meetings demonstrates the broad variety of collaborative arrangements that have been put in place to support preparedness across the African continent. These entail examples of arrangements for addressing different policy issues (security being the most prominent issue), a combination of formalized and *ad hoc* arrangements, and meetings devoted to different tasks, including information sharing, analysis, and decision making. Across the period investigated (2014–2016), only the minority of the meetings examined were devoted to acute crisis events, focusing on, for example, epidemics, terrorism, and armed conflicts.

In some of the cases studied here collaboration has been coordinated, or "mandated," in a top-down fashion. Sometimes collaboration is depicted in terms of self-organization, as a process where autonomous organizations come together on equal terms in efforts to work together to formulate and implement shared goals based on voluntary participation (O'Leary and Bingham 2009). In the literature on collaborative governance and crisis management, this model of self-organization is sometimes juxtaposed to an alternative model based on a pre-planned and semi-hierarchical system for creating authority across organizational and jurisdictional boundaries. For instance, self-organization is assumed to be more apt to flexibility, adaptation, innovation, and improvisation – qualities that are often associated with effective crisis management – while hierarchical models have been deemed less suitable for achieving these qualities (Ansell, Boin, and Keller 2010; Farazmand 2007; Waugh and Streib 2006).

The evidence collected for the purpose of this book is, however, not sufficient for drawing any robust conclusions regarding the relationship between forms of collaborative arrangements and crisis management performance. This issue brings considerable analytical challenges, including collecting empirical evidence to document the impact of arrangements on performance across cases. Nevertheless, the chapter comparing wildfire responses between Canada and Sweden (Nohrstedt et al., this volume) gives some insight into how institutional features may condition the response. Nohrstedt and colleagues found that although the crisis management systems of Canada and Sweden display considerable differences in terms of system design, both wildfire responses gave rise to similar challenges. Actors in both cases faced the issue of when to scale up the response to the next level. Also, in both Canada and Sweden regional level actors shared a concern that local actors were short of resources but did not ask for assistance in managing the wildfires from the regional level. Although these examples do not inform the broader issue of system effectiveness, they do suggest that the same managerial challenges tend to emerge regardless of system design.

Inclusiveness and Trust

The "inclusiveness" of processes and arrangements for collaborative crisis management also presents a potential tradeoff between incorporating too many actors and too few. Throughout this book we have seen several examples of collaboration involving a large number of individuals from many different organizations. For instance, actors engaged in the response to the 2014 Västmanland wildfire in Sweden had to devote considerable time and energy to achieve coordination, including finding appropriate organizational forms and routines for ensuring effective communication and information sharing across organizational boundaries (Bynander, this volume). This challenge is evident in cases where there is no preexisting institutional structure in place (the Swedish wildfire response) but also in cases where institutional structures and routines are in place but have to be "activated" (for example, the Canadian wildfire response) (Nohrstedt et al., this volume; Bodin et al. 2019). In contrast, in other cases the circle of participants is drawn too narrowly, which brings other problems when actors with competence, skills, and decision authority are excluded from collaboration (Boin and 't Hart 2010). For example, it was noted that in the Dutch response to the ISIS threat during 2013 and 2014, schools and welfare organizations were largely excluded from the multi-organizational coalitions that were formed to coordinate local level responses, which led to more security-focused interventions (Scott, Bos, and Noordegraaf, this volume).

It is often argued that viable collaboration generally depends on reciprocal trust between individuals, which is needed to ensure that individuals will not defect or freeride on others (Berardo 2009; Huxham et al. 2000; Klijn, Edelenbos, and Steijn 2010). Relationships based on trust are certainly a key ingredient in many examples of crisis management, including cases where individuals rely upon preexisting relationships with other individuals as the basis for ensuring a coordinated response to turbulent events. Building and maintaining such networks of interpersonal relations is a way to prepare for extreme events through efforts to reduce transaction costs; that is, to remove some of the potential hurdles for achieving collaboration in response to extreme events. This was noted, for instance, by Hermansson (this volume) in the chapter on collaborative crisis management in Turkey, which demonstrated that regular joint training helped in building relationships that facilitated collaboration among regional state actors and NGO representatives in response to the 2011 Van earthquake. However, in some situations actors have no choice but to initiate new relationships with individuals with whom they have no previous contact. It can also be noted that the very same event is likely to entail a significant number of new relationships. The two wildfires in Canada and Sweden, for example, illustrated that many actors had to establish collaboration with individuals with whom they had no preexisting relationships (Nohrstedt et al., this volume). One interviewee in the Canadian case estimated that during the Fort McMurray wildfire, approximately 30% of all relationships were among individuals who had not collaborated before. Hence, in these cases, many instances of collaboration are not based on trust established through prior interactions among individuals.

These experiences illustrate the breadth of relationships emerging during complex extreme events, ranging from the "activation" of pre-established relationships among actors who already know each other, to the formation of entirely new collaborative ties between actors who have never worked together before (Bodin et al. 2019). This observation has some immediate practical implications concerning planning and preparing for collaborative crisis management, which ideally should strike the right balance between training and education of predetermined clusters of actors and other actors that are typically not considered for crisis management. In terms of planning and preparedness, this means that it is important to consider both the range of known risks that are more or less likely to materialize as well as events that are more unknown, or even unknowable, which helps to ensure a relatively inclusive approach to collaborative crisis management (Boin and 't Hart 2010).

The mixture of preexisting and new relationships also brings intriguing new research questions regarding the formation, maintenance, and performance of collaborative crisis management. One way to enhance knowledge about these aspects of collaboration is to view collaboration as the result of the choices that individual actors make. In theory, every individual that is involved in responding to an extreme event will face multiple choices about what other individuals they should collaborate with, what forums to participate in, and what tasks to engage with. Due to resource scarcity, these choices imply making strategic decisions concerning how to spend time, energy, and other resources wisely. What motives guide these choices represent an interesting area of future work. This is particularly interesting in the context of crisis management where uncertainty and urgency impose constraints on individual choice. For example, recent studies suggest that actors have a tendency to select their collaboration partners based on risk aversion and uncertainty about costs and benefits that in turn appear to be shaped by the organizational context in which collaboration unfolds – specifically whether collaboration unfolds between individuals within the same organization, across organizations at the same scale, or across scales (Bodin et al. 2019; Bodin and Nohrstedt 2016; Nohrstedt and Bodin 2019). Exploring further how these factors influence collaboration constitutes an important topic for advancing our understanding of collaboration. Yet, this also brings significant methodological challenges concerning the collection of data about collaborative ties among many different individuals and organizations as well as measurement of the outcomes and impacts of collaboration.

Uncertainty and Conflict

Our book also corroborates insights in the broader literature on collaborative governance and public management about uncertainty and conflict. It has been noted that, in theory, collaboration is both a strategy to reduce uncertainty about complex problems as well as a source of uncertainty related to interactions among individuals representing different organizations. While collaboration is essential to pool resources and facilitate coordination, it is also likely to be accompanied by considerable uncertainty about other actors' capacities, intentions, and actions. Uncertainty may also emerge as the result of differences in language, rules, opinions, and tasks (Koppenjan and Klijn 2004). This observation again corroborates the insight that collaboration may create additional demands in the midst of crisis that have to be addressed so that it can be turned into an asset for collectively mitigating risks and threats.

The chapters in this book convey several examples where efforts to achieve collaboration have resulted in frictions, tensions, and conflicts among actors. A recurrent pattern among the cases studied here is that these conflicts emerged as the result of divergent views among stakeholders concerning proper organizational forms for addressing acute problems effectively. For example, Kuipers and Swinkels (this volume) show that during preparations for the Nuclear Security Summit in The Hague, an intense dispute erupted between the local police and the special police forces about the integration of command centers on the site of the summit. Similarly, Hansén and Deverell (this volume) noted that friction emerged between the local governments and the national level authorities concerning the coordination of the response to the 2015 migration crisis in Sweden. Some tensions between actors at different levels of authority were also noted in the chapter on the response to the 2014 wildfire in Sweden, where disagreements emerged between representatives of the municipalities and the regional level actors concerning the role of the different organizations involved in the response (Nohrstedt et al., this volume; Bynander, this volume).

Such tensions may clearly hamper crisis management performance. For example, in the case of the 2011 earthquake in Van, Turkey, Hermansson (this volume) observed that the lack of collaboration between the municipal and provincial actors caused problems that forced many residents to leave the city. In this case, the conflict originated in a deeper political controversy, which also led to other problems – such as poor assessments of houses and of the building stock after the 2011 earthquakes. Meanwhile, we noted in several chapters that these conflicts did occur but did not seem to have a negative effect on the outcome of the collective crisis response. Taken together, the evidence presented by the chapters suggests that conflict is a recurrent feature of collaborative crisis management, yet actors often find ways to overcome it – or at least take action to ensure that it does not have a negative impact on collective action.

This insight regarding conflict is not new; on the contrary, it is consistent with the observation in the literature that tensions among participants in collaborative networks are inevitable and thus something that demands continuous attention among managers and leaders (O'Leary and Bingham 2009). Indeed one should recognize that some of these conflicts can have negative consequences by constraining or even paralyzing collective-action. This is also true for episodes of crisis management, which may give rise to bureau-political rifts during planning, response, and recovery (Rosenthal, 't Hart, and Kouzmin 1991), as well as contests among broader coalitions of policy actors and stakeholders concerning the appropriate approach for crisis resolution (Boin, 't Hart, and McConnell 2009; Nohrstedt 2013), including learning and the need for policy change and reform (Ingold and Gavilano, this volume).

The potential costs that emerge following such conflicts can be high, since they may reduce the early warning and response capacity of a system. In return, considerable effort may be devoted to prevent conflict from occurring (O'Leary and Vij 2012). Yet, one of the lessons that can be drawn from this book is that conflicts may not necessarily hamper collective efforts to cope with crisis and reduce risks. For instance, Kuipers and Swinkels (this volume) shared an example from the preparations for the Nuclear Security Summit network in The Hague, where an intense conflict erupted between the local police and the special police force concerning the inclusion of local emergency services in the operational command center inside the secured zone. In this particular episode, according to Kuipers and Swinkels, the disagreement initially harmed the reputation of the police, among other emergent response organizations; however, in the end the integrated command center worked well.

Future Research

Issues of collaborative governance and management attract considerable scholarly attention across fields and issue areas. Collaborative crisis management is no exception, and the field is constantly evolving with the addition of new cases, methodological advances, and theoretical insights. We end this book by looking forward and discussing briefly what avenues of future research may emerge from the chapters presented here and what may be the next important steps to push the knowledge frontier.

We recently conducted a systematic literature review to identify some of the dominating themes and avenues for future research in collaborative crisis management (Nohrstedt et al. 2018). The cases reviewed in this book may be seen as an initial evaluation to probe the plausibility of the questions and themes that emerged from the review. Hereby we can draw on the insights presented in our book to advance this research agenda further by proposing theoretical specifications as well as identifying more general themes and issues that deserve future empirical work. Taking our review as the point of departure, we identified seven areas that emerged as particularly interesting and promising as a basis for pushing the research frontier regarding collaborative crisis management:

1. **Examine emergent *ad hoc* collaborative arrangements to draw lessons and insights about ways to speed up processes of network formation and collective action.** This book entails several examples of *ad hoc* arrangements that formed and evolved in the heat of the moment to support and facilitate inter-organizational collaboration for mitigating urgent threats and risks. We have also seen examples of collaboration that developed gradually through trial-and-error in response to drawn-out risks and threats such as the ISIS threat in the Netherlands (Scott, Bos, and Noordegraaf, this volume). These examples are interesting in light of the longstanding observation concerning the role of trust as an essential feature of well-functioning collaborations. In some of the cases reviewed here, the actors did not have the luxury of time to build relationships based on repeated interactions through joint planning and preparation prior to the event. In other cases, the crisis experience exposed institutional gaps where arrangements for collaboration were largely lacking. But despite this, one observation that we make here is that actors are relatively skilled at overcoming transaction costs and engaging in well-functioning collaboration even under the most pressing conditions and in the absence of preexisting interpersonal relationships based on trust. Thus, we expect that future work will continue exploring how institutional conditions (combinations of formal rules and informal norms), different types of collaborative networks, and the attributes and skills of individual actors may make or break emergent collaborative arrangements for crisis management.
2. **Develop, refine, and apply evaluation frameworks for assessing both crisis response performance at large and collaborative performance in the context of both situational and institutional crises.** None of the chapters in this book have explicitly investigated issues associated with crisis management performance. Some of the authors nevertheless discuss, based on their detailed knowledge of the cases, aspects of collaboration that worked well, as well as instances of failure or suboptimal solutions and actions. These observations include diverse experiences from, for instance, processes of resource mobilization, communication, coordination, and joint decision making. What remains here, though, is to come up with ways to systematically assess collective performance in different types of cases. In this regard, the approach by Parker and Sundelius (this volume) is helpful as a basis for identifying potential sources of failure in collaborative crisis management as well as prescriptions for

diminishing their occurrence. Scholars and students can also build from preexisting frameworks and approaches using insights from the study of successes and failures in public policy in general and in crisis management in particular. These approaches offer clearly defined concepts and criteria for evaluating specific aspects of collaboration associated with processes (concerning, e.g., contingency planning and early warning), decisions (by individuals at strategic and operational levels to intervene or not in an event or situation and the timing for doing so), and politics (efforts to manage the potential impacts of crises on the reputation of actors and institutions and on policy agendas) (McConnell 2011). One interesting implication from this work is that performance may differ across the different dimensions of collaboration; for instance, the process of collaboration may work well, while the end result might not be depicted in a positive light, and vice versa. In addition, other important insights concerning the evaluation of collaborative crisis management can be gained by combining this approach with evaluation frameworks associated specifically with collaborative governance and management (see, e.g., special issues in *Public Performance & Management Review* [2014–2015, Vol. 38] and *Public Management Review* [2008, Vol. 10]). These frameworks may also be combined with approaches for assessing crisis and emergency management specifically (Boin and 't Hart 2010; Henstra 2010; Quarantelli 1997).

3. **Enhance knowledge of the obstacles that managers confront when attempting to change and improve institutional arrangements to facilitate collaboration in crisis management.** The scientific literature has documented a long list of barriers and hurdles that obstruct managers from engaging in and facilitating collaborative governance. The context of crisis brings a unique set of challenges associated with, for example, diagnosing fast-moving situations, formulating and deciding a response, mobilizing operational resources, and communicating across organizational boundaries and to the general public (Boin and 't Hart 2010). As suggested by the chapters in this book, managers are likely to face several obstacles that may prevent them from addressing these challenges effectively through collaboration. These obstacles include, for instance, legal requirements, lack of shared experience (Hansén and Deverell, this volume), disagreements concerning proper organizational forms for supporting collaboration (Nohrstedt et al., this volume), narrow problem framing (Scott, Bos, and Noordegraaf, this volume), divergent perceptions concerning the meaning of collaboration (Hermansson, this volume), culture clashes between organizations (Kuipers and Swinkels, this volume), and economic considerations (Larsson, this volume). These insights are not novel or unique to these cases, yet they do confirm the multiplicity of obstacles that work against collaboration in different contexts. At the same time, we have noted instances of well-functioning collaboration in situations where it was perhaps not expected, given our knowledge of obstacles. Consequently, we theorize here that there is perhaps a hierarchy among those obstacles where some are more difficult to overcome than others. Identifying what these obstacles are and what strategies or approaches actors utilize to overcome them is one intriguing area for future work. Here we particularly recommend the chapter by Parker and Sundelius (this volume), which proposes several prescriptions for overcoming sources of failures associated with collaborative crisis management. Their suggested prescriptions – for example institutionalizing and exercising imagination as a means of building collective capacity to detect, diagnose, and respond to surprise events – can serve as a guide for examining obstacles to collaborative crisis management and ways to overcome them in various settings.

4. **Expand the empirical focus beyond single networks or venues to consider coordination across multiple networks that engage in linked collective-action problems and overlapping policy issues.** The issue of institutional complexity – the diverse mix of collaborative institutions, collective-action problems, and actors – is a central feature of many policy issues, including matters associated with crisis management. As noted by Lubell, Robins, and Wang (2014, 1), this complexity is "not a hypothesis; it is the everyday reality faced by policy makers." Several of the chapters in this book confirm that risks and extreme events are managed by multiple actors working together within relatively complex settings of interdependent problems, overlapping venues for deliberation and decision making, and networks. Traditionally, crisis (emergency and disaster) management scholars have taken a narrow perspective on collaboration by studying single networks at each time. Obviously, there are some practical reasons for doing so since institutional complexity brings major methodological challenges to analysts interested in reconstructing and examining patterns of collaboration *postmortem*. Also, empirically documenting cases of institutional complexity in the context of rapidly evolving events is perhaps even more demanding compared to cases where there is less urgency. Nevertheless, the chapters presented here provide some insight into what these "networks of networks" may look like concerning participation, coordination, and performance. Here loom several important questions for future research. For example, how do individual actors make decisions concerning what collaborative venues to participate in given the scarcity of time and other resources and the complex set of arrangements available to them? How can effective communication across collaborative forums be ensured to achieve coordination and implementation of decisions? A handful of studies (McAllister et al. 2015; Nohrstedt 2018b) have begun to empirically investigate coordination between actors across forums in more acute events and situations, yet this remains an important topic for more research.

5. **Engage in comparative studies of how governmental actors meta-govern (design, authorize, steer, steward) crisis management networks and to what effect.** Although meta-governance has not been the main topic for the chapters in this book (except the chapter by Oscar Larsson, which goes into some depth with meta-governance in relation to implementation of communication systems) several of them offer examples and insights for advancing research concerning the forms and effects of network governance in the context of collaborative crisis management. One recurrent observation concerns the active participation and involvement of governmental actors in processes and structures for collaboration. These activities come in different forms, from "hands-on" efforts to directly promote collaboration among diverse sets of stakeholders to "hands-off" measures to influence the political and organizational context for collaboration via framing and provision of support and facilitation (Sorensen and Torfing 2009). The diversity of these governance approaches and the reasons for adopting them in cases of crisis management deserves further theoretical and empirical scrutiny. By extension, the topic of meta-governance is also highly relevant when connected with types of collaborative arrangements (theme 1) and crisis management performance (theme 2). As recognized elsewhere and in our introductory chapter (Bynander and Nohrstedt, this volume), societies face a broad range of risks and threats, which when they materialize also result in different crisis trajectories. One important topic to investigate further concerns the flexibility and adaptive capacity of meta-governance arrangements, including the extent to which state actors that participate in collaborative crisis management can switch from steering (hands-on) to facilitation (hands-off).

6. **Examine how crisis actors can co-construct productive forms of crisis-induced policy learning and institutional consolidation and adaptation.** Issues associated with the evolution of collaboration, including learning and change, remain one of the most understudied aspects of collaborative governance in general (Gerlak and Heikkila 2011) and collaborative crisis management in particular (Nohrstedt et al. 2018). Based on the findings reported in the chapters in this book, we are able to identify some useful lessons and insights that can help advance the understanding of these issues. One interesting observation is that collaboration does not necessarily evolve as the result of deliberate reforms but rather emerges as individual actors deepen and cultivate interpersonal relationships through time. Some examples described in this book – for example in the chapter on collaboration in the wake of earthquakes in Turkey (Hermansson, this volume) – indicate that such relationships can emerge from shared experiences of dramatic events. We have also seen examples of intra-crisis learning (Moynihan 2008) where actors in the midst of an unfolding crisis take action to adapt collective responses and correct mistakes or systemic flaws. Some evidence reported in this book suggests that such "adaptation" may be driven by the intervention of a hierarchically superior actor as well as initiatives by single organizations to address voids in the collaborative response (see, for example, Hansén and Deverell, this volume). Besides learning and adaptation during an event, clearly more work is needed to examine the role of collaboration in fostering learning *after* or *from* events. This is another aspect that has received sparse attention in this book, except for the chapter by Ingold and Gavilano (this volume) on the role of major flooding events in shaping paradigm shifts in Swiss flood risk management policy. Some prior work on the topic of learning in the context of collaboration and crisis management suggests that the process of drawing lessons and thinking about ways to transform those lessons into new guidelines, rules, or practices is likely to take place away from the media spotlight and with limited public interest and insight (Boin and 't Hart 2010). The result, however, may be profoundly important, as collective efforts to draw lessons may strengthen relationships, correct flaws, and improve the overall capacity of a response system. Hence, we hope more empirical work can be devoted to examining how such learning processes unfold, focusing on participation and influence, ways of overcoming destructive blame games and accountability processes, what results may come out of efforts to draw lessons, and how lessons learned and implemented can enhance performance in subsequent events (Nohrstedt and Parker 2014).

7. **Enhance the understanding of how actors overcome real or perceived costs of engaging in collaboration toward building generic capacity in preparation of uncertain future events.** The issue of overcoming transaction costs is one of the most widely studied topics in the vast literature on collective-action and collaborative governance. Questions regarding how transaction costs constrain collective action during major crises, emergencies, and disasters are also relatively well covered by the literature, including recent work studying collaborative crisis management as institutional collective-action dilemmas (Jung, Song, and Feiock 2019). Again, obstacles to collaboration have also been studied in depth in the chapters in this book. Based on these insights, we have already come a long way in developing the understanding of how various costs impose constraints on collaborative crisis management and what strategies may be employed to effectively prevent these costs from constraining collective-action. Several issues deserve closer attention in order to advance this understanding further. The starting point for addressing some of these issues is the recognition of the unique features of crisis management as an area of decision making and governance. From a

planning perspective, preparing for a crisis involves major costs (time, money, organizational capital, etc.), yet the end goal of community preparedness, resilience, safety, and security is relatively diffuse. Furthermore, individuals' perceptions of the meaning and importance of collaboration are likely to vary (see Hermansson, this volume). In research and practice alike, there is a strong claim being made that these goals require an inclusive approach based on ideals associated with participatory governance and voluntarism. In addition, a strong case is also being made that crisis management needs to build on innovation, improvisation, and adaptation (Farazmand 2007; Waugh and Streib 2006). These attributes sometimes clash, and it might be difficult for some actors to justify why they should bear the costs of collaboration. How actors in different sectors, at different levels of authority and within different jurisdictions, weigh the costs and benefits of collaboration in preparation for a crisis will continue to be an important issue for theory and practice.

The next step is for researchers and students with an interest in collaborative approaches to societal security, resilience, and crisis management to take an active part in developing, expanding, and specifying this research agenda further. The seven themes detailed here are by no means an exhaustive list of topics that define the field, and there are definitely other issues and questions that also deserve more attention in order to enhance the understanding of collaborative crisis management. Dialogues and interactions with practitioners also hold great potential as a source to elaborate new insights and lessons concerning the meaning, role, and effects of collaboration in different settings. This includes, for example, different understandings of what collaboration actually means to different stakeholders and what strategies may be employed for achieving viable collaboration given time and other resource constraints. Conversely, it is our experience that practitioners are often genuinely interested in what research has to offer in terms of the conceptual understanding of collaboration, what factors may condition collaboration in different contexts and cases, and how it can be evaluated and improved through time. Engaging in such dialogues is one important strategy for pushing the research frontier and supporting the practice of collaborative crisis management.

Note

1. We refer readers interested in integrated frameworks of collaborative governance arrangements to any of the following references: Ansell and Gash (2007); Bryson, Crosby, and Stone (2006); Emerson and Nabatchi (2015); Leach, Pelkey, and Sabatier (2002); Mandell and Keast (2008); Newig et al. (2017); Provan and Kenis (2007); Turrini, Cristofoli, and Nasi (2009).

References

Agranoff, Robert. 2012. *Collaborating to Manage: A Primer for the Public Sector.* Washington, DC: Georgetown University Press.

Ansell, Chris, Arjen Boin, and Ann Keller. 2010. "Managing Transboundary Crises: Identifying the Building Blocks of an Effective Response System." *Journal of Contingencies and Crisis Management* 18 (4): 195–207.

Ansell, Chris and Alison Gash. 2007. "Collaborative Governance in Theory and Practice." *Journal of Public Administration Research and Theory* 18 (4): 543–71.

Berardo, Ramiro. 2009. "Generalized Trust in Multi-Organizational Policy Arenas." *Political Research Quarterly* 62 (1): 178–89.

Bodin, Örjan and Daniel Nohrstedt. 2016. "Formation and Performance of Collaborative Disaster Management Networks: Evidence from a Swedish Wildfire Response." *Global Environmental Change*: 41: 183–94.

Bodin, Örjan, Daniel Nohrstedt, Julia Baird, Ryan Plummer, and Robert Summers. 2019. "Working at the 'Speed of Trust': Pre-Existing and Emerging Social Ties in Wildfire Responder Networks in Sweden and Canada." *Regional Environmental Change*, first online version: 1–12.

Boin, Arjen and Paul 't Hart. 2010. "Organising for Effective Emergency Management: Lessons from Research." *Australian Journal of Public Administration* 69 (4): 357–71.

Boin, Arjen, Paul 't Hart, and Allan McConnell. 2009. "Crisis Exploitation: Political and Policy Impacts of Framing Contests." *Journal of European Public Policy* 16 (1): 81–106.

Bryson, John M., Barbara C. Crosby, and Melissa Middleton Stone. 2006. "The Design and Implementation of Cross-Sector Collaborations: Propositions from the Literature." *Public Administration Review* 66 (S1): 44–55.

Emerson, Kirk and Tina Nabatchi. 2015. *Collaborative Governance Regimes*. Washington, DC: Georgetown University Press.

Farazmand, Ali. 2007. "Learning from the Katrina Crisis: A Global and International Perspective With Implications for Future Crisis Management." *Public Administration Review* 67 (S1): 149–59.

Gerlak, Andrea and Tanya Heikkila. 2011. "Building a Theory of Learning in Collaboratives: Evidence from the Everglades Restoration Program." *Journal of Public Administration Research and Theory* 21 (4): 619–44.

Henstra, Daniel. 2010. "Evaluating Local Government Emergency Management Programs: What Framework Should Public Managers Adopt?" *Public Administration Review* 70 (2): 236–46.

Hicklin, Alisa, Laurence O'Toole, and Kenneth Meier. 2007. "Serpents in the Sand: Managerial Networking and Nonlinear Influences on Organizational Performance." *Journal of Public Administration Research and Theory* 18 (2): 253–73.

Huxham, Chris, S. Vangen, C. Huxham, and C. Eden. 2000. "The Challenge of Collaborative Governance." *Public Management: An International Journal of Research and Theory* 2 (3): 337–58.

Jung, Kyujin, Minsun Song, and Richard Feiock. 2019. "Isolated and Broken Bridges from Interorganizational Emergency Management Networks: An Institutional Collective Action Perspective." *Urban Affairs Review* 55 (3): 950–75.

Klijn, Erik-Hans, Jurian Edelenbos, and Bram Steijn. 2010. "Trust in Governance Networks." *Administration & Society* 42 (2): 193–221.

Koppenjan, Johannes, Franciscus Maria, and Erik-Hans Klijn. 2004. *Managing Uncertainties in Networks : A Network Approach to Problem Solving and Decision Making*. London: Routledge.

Leach, William D., Neil W. Pelkey, and Paul A. Sabatier. 2002. "Stakeholder Partnerships as Collaborative Policymaking: Evaluation Criteria Applied to Watershed Management in California and Washington." *Journal of Policy Analysis and Management* 21 (4): 645–70.

Lubell, Mark, Garry Robins, and Peng Wang. 2014. "Network Structure and Institutional Complexity in an Ecology of Water Management Games." *Ecology and Society* 19 (4): 23.

Mandell, Myrna P. and Robyn Keast. 2008. "Evaluating the Effectiveness of Interorganizational Relations Through Networks." *Public Management Review* 10 (6): 715–31.

McAllister, Ryan R.J., Catherine J. Robinson, Kirsten Maclean, Angela M. Guerrero, Kerry Collins, Bruce M. Taylor, and Paul J. De Barro. 2015. "From Local to Central: A Network Analysis of Who Manages Plant Pest and Disease Outbreaks across Scales." *Ecology and Society* 20 (1): 67.

McConnell, Allan. 2011. "Success? Failure? Something in-Between? A Framework for Evaluating Crisis Management." *Policy and Society* 30 (2): 63–76.

Meier, Kenneth J. and Laurence J. O'Toole. 2003. "Public Management and Educational Performance: The Impact of Managerial Networking." *Public Administration Review* 63 (6): 689–99.

Moynihan, Donald P. 2008. "Learning Under Uncertainty: Networks in Crisis Management." *Public Administration Review* 68 (2): 350–65.

Newig, Jens, Edward Challies, Nicolas W. Jager, Elisa Kochskaemper, and Ana Adzersen. 2017. "The Environmental Performance of Participatory and Collaborative Governance: A Framework of Causal Mechanisms." *Policy Studies Journal* 46 (2): 269–97.

Nohrstedt, Daniel. 2018a. "Networking and Crisis Management Capacity." *The American Review of Public Administration* 48 (3): 232–44.

———. 2018b. "Bonding and Bridging Relationships in Collaborative Forums Responding to Weather Warnings." *Weather, Climate, and Society* 10 (3): 521–36.

———. 2013. "Advocacy Coalitions in Crisis Resolution: Understanding Policy Dispute in the European Volcanic Ash Cloud Crisis." *Public Administration* 91 (4): 964–79.

Nohrstedt, Daniel and Örjan Bodin. 2019. "Collective Action Problem Characteristics and Partner Uncertainty as Drivers of Social Tie Formation in Collaborative Networks." *Policy Studies Journal*, Online First version: 1-12.

Nohrstedt, Daniel, Fredrik Bynander, Charles Parker, and Paul 't Hart. 2018. "Managing Crises Collaboratively: Prospects and Problems-A Systematic Literature Review." *Perspectives on Public Management and Governance* 1 (4): 257–71.

Nohrstedt, Daniel and Charles Parker. 2014. "The Public Policy Dimension of Resilience in Natural Disaster Management: Sweden's Gudrun and Per Storms." In *Disaster and Development*, edited by Naim Kapucu and K. T. Liou, 235–53. Cham: Springer International Publishing.

O'Leary, Rosemary and Lisa Bingham. 2009. *The Collaborative Public Manager: New Ideas for the Twenty-First Century*. Washington, DC: Georgetown University Press.

O'Leary, Rosemary and Nidhi Vij. 2012. "Collaborative Public Management: Where Have We Been and Where Are We Going?" *The American Review of Public Administration* 42 (5): 507–22.

Provan, Keith and Patrick Kenis. 2007. "Modes of Network Governance: Structure, Management, and Effectiveness." *Journal of Public Administration Research and Theory* 18 (2): 229–52.

Quarantelli, Enrico. 1997. "Ten Criteria for Evaluating the Management of Community Disasters." *Disasters* 21 (1): 39–56.

Rosenthal, Uriel, Paul 't Hart, and Alexander Kouzmin. 1991. "The Bureau-Politics of Crisis Management." *Public Administration* 69 (2): 211–33.

Sorensen, Eva and Jacob Torfing. 2009. "Making Governance Networks Effective and Democratic through Metagovernance." *Public Administration* 87 (2): 234–58.

Turrini, Alex, Daniela Cristofoli, and Greta Nasi. 2009. "Networking Literature About Determinants of Network Effectiveness." *Public Administration* 88 (2): 528–50.

Waugh, William L. and Gregory Streib. 2006. "Collaboration and Leadership for Effective Emergency Management." *Public Administration Review* 66 (S1): 131–40.

Index

Note: Page numbers in *italics* and **bold** indicate figures and tables, respectively.

9/11 Commission 120

actors: collaborating with 76; collaboration between 83; community 6; cooperation of 29; in crisis response *110*; developing relationships with 14; in event subsystems 134; excluded from collaboration 151; familiarity and trust between 101–2; in flood events 139; formal relationships of 111; friction between 52, 85–6, 153; meta-governance and 156; overcoming costs of engagement 157–8; regional 22; tensions between 109–10, 153; in transregional crisis management 100; types of 6
ad hoc collaborations 154
ad hoc demonstrators 30
ad hoc meetings 93, 96, 99, 101, 102n3, 150
ad hoc networks 13–14, 28, 95, 97, 101–2
ad hoc organizations 20–1
Advocacy Coalition Framework 134
Africa: disaster agreements in 92; transregional networks in 150; *see also* transregional crisis management
African Union (AU) 92
anti-establishment groups 31
asylum seekers 43, 47–9

black bloc tactics 32
blame game dynamics 120, 125–6, 157
border controls 49–50
Boxing Day Tsunami 120, 125
BP Deepwater Horizon oil disaster 125
Bronze-Silver-Gold structure (UK) 124

Canada: communication challenges 23; delegation of authority 16; Emergency Management Act 14; Fort McMurray Wildfire 14–18; G20 Toronto Summit 32–5; municipal/provincial wildfire responses 15; provincial operations center (POC) 15, 22–3; Provincial State of Emergency 16; upscaling 22
capacity building 122–3
cathartic crises 5, 105, 106

Civil Protection Act (Sweden) 19
collaborating partners 57
collaboration: definition of 7; intensity of 149; obstacles to 157; supporting interactions 150
collaboration modes 6–7, 111
collaboration performance indicators 75–8
collaborative arrangements and efforts 5–6, 150
collaborative crisis management: definition of 1; failures (*see* failures of collaborative crisis management); future research 154–8; meta-governance in 57, 62, 67, 156; modes of 6–7
collaborative crisis management networks *see* networks
collaborative emergency management 4
collaborative governance: cross-sectoral 84; disaster management and 87; fast-burning crises and 80; in flood prevention 142; future research on 154, 155, 157; G20 Toronto Summit and 37; in paradigm shifts 141; in political-administrative context 87; self-organization and 150; in Swiss flood risk management 9, 132, 134, 139; system context and 81; uncertainty and conflict 152
collaborative learning 51
common operational picture (COP) 21
communication: challenges to 23; failures in 123–4; interpersonal networks 23–4; management of 58; meaning-making and 126; network brokers 23, 24; public announcements 77; restrictions in 58; upscaling and 18; during Västmanland Wildfire 77
communication systems: benefits of 57; financial aspects of 58; RAKEL 57–8
community actors 6
Community Relations Group (CRG: Toronto) 37–8
conceptual dimensions 5, 6, 93
conflicts 152–3
cooperation: of actors 29; definition of 7; failures of 123–4; network 29–30

162 Index

coordination: definition of 7; in disaster and emergencies 2–3; failures of 123–4; formal 53; of networks 5, 50, 93, 96
County Administrative Board (Sweden) 18–21, 22, 51
credibility failures 124–6
credible crisis response 125–6
crisis communications *see* communication
crisis coordination secretariat 71
crisis management: collaborative approaches to 2; communication (*see* communication); generalized patterns 149–53; obstacles 155; single networks and 156; in a societal sense 43–4; temporal perspective on 5; whole-of-society approach to 43
Crisis Preparedness Act (Sweden) 18–19; *see also* preparedness activities
crisis responder networks 2, 13–14, 23; *see also* networks
crisis response operations 22
crisis response organizations 14
crisis response performance 18, 93, 154–5; *see also* transboundary crises, transregional crisis management
crisis situations: categorizing 105–6; conceptual categories 105; phases of 105; response phases 107–8; stress test for 119; surprise attacks 120–2; theoretical categories of **106, 108**; *see also* transboundary crises
crisis trajectories 5, 105, 106–7
culture clashes 37–8

delegation of authority 16
Department of National Operations (NOA: Sweden) 49–50
deradicalization programs 107–9, 111
Disaster and Emergency Management Presidency (AFAD: Turkey) 83–4
disaster response, preparedness activities vs. 4
disaster risk reductions 83, 87
distributed sensemaking 5, 93, 94, 96, 98, 100
Dutch Ministry of Foreign Affairs 35
Dynes' boxes 30

Emergency Management Act (Canada) 14
emergency management organizations, operational levels for 14–15
emergency managers 2, 4
emergency response requirements 2
emergency response systems 13
emergent organizations 3, 30, 93
established organizations 3, 30
European Telecommunications Standards Institute (ETSI) 58
European Union: Community Mechanism for Civil Protection 70; rescEU 124; Union Civil Protection Mechanism 124
expanding organizations 3, 4, 30
extending organizations 3, 30

Extra-Parliamentary Commission for Natural Hazards (PLANAT) 137
Eyjafjallajökull ash cloud crisis 127

failures of collaborative crisis management: after-action learning 126–7; coordination and cooperation 123–4; credibility 124–6; future research on 154–5; imagination 120–2; initiative 122–3; post-crisis investigations 126–7; shared sensemaking and 121–2
fast-burning crises 5, 105, 106
fault lines: culture clashes 37–8; focus on 29–30; inclusive approach 39; moving to slack lines 40; problem framing 36; security planning 36; single perspectives rule 36–7
fire risk assessments 70
first responders 3
flood events **135–6**; becoming focusing events 135–6; characteristics of 138–9; economic damages *141*; geographic outreach *140*; objective magnitude of 138–9, *141*; subsystem properties 139; Swiss Confederation 135
flood risk management: hypotheses 133–4; pro-infrastructure coalition and 139; subsystem dynamics 141; theory 132–3; *see also* flood events; Swiss flood prevention
focusing events: absorbed by a subsystem 134–5; definition of 133; flood events as 135–6, 137–8; policy change and 133; provoking subsystem structure changes 134
forest fire depots 76
formal coordination 53
Fort McMurray Wildfire 14–18, 23, 152
frontline capacity 114
Fukushima nuclear disaster 125

G20 Toronto Summit 32–5
geographical area responsibility 71
global summits 27–8
Grimsvötn volcano 127

Hague summit, The 36–7; *see also* Nuclear Security Summit
heroism 83–4
hierarchical bureaucracy 1
high security events 27, 33, 35; *see also* summits
high stakes crises 30, 122, 123, 128
Homeland Security, U.S. Department of 128–9
horizontal cooperation 3, 29–30, 39, 46, 50–4, 124
Hurricane Andrew 123
Hurricane Katrina 122, 123, 125
Hydraulic Engineering Inspectorate Act (Switzerland) 137

imagination: exercising 155; failures of 120–2; sensemaking capacities 121–2

Incident Command System (ICS) 15, 124
inclusiveness 39, 151–2
Information Communication Technology (ICT) 58–9
information sharing 121
information tools 124
initiating leadership 86, 87–8; *see also* system context
initiative failures 122–3
institutional structures 150, 155–6
Intelligence Community (US) 125
interconnectedness, technological 123
Intergovernmental Panel on Climate Change (IPCC) 128
inter-governmental tensions 23
Internationally Protected Persons (IPPs) 34
inter-organizational collaboration 4, 19, 53, 123
interpersonal networks 23–4
inter-regional collaborative arrangements 93
interventions, transboundary crises 113–14, 116
intra-crisis collaborative learning 51, 157
involuntary networks 29–30
ISIS: crisis in Netherlands (*see* transboundary crises); deradicalization programs 107–8; domestic danger from 104; Dutch response to 150, 151; threats posed by 116

Joint Intelligence Group (JIG) 37

KBM 60–3
knowledge, science-based 128–9

Law on Accident Mitigation (Sweden) 71, 75
learning failures 126–7
long-burning crisis 104
long-shadow crises 5, 105, 107

meaning-making 125–6
meta-governance of collaborative crisis management 57, 62, 67, 156
Metro Toronto Convention Centre (MTCC) 34
migrant crisis, Sweden: border controls 49–50; bureaucratic barriers 52; conflicts 54; extraordinary measures 47; future research on 153; media sources 45; obstacles 54; ownership, sense of 52–3; refugee housing 46–7; responsibility loophole 52; unaccompanied minors 47–9
Migration Agency (Sweden) 43, 46–7, 50, 53
Ministerial Committee (Netherlands) 35
modes of collaboration *see* collaboration modes
MSB (Swedish Civil Contingencies Agency) 63–6
muhtars 82–3
multidimensional pan-regionalization of Africa 100–1

Multidisciplinary Case Assessment meeting *113*, 115
multidisciplinary scientific knowledge 128–9
multi-organizational crisis responder networks 2
multiplex networks 25

National Counterterrorism Strategy (Netherlands) 107
National Medical Rescue Teams (UMKE) 89n3
National Response Plan (NRP: US) 122
Natural Hazard Strategy (Switzerland) 137
Netherlands: Action Program 113–14; Comprehensive Approach (policy) 110–11; ISIS domestic danger (*see* ISIS); local government's deradicalization responsibilities 109; local government subsidies 107; National Counterterrorism Strategy 107; Polarization and Deradicalization Program 107; transboundary crises (*see* transboundary crises)
Network Administrative Organization (NAO) 30
networks: adaptiveness 51–2; ad hoc 101–2; brokers 23, 24; coordination of 5, 50, 93, 96, 97; emergence of 57; formal 93; overlapping 50–1, 77–8; performance of 17–18, 20–2
new emergency management 4
non-governmental organizations (NGOs) 82–5, 86–7
Nuclear Security Summit: administrative backbone of 35; command center integration 38; culture clashes 37; description of 32; informal marketing campaign 37–8; PGV group 35–7; security planning 36; self-reported activism 32

Obama administration 125
objective magnitude of floods 138–9, 141
Ontario Provincial Police (OPP) 34
operational synchronization 111
organizational systems 3

pan-regionalization of Africa 100–1
paradigm shift 132–3, 136–8
Peel Regional Police (PRP) 34
policy communities/subsystems 133–4
policymaking, evaluating success and failure in 28
policy process theories 132–3
political-administrative systems 81–2, 88
post-crisis accountability 120, 126–7
post-incident assessment reports 16
power balance in collaborations 87
preexisting relationships 13, 23–4, 81, 84, 151–2, 155
preparedness activities: avoiding known failures 127; capacity building 122–3; collaborative

164 Index

arrangements and efforts 150; disaster response vs. 4; lessons learned 127; meaning-making 125–6; scenario-based training exercises 121–2; training exercises 127; transboundary crises coordination 123–4; for uncertain future 157–8
problem framing 36
provincial operations center (POC) 15, 22–3
public announcements 77
public service networks, involuntary participation in 30–1

radicalization: case review process *113*; children involved in 111; knowledge of 108
RAKEL 57–8
RAKEL communications system: accession efforts 64; annual RAKEL Day 64; Collaboration Forum 64; construction of 65; development of 60; encouraging participation in 62; end-users of 60–2; financial model for 61–3, 66–7; functionality of 66; KBM and 60–3; lack of interest in 61–2; methods and materials 59–60; MSB managing 63–6; municipality's hesitation to use 60; national strategy for 63; subscriptions to 64–5, **65**; technical problems with 61, 67; user categories **65**; user-friendliness of 66; Västmanland Wildfire 76
RAKEL Council 63–4
real collaboration, definition of 87
Regional Economic Communities (RECs) 92
regional emergency operations center (REOC) 15
Regional Municipality of Wood Buffalo 15
rescEU 124
responder network performance 17–18, 20–2
response network, functionality of 17
risk reduction paradigm 2
routine emergencies 1
Royal Canadian Mounted Police (RCMP) 34

SALAR (Swedish Association of Local Authorities and Regions) 150
scaling procedures 5, 14–15, 18–19, 124
scenario-based training exercises 121–2
science-based knowledge 128–9
Scientific Advisory Group for Emergencies (SAGE) 128
security communication *see* communication
Security Communications System (SCS) 57–8; *see also* RAKEL communications system
security planning, integrated approach to 36
security privatization 6
Security Project Group – PGV 35–8
see also transregional meetings, Africa: ad hoc and formal **98**; frequency of topics 97; topics discussed at **95**–6, **97**, **98**
self-organization 150
sense-giving 122

sensemaking *see* distributed sensemaking
sensemaking capacities 124
sequences 142
shifts in policies 133
short-fuse crisis 104
situational awareness 21, 75
slack lines 40
slow-burning crises 5, 105, 107
societal crisis 43–4
societal resilience 2
societal security 2, 119
SOS Alarm 72
spatial planning regimes 137–8
spatial scales 6
standard operating procedures (SOPs) 94, 122
street-level synchronization 111
subregional meetings *see* transregional crisis management
Summit Management Office (SMO) 34
summits: characteristics of 33; as crises 28–9; G20 Toronto Summit 32–5; global 27–8; Nuclear Security Summit 32; protestors 32; security failure of 28–9; success assessment 29; unrest outcomes 34; violent protests during 27
supply chain management 94
surge capacity 5, 93, 94, 97, 98–9, 100
surprise attacks/events 120–2
Sweden: Armed Forces 76–7; asylum seekers 43, 47–9; Civil Protection Act 19; Coast Guard 77; communication challenges 23; County Administrative Board 18–21, 22, 51; crisis coordination secretariat 71; crisis preparedness 71, 76; Crisis Preparedness Act 18–19; Department of National Operations 49–50; Law on Accident Mitigation 71, 75; Migration Agency 43, 46–7, 50, 53; migration crisis (*see* migrant crisis, Sweden); National Traffic Agency 77; Police Authority 52; principle of responsibility 18, 71; reintroducing border controls 49–50; vertical crisis collaboration 77–8; wildfires in (*see* Västmanland Wildfire)
Swedish Association of Local Authorities and Regions (SKL) 46, 51, 150
Swedish Civil Contingencies Agency 52, 53–4, 63–6, 70, 76
Swedish National Board of Institutional Care 48
Swiss Federation Institute for Forest, Snow and Landscape Research 136
Swiss flood prevention: paradigm shift in 136–7; pro-infrastructure coalition 139; sequences 142; subsystem characteristics 142; subsystem properties 139; *see also* flood risk management
Switzerland: flood prevention *138*; Hydraulic Engineering Inspectorate Act 137; Hydraulic Engineering Ordinance 137; integrated risk

management 137; Natural Hazard Strategy 137; Spatial Planning Regime 137; Water Retaining Facilities Ordinance 137
system architecture 57
system context: in collaborative government framework 84; definition of 81; drivers and 87
system integration 121

technological interconnectedness 123
temporal perspective on crisis management 5
terrorist attacks 123
TETRA (Terrestrial Trunked Radio) 58
top-down collaboration *see* vertical cooperation
Toronto Police Service (TPS) 34–5
training exercises 121–2
transboundary coalitions 112, 115–16
transboundary crises: analyzing 94; coordination 123–4; creating coalitions 112–13; creating spaces 115–16; dimensions of 4–5; initiatives 104; interventions 113–14; management tools 112–16; managing 92; observations from **112**; policy domains 110–11; responses to 116; transcending levels of government 109–10; *see also* transregional crisis management
transboundary spaces 115–16
transit refugees 46
transregional crisis management: actors participating in 100; analyzing 93–4; categories 93–4; distributed sensemaking 93, 94, 96, 98, 100; mapping **94**; network coordination 93–4, 96, 99–100; networks, significance of 100; pan-regionalization and 100–1; potential for 101; preparedness 92; surge capacity 93, 94, 97, 98–9, 100; *see also* transboundary crises
transregional networks *see* networks
trial-and-error collaboration 154
trust building 101–2, 151–2
Turkey: crisis coordination centers 82; cross-sectoral collaboration 84–7; damage

assessment activities 86; Disaster and Emergency Management Presidency agency 82–3; Disaster Management System 82–3; as "father state" 82; muhtars 82–3; national earthquake strategy and action plan 83; non-governmental organizations 82–5, 86–7; polarized political system of 88; political-administrative system in 81–2, 88; risk management system 82–3; society polarization 85; state's dominance over civil society 82; as transcendental state 81

uncertainty and conflict 152–3
Union Civil Protection Mechanism (UCPM) 124
upscaling: challenges to 13; communication as hurdle in 18; flow of information 21–2; formal process of 14–15, 18–19; managerial challenges 22; organizational 22–3; in practice 15–17, 19–20; uncertainty of 23
USAM regional forum 19–20, 23
U.S. Department of Homeland Security 128–9

Västmanland Wildfire 18–22; actors and 153; Coast Guard 77; collaboration performance indicators 75–8; command center authority 75–6; communications 77; first casualty of 73–4; information coordination 72–4, 151; local actors 76; national actors collaboration 76–7; National Traffic Agency 77; situational awareness 21, 75; Swedish Armed Forces during 76–7; USAM framework 72–3; vertical cooperation during 73–4; *see also* Sweden
vertical cooperation 29, 50–4, 86, 109–10, 124
vertical crisis collaboration 77–8

whole-of-society approach: to crisis management 43; for societal security 2
wildfires *see* Västmanland Wildfire
within-case observations 9, 45–6, 52, 54

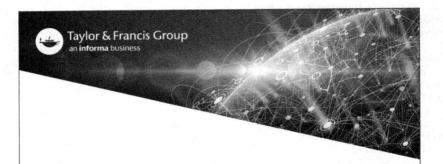